WHAT
ANTHROPOLOGISTS
DO

WHAT ANTHROPOLOGISTS DO

Veronica Strang

Illustrations by
Blue Powell

Oxford • New York

English edition
First published in 2009 by
Berg
Editorial offices:
First Floor, Angel Court, 81 St Clements Street, Oxford OX4 1AW, UK
175 Fifth Avenue, New York, NY 10010, USA

Berg is the imprint of Oxford International Publishers Ltd.

Library of Congress Cataloging-in-Publication Data

Strang, Veronica.
 What anthropologists do / Veronica Strang ; illustrations by Blue Powell.—English ed.
  p. cm.
 Includes bibliographical references and index.
 ISBN-13: 978-1-84520-355-9 (pbk.)
 ISBN-10: 1-84520-355-0 (pbk.)
 ISBN-13: 978-1-84520-354-2 (cloth)
 ISBN-10: 1-84520-354-2 (cloth)
 1. Anthropology—Vocational guidance. 2. Anthropology—Research. 3. Anthropology
—Methodology. I. Powell, Blue, ill. II. Title.

 GN41.8.S77 2009
 306.023—dc22

                                                                    2009011242

British Library Cataloguing-in-Publication Data

A catalogue record for this book is available from the British Library.

ISBN 978 1 84520 354 2 (Cloth)
      978 1 84520 355 9 (Paper)

Typeset by JS Typesetting Ltd, Porthcawl, Mid Glamorgan
Printed in the UK by the MPG Books Group

www.bergpublishers.com

CONTENTS

ACKNOWLEDGEMENTS

This book arose out of discussions between the executive committees of the Association of Social Anthropologists of the UK and the Commonwealth, and the Royal Anthropological Institute. Both have long observed that, with little anthropology offered in schools, school leavers have little idea about what anthropologists do, and no idea at all about the broad potential for interesting (and viable) careers that studying anthropology provides. It is apparent that many potential research users are equally unsure about what anthropology can offer. As a result of these discussions Berg's managing director, Kathryn Earle, asked me to review the 'applied anthropology' literature, collect a range of examples and describe these in a form accessible to a younger audience. This turned out to be an intriguing project, enabling me to discover what my colleagues around the world *are* doing in many areas of research far removed from my own. I am grateful for this opportunity, and for the support of the ASA and the RAI in the process. Other anthropology associations and journals were also very helpful in circulating my requests for information. I would like to thank them, and in particular those colleagues from around the world who responded with lively accounts of their professional experiences.[1]

There are some excellent texts aimed at introducing first-year anthropology undergraduates to the discipline and providing career advice for graduates. These describe ways of applying anthropology that are now well established, as well as pointing to emerging areas. I am greatly indebted to the authors of these texts, and hope this volume will provide a stepping stone to their work.

A number of people assisted this project directly. I would particularly like to thank my research assistant, Mira Taitz, who did a sterling job helping to collect diverse examples of anthropological application; Blue Powell who undertook the large and challenging task of illustrating the text; Aran Yardley and April-Rose Geers who acted as my 'guinea pigs' for final drafts; and the various colleagues and anonymous referees who took the time to read and make comments on the manuscript. And it was, as ever, a pleasure to work with the team at Berg.

INTRODUCTION

WHAT DO ANTHROPOLOGISTS DO?

'What anthropologists do' seems to be a bit of a mystery to many people, and there are several reasons for this. One is that anthropologists are involved in such a wide variety of things that the most accurate answer to the question 'what do they do?' is 'just about anything that involves understanding human social behaviour'. Another is that people's ideas about anthropology are often gleaned from portrayals in literature, film and television, which tend to favour rather dramatic stereotypes: pith-helmet-wearing colonial adventurers living with (equally stereotypical) 'hidden tribes' in the jungle; crime-busting forensic anthropologists (who always find the murderer); or bearded, sandals-with-socks obsessives going bonkers somewhere in the outback.[1]

My personal view is that we need to challenge these stereotypes for several reasons: because the facts are more interesting than the fiction; because, in an ever more complex world, anthropology has a vital contribution to make; and because, contrary to the stereotypes, anthropological training is immensely applicable in a very wide variety of careers. So the purpose of this book is to describe what anthropologists actually do, with examples from a range of areas. It is not a comprehensive account: just a brief introduction to the kind of work that anthropologists undertake, and the multiple directions open to practitioners.

It is probably useful to start by talking about what anthropology *is*.[2] The broadest definition is that it is a social science that involves the study of human groups and their behaviour: their interactions with each other, and with the material environment. Most anthropologists study contemporary societies (or smaller groups within them), although in some countries anthropology also includes archaeology and the study of past societies.[3] It sits alongside related social sciences like sociology (which tends to be more quantitative), and psychology (which focuses more on individuals).

Anthropology itself is a very broad discipline[4] with large sub-disciplinary areas: for example, social anthropology, cultural anthropology, political anthropology, economic anthropology, the anthropology of religion, biological anthropology, medical anthropology and my own field, environmental anthropology. There are other 'offshoots' too, crossing into development studies, social policy, and studies of art and material culture. And, as a glance at the diverse list of contents for this book illustrates, there is a host of smaller, even more specialized areas.

What unites this diversity? Anthropology has several key characteristics: it is holistic, placing whatever behaviour it is examining within its social and environmental context, and considering the range of cultural beliefs and practices that direct people's activities. It is largely qualitative, recognizing that most of these things are not readily measurable. It aims to be 'in-depth', getting under the surface of social life to make its underlying dynamics visible. It engages fully with the complexities of human 'being'.

In effect, 'what anthropologists do' is try to understand and represent the realities of particular cultural and sub-cultural worldviews, encapsulating their key features and underlying principles, in order to 'make sense' of human behaviour. They try to do this in such a way that this understanding can be communicated cross-culturally, acting as a translatory bridge between groups whose beliefs, values and practices may be completely different.

Anthropological research generally involves working with a host group or community to create an 'ethnography'. This can be described as a portrait of that group and its dynamics, which is usually in text form, although some anthropologists also use visual media. Most ethnographies contain a set of core elements: the composition of the group; its history; its ways of making a living in a particular environment; its social and political institutions; its belief systems and values. A good way to imagine this ethnographic portrait is that the particular issue the anthropologist is studying will be in the foreground, in detail, but these contextualizing elements that shape how people live will be there too, as an explanatory background (see Agar 1996, Pawluch *et al.* 2005).

An ethnography is the result of the two key things that underpin any science: theory and method. Like other sciences, anthropology has, over many years, developed a set of theoretical principles. Being part of an ongoing international and inter-cultural scientific 'conversation', these are always moving forward, increasing our understanding. Again like other sciences, anthropology is fundamentally comparative: we compare different social and cultural groups and, by examining their differences and similarities, we are able to tackle broader questions about human beings and the patterns of behaviour that they share.

Anthropology theories have been described in various ways: for example, by James Peacock (1986) as a 'lens' that helps to bring human life into focus. As a keen scuba diver, I tend to think of the in-depth immersion of ethnographic research as a way of seeing under the surface. Theories are also presented as a sort of 'tool kit' for analysis, and that's quite a good analogy too, as it underlines the reality that theory is a practical thing: a set of useful 'idea tools' that help us to open up what is often regarded as the 'black box' of human behaviour.

Of course any sensible analysis requires data. Anthropology is fundamentally empirical, in that it relies on data collected 'in the field'. Let me have another swipe at the stereotypes here, and say that 'in the field' doesn't have to be somewhere far away, or even somewhere else. As anyone who has travelled will know, being a long way from home is certainly useful, in terms of coming into contact with (and being able to compare) very different perspectives on life. But highly diverse social groups and cultural ideas can also be found on the doorstep, and there are many anthropologists for whom 'the field' is at home, working with particular communities, sub-cultural groups, organizations or networks.

EMPLOYING ANTHROPOLOGY

Anthropologists are supported in their work in a variety of ways. Some are employed by universities, and therefore combine teaching with research. Both of these activities are important to universities, and most hope that their academic staff will devote their time fairly equally to both. In reality, most university-based anthropologists probably spend a higher proportion of their time teaching and doing administration, but they are still expected to keep up with what is going on in their field, and to conduct some research. At a tertiary level, there is (or should be) a symbiotic relationship between teaching and research, with original research findings feeding into the curriculum. This makes additional use of the external research that academics do, and ensures that students receive teaching that is intellectually fresh and up-to-date.

For anthropologists who like teaching, and who can tolerate the (considerable) administrative demands of university life, an institutional post has a number of advantages. The teaching itself is often very rewarding; a good academic department provides a lively and supportive intellectual environment and – with luck – congenial colleagues; and, where tenure or long-term contracts are available, there is a greater degree of security than may be provided by more independent career paths. Universities often provide some financial support for research, or at least regular sabbatical time to enable bursts of research activity, and university-employed anthropologists also write research proposals and compete for funding from national or international funding bodies. Most countries have a research council, and there are other (national and international) funding bodies, such as the Royal Anthropological Institute or the Wenner-Gren Foundation, whose aim is to support original research in the discipline.

Some university-based anthropologists also do consultancy work, and some combine part-time teaching posts with other forms of employment or freelance research. As the case studies in this book illustrate, anthropological CVs often contain a mixture of ways to make use of anthropological training, and there is considerable scope for people to shape their careers in accord with their particular interests and preferences.

Although teaching is an obvious avenue of employment for anyone trained in a scientific discipline, there are probably greater numbers of anthropologists either employed as full-time researchers or working as freelancers for government departments, non-governmental organizations, charities, industries, legal bodies, indigenous communities and so forth. There are significant advantages to employment outside the academy, although it is sometimes less secure: an ability to focus on research (rather than spending a large proportion of time on teaching and administrative duties); the opportunity to follow specific areas of interest, for example in politics, health, or development; and, of course, independence from the strictures of institutional employment.

CONDUCTING RESEARCH

However anthropologists make a living, they have a responsibility, not only to their employers or sponsors, but also to anthropology as a discipline, in terms of maintaining professional standards, academic independence, and ethical principles. Ethics are central to practitioners' relationships with the groups or communities in which they conduct research (see Caplan 2003, Fluehr-Lobban 2003). Professional anthropology associations expect their members to conform to detailed and rigorous codes of practice, which ensure that the interests of the host group or community are carefully protected throughout the research.[5] Projects are therefore designed with two key questions in mind: 'how will this research produce new knowledge that answers a particular question?' and 'how will it benefit the group in which it is conducted, and society in general?' In many cases, the host group is involved in the research design from the very beginning. At the very least, there will be a process of asking permission from them; of seeking input on the proposed work; and of getting feedback on the research findings as these emerge.

Many anthropologists maintain long-term relationships with communities, returning regularly to extend earlier research, or to do new projects. As well as allowing researchers to develop productive collaborations with individuals and groups, these lengthy relationships also permit shorter research projects, building on accumulated background ethnographic data. In many professional contexts, the realities of research funding do not permit a great deal of time for fieldwork, and anthropologists have to build on former (or other people's) datasets and experience. Nevertheless, the major objective is still to create as complete a picture as possible, so that the research question is always given an ethnographic context that will help to explain what is going on.

Anthropologists tend to collect a lot of data, and it is this meticulous depth and detail that gives strong foundations to their analyses. Preliminary literature reviews can take many weeks, and it is common for fieldwork to take from six months to a year. In a sense, anthropology is the 'slow food' of the social sciences, because it tends to be quite painstaking and cannot be 'whipped up' instantly. Fortunately, this willingness to be very thorough generally pays off, providing genuine and useful insights into human behaviour.

Ethnographic data are collected in a variety of ways. A core method is 'participant observation', which – as its name implies – involves participating in the everyday life of the host community, and carefully observing and recording events. The other major method is to conduct interviews with individuals and groups, and this usually means a mixture of long in-depth interviews and shorter, more opportunistic ones. Interviews might be formal (with a specific list of issues to explore) or more exploratory and informal. Ethnographers often interview people a number of times, and spend a lot of time with them, in particular those members of the host group willing to work collaboratively on the research.

Fieldwork is followed by a process of analysis, which means organizing the data coherently and employing theory to make sense of the picture that emerges. This can take a while too: there will be a lot of data to consider and there are no easy answers. Humans are complex creatures, and while biological and ecological factors may play a part, behaviour is greatly complicated by social and cultural complexities. The art of producing a good ethnographic account is to crystallize the issues succinctly but not to reduce them to the point where they cease to be meaningful, and to leave sufficient explanatory context so that it is possible to see consistent patterns, to understand what is going on, and thus to offer practical, helpful insights that can be applied to the problems and challenges that people face.

Many people assume that anthropology divides into 'applied' work (by which they usually mean research with an intended practical outcome taking place outside the academe), or more 'theoretical' work, which supposedly takes place in the 'ivory tower' of a university. There are various societies of 'applied anthropologists', and these are immensely helpful and supportive to practitioners who freelance, or whose institutional base does not contain many anthropological colleagues. However, although this applied/theoretical dichotomy is a functional shorthand, it is a little misleading. It encourages an assumption that 'ivory-tower' research and the development of theory is rather exclusive and not very practical and that anthropologists working elsewhere are somehow 'outside' the main part of the discipline.

My own view is that both of these assumptions are wrong. Good 'applied' research, wherever it is based, requires a strong theoretical framework and a rigorous 'academic' approach; and theoretical development itself is greatly strengthened by information gleaned directly from empirical data (based on evidence) and field experience. The nature of anthropological research, with its grass-roots focus and its immediate involvement with human communities, is very grounded in any case. So however esoteric a research question may seem, understanding 'why people do what they do' always has some practical value, and even seemingly abstract research generates ideas and proposes new theories that – if they are robust – will filter, through wider discourse, into practice.

In essence, the process of anthropological research entails the following steps (although probably in a much less neatly defined order, with lots of feedback loops and sidetracks):

- Designing: outlining the research question and the aims of the research.
- Seeking funds: writing grant proposals.
- Reviewing: trawling the theoretical and ethnographic literature to see what has been done on the research topic to date.
- Defining and refining: developing the project aims and hypotheses.
- Doing ethnographic fieldwork: collecting data through, for example, participant observation and interviews (some preliminary fieldwork is often done at an earlier stage too).
- Analysing the data: making sense of the picture through the 'lens' of anthropological theories, testing hypotheses.
- Finding answers: drawing conclusions from the research.
- Disseminating the findings: writing texts, giving presentations, making films, or producing other outputs, such as exhibitions.
- Participating in international conversations: adding input to wider debates on research questions, contributing to theoretical development.

And often . . .

- Making recommendations: advising policy and decision makers, research users.
- Following through: assisting the implementation of the findings.
- Evaluating: conducting further research on the effects of this implementation.

As this list suggests, anthropological research produces outcomes in several potential directions: towards theoretical developments within the discipline, and into practical recommendations for research users. It also illustrates the important feedback relationship between theory and practice, underlining the artificiality of the division between 'theoretical' and 'applied' work.

This division is equally artificial in defining people's career identities. As noted above, anthropologists' careers frequently involve a mixture of teaching/university posts and other roles, and most have research interests that engage with issues far removed from any kind of 'ivory tower'. Typically, anthropologists' web sites or lists of publications (including those found on university web pages) describe a range of work, some of which could readily be described as 'applied' and some of which is more obviously focused on contributing to theoretical debates. They also reveal an extraordinary diversity of interests: a profession investigating a host of intriguing questions about human behaviour in an equally varied range of groups.

Anthropology is not only fascinating but also rather addictive. Many people start by studying a bit of anthropology but then find they want to go on. That is more or less what happened to me: after more than a decade of working as a freelance writer and researcher in various parts of the world, I was sufficiently intrigued by a stint in the Australian outback to spend a year doing a masters' course in anthropology. A doctorate, several teaching posts and numerous research projects later it remains endlessly absorbing.

This raises a question as to why there are not more people doing anthropology. After all, there are plenty of souls with incurable curiosity, the flexibility to work with different cultures and ideas, and enough patience to do in-depth research. A major obstacle is that anthropology is not generally taught in schools, so most people don't come into contact with it.[6] This leaves them with only the stereotypes to consider, and part of the problem with those (quite apart from the fact that they are inaccurate and outdated), is that they don't seem to point either to potential careers in anthropology, or to many 'practical' uses of anthropological research.

So this book is intended to show that anthropology can lead to a vast choice of careers, and that it has an equally diverse range of potential applications. I have divided the material into some broad areas, but these are fairly arbitrary and there is considerable overlap and flow between them. In each area, however, the purpose of anthropological research remains constant: to gain a real understanding of a particular social reality, its beliefs values and practices, and to communicate this understanding across cultural and sub-cultural boundaries.

1 ANTHROPOLOGY AND ADVOCACY

BALANCING ACTS

A lot of the work that anthropologists do involves acting as cultural translators: creating bridges between societies or more specific social groups that have quite different worldviews. Being able to understand various points of view, and translate ideas in a non-judgemental way, is a key aspect of the training that they receive, and this rests on a combination of rigorous in-depth research and a theoretical framework that enables them to step back and consider situations analytically. In many situations, having a 'neutral' but empathetic outsider, who has taken the trouble to gain insights into the complexities of people's lives, can greatly assist cross-cultural interactions. Scientific neutrality can be particularly important in legal contexts, where courts or tribunals depend on the testimony of 'disinterested' expert witnesses to present evidence, but there are many situations in which cultural beliefs, values and practices clash, and tensions arise. For example, the translatory skills of anthropologists may be used in conflicts between religious groups; in quarrels between managers and workforces; in defusing racial or ethnic hostilities; in mediating between organizations competing for the control of heritage sites and national parks; or in facilitating communication between local groups and government agencies.

For some practitioners, advocacy is a logical extension of long-term working relationships with host communities. It is, after all, virtually impossible to work closely with people and not develop some sympathy for their concerns. Even in the early 1900s, when Bronislaw Malinowski first established in-depth fieldwork as a core anthropological method, he suggested that 'as a scientific moralist fully in sympathy with races hereto oppressed or at least underprivileged, the anthropologist would demand equal treatment for all, full cultural independence for every differential group or nation' (Hedican 1995: 45). Malinowski carried through with these views, presenting evidence to the Australian government about the labour conditions people were experiencing in the western Pacific, and criticizing colonial administrations for appropriating the land of indigenous people and disregarding their customary practices. 'Malinowski thereby laid the foundation for an advocacy role in anthropology very early on in the history of the discipline' (Hedican 1995: 45).

> It is almost inevitable that sustained contact with a given people will involve the ethnographer in disputes emerging from the contradictions between ethnic, regional, national and international interests... The profession's commitment to the non-academic world, is especially evident in the context of indigenous human rights... Countries such as Australia, Canada, Brazil, and most of Hispanic America have conferred a great deal of weight on the work of ethnographers. Both the State and the public at large, credit these professionals for their anthropological knowledge but, perhaps more explicitly, for the kind of complicity bred between researchers and research subjects, a complicity that comes from sharing the vicissitudes met by indigenous people in their interethnic lives. (Ramos 2004: 57–8)

Anthropologists have always had to make delicate judgements about where to position themselves on a continuum between striving for as much scientific 'impartiality' as can be achieved (recognizing that all scientific activity contains value choices), and taking up a more partisan role as direct advocates for the people with whom they work. There has been much debate in the discipline about how relationships with host communities and other research users should be constructed, and about the potential for direct advocacy to undermine perceptually neutral scientific 'authority', which is, in its own way, highly effective in assisting people.

The ethics of working with people, whoever and wherever they are, require social researchers at the very least to 'do no harm' to them. As noted in the introduction, many anthropologists think that this ought to go further, believing that research should not be a one-way street that merely benefits the funding agency or the social scientist, but should entail a reciprocal relationship in which there is also some benefit to the group concerned. This 'benefit' may lie in the usefulness of the research, rather than in direct advocacy, but the principle of reciprocity is now well embedded in the ethical codes that guide the discipline and much contemporary anthropological research is based on principles of partnership with host communities.

In reality, every anthropologist has to decide how best to do rigorous and useful research, while also meeting ethical and moral imperatives. Anthropologists are not *just* social scientists – they are also individuals with their own values and political beliefs, and they have often chosen to do this kind of work because they feel that it can make a difference. 'Advocacy, in its choice of an issue, is often highly charged and personal' (Ervin 2005: 151). Anthropology therefore enables its practitioners not only to follow their intellectual curiosity about why people do what they do, and produce research that reveals this in scientific terms, but also to take social action upon issues that they care about, and to give real help to the communities in which they work.

In becoming involved in people's lives, anthropologists perform many kinds of community service, and this can be very informal. For example, Mitzi Goheen, who has worked with the Nso' community in western Cameroon so extensively that they have given her a local title

> ...often puts her topical and geographical expertise to practical use in serving the people among whom she lives and works. As a titled leader, for example, Dr Goheen has certain obligations to her Cameroonian friends, which she fulfills by taking care of them in direct, practical ways. She is godmother to a Cameroonian child, helps young men of the community negotiate bridewealth payments, and maintains a fund at the local Baptist mission hospital to pay her friends' medical bills... She also helps villagers make hospital care decisions – and often transports them to the hospital as well. (Gwynne 2003a: 144)

In addition, Goheen is a director of a local lending organization, which gives small loans to women to enable them to become players in the local economy.

These kinds of activities are common: anthropologists in the field typically try to make themselves useful in whatever way seems to fit. 'One need not hold the title of applied anthropologist to put anthropological theory, method and expertise to good use, nor the title advocacy anthropologist to provide support for the members of small-scale communities' (Gwynne 2003a: 145). In this sense, the concept of anthropology as 'community service' underpins a lot of the work described in this book. However, this chapter focuses particularly on the situations in which the role

of advocacy in anthropology comes to the fore, becoming what David Maybury-Lewis (who went on from Harvard to become the president of Cultural Survival Inc.) called 'a special sort of pleading' (in Hedican 1995: 73).

FACILITATING CROSS-CULTURAL COMMUNICATION

Sometimes 'special pleading' articulates the concerns of a group who may otherwise not be heard. For instance, Jacqueline Solway works in Botswana as an advocate for minority language groups who, even in a peaceful multi-party democracy, remain somewhat disenfranchised. By communicating the realities of their lives to decision makers in the political arena, her work seeks ways to assist the state in becoming more inclusive to these groups (Solway 2004).

Elizabeth Grobsmith works with Native-American inmates in prisons in Nebraska who, although their community comprises only 1 per cent of the population as a whole, make up 4 per cent of the prison population. Her work began in the 1970s, when the courts upheld prisoners' rights to religious freedom and education, and she was employed to teach a programme in American Indian studies. As she says, 'prisoners stand to profit both from an academic perspective and from the increased self-respect which education affords. Their culture gains credibility by being the subject of a prison college class' (Grobsmith 2002: 166). Thus she was able to allay the authorities' anxieties about religious practices, such as pipe smoking:

> The contribution of the anthropologist can be great here, serving as a consultant to correctional authorities and guiding them as to the legitimacy and meaning of these religious practices. Absence of regular training programs and turnover of employees result in ignorance and insensitivity on the part of correctional officers and continual mistakes which prisoners deeply resent... Anthropological expertise is of benefit not because the inmates are incapable themselves of explaining their traditions. Rather the use of an 'outside expert' or consultant affords legitimacy to the entire process. (Grobsmith 2002: 167)

Grobsmith was also involved in the design of treatment programmes to tackle drug and alcohol problems in the prison population, pointing out that 'the consequences of ignoring Native American prisoners' needs is the ultimate return of most Indian inmates to incarceration' (Grobsmith 2002: 168). She advised the parole board on indigenous cultural approaches to rehabilitation, and acted as an expert witness in disputes on prisoners' rights.

> There is a tremendous need for anthropologists in correctional affairs. With the largest number of inmates representing minorities, and correctional staff rarely

representative of those same groups, anthropologists are frequently sought as liaisons, cultural resources persons, and simply savvy outsiders who can help minority individuals interact with the complex, legal world in which they live. Correctional authorities benefit from this interaction as well, through improved inmate-staff relationships, decreased litigation, and prison accreditation standards which reward institutions that permit and cooperate with research. (Grobsmith 2002: 170)

As she concludes: 'few activities are more satisfying than helping to mend an intercultural communication network that has broken down' (Grobsmith 2002: 171).

Communication problems have been similarly central to Barbara Jones' advocacy work with Native-American Bannock and Shoshoni women. When some of the women were prosecuted for withholding information from social services, her research showed that cultural misunderstandings had occurred because of different usages of English by the women, and by the social services staff. The presiding Judge ruled that the women were innocent, and that, in the future, an interpreter should be used to ensure clarity in communications (in Ervin 2005: 106).

Facilitating culturally appropriate forms of communication is also at the heart of Kevin Avruch and Peter Black's work on the role of anthropology in 'alternative dispute resolution' (ADR), which has become increasingly popular as an informal 'alternative' to legal action in America (Avruch and Black 1996). They point out that anthropology actually provided the inspiration for ADR, because 'some reformers from within the legal profession read ethnography and thought they had found the perfect template for their reform: dispute resolution in "tribal societies"' (Avruch and Black 1996: 50). Anthropologists themselves, however, have been quite critical of the misuse of ethnography to construct an idealized image of tribal social life, and of the idea that particular methods of resolving disputes can simply be 'lifted' from one cultural context and plonked down in another. As ADR has become entrenched in American legal culture there have been increasing efforts to commodify and export it, and Avruch and Black note that for the modern ADR 'missionaries ... a concern with possible cultural differences as having significant effects does not seem to detain them for very long' (Avruch and Black 1996: 53). Their research examines attempts to introduce alternative dispute resolution in the Pacific island of Palau:

> There is perhaps something ironic in bringing ADR, an ideological formation partly inspired by misread ethnography ... *back* to the sort of cultural setting people ... thought it came from in the first place. But to revel in that irony is perhaps to underestimate the costs that such a disingenuous export can inflict... It is important that if ADR is introduced to Palau, it be done in a manner that makes good local sense. In our opinion, this is not something that can be written in by consultants drawn from the American ADR community, no matter how culturally sensitive they may be. Those designing ADR for Palau will do well to predicate it on *Palauan* assumptions about conflict and its management, assumptions that are part of Palauan culture... One way to ensure that this happens is to put the design of the process firmly in Palauan hands... The contribution that anthropological outsiders can make is to offer suggestions about the design of the process. (Avruch and Black 1996: 54–9)

From their point of view, 'the greatest contribution anthropology can make to the creation of a humane fit between ADR and Paluan society may lie in its insistence on the importance of culture' (Avruch and Black 1996: 47), and they have gone on to insist as best they can.

DEFENDING LIVELIHOODS AND KNOWLEDGE

'The importance of culture' also underlies the work that Alexander Ervin does in assisting rural farming communities in protecting their way of life. As he says: 'The industrialization of agriculture has long been a threat to rural North Americans. It undermines the family farm and community, erodes rural self-sufficiency and self-determination, and can negatively affect health and the environment' (Ervin 2005: 154).

Anthropologists have been speaking up for many decades about the social effects of industrialization in agriculture, beginning with Walter Goldschmidt's work in the 1940s. Goldschmidt compared two Californian farming communities: one was largely dominated by factory farms owned by large corporations based elsewhere. The labour force was migratory and poor, and the local town had a high crime rate. The other community was largely composed of independent farmers. They achieved higher levels of production, had higher household incomes, and their local town had prospering businesses, churches and family clubs. The research showed the benefits of protecting community life in rural areas. However, disruptive patterns of development have often been repeated:

For rural peoples, the decline of community is reinforced by federal and state agricultural policies that favor the goals and profit motives of major agribusiness corporations in the supposed interests of efficiency and the untested assumption that only industrialized agriculture can cheaply feed the world. (Ervin 2005: 154–5)

Kendall Thu and Paul Durrenberger's research is similarly critical of the social and ecological effects of industrial farming, showing how pig factories in Iowa and North Carolina created enormous stenches for miles, lowered property values and impinged on social life, as well as polluting rivers, and damaging fish and fisheries. They provide an account of the social costs of these changes: the loss of family farms; the environmental and health risks; the greater uncertainties in employment; and the way that these pressures lead to social division and conflict. Kendall Thu therefore sees a clear need for research to lead to advocacy:

My applied work involves a strategy combining research with advocacy through the media, public speaking, legislative testimony, expert witness work in the courtroom, holding industries publicly accountable for co-opting science, work with non-profit organizations and cooperation among community groups… Research and advocacy are necessary partners. Science never has, nor ever will, exist in a political vacuum. If we do not advocate based on the rigor of our ethnographies, by default we have made a decision affecting the lives of those whose knowledge provided for our professional careers. (Ervin 2005: 157)

In a contemporary context, one of the major issues in agriculture is the introduction of genetically modified crops. Some of these carry 'terminator' genes that, by preventing the plants from producing viable seeds for further crops, make the farmers heavily dependent on the large corporations that supply GM seed and the pesticides that these require. Genetically modified crops also marginalize local knowledge about plant breeding: for example, Glenn Stone's work in India (Stone 2002, 2007) examines how the introduction of GM cotton has destablized local knowledge and social exchange systems, placing immense pressure on farmers and leading to a rapid rise in the suicide rate among them (carried out, ironically, by drinking pesticides). Stone (2007: 67) describes: '…symptomatic disrupting of the process of experimentation and development of management skill. In fact, Warangal cotton farming offers a case study in agricultural deskilling [which] severs a vital link between environmental and social learning.'

Plainly this work is important in the ongoing debates about GM crops, and in wider concerns about the need to maintain local knowledges. This is both a matter of making sure that they are maintained through use, and protecting the ownership of this expertise. As well as having a way of life that they hope to protect, local communities – whether they farm or make a living from other economic modes – often have valuable ecological knowledge, and another area of advocacy in anthropology is concerned with the protection of intellectual property rights. Working for the International Potato Center (which in Spanish is called the *Centro Internacional de la Papa* (CIP)), Robert Rhoades observes that with scientists and pharmaceutical and food corporations on the lookout for new plant breeding opportunities, 'the topic of ownership of plant genetic resources is an international minefield of controversy because it concerns profits, power and politics at the highest levels of international government' (Rhoades 2005: 77). Since the mid-1980s, anthropologists have assisted local communities and the Centre in protecting indigenous intellectual property:

> As the traditional curators of cultivated species … indigenous people have become more aware of their own rights and their crucial role in conservation. This connection between indigenous cultures and crop diversity has increased the demand for anthropologists, especially ethnobotanists,[1] in agricultural research… Anthropological contribution to this area took place in several ways. First, field-level studies demonstrated that farmers possessed a complex folk nomenclature of native potatoes… Ethnobotanical studies provided basic information on farmer selections to assist with the center's efforts… An approach called 'memory banking' pioneered by anthropologist Virginia Nazarea … demonstrated how cultural knowledge should be conserved along with the conventional gene bank 'passport' data… Anthropologists have served on panels and international commissions to encourage implementation of farmers' rights as a way to maintain germplasm diversity. An effort has been made to lobby legislative bodies and get the message about genetic erosion and indigenous cultures to the general public… Today several international centers – including the Rome-based International Plant Genetics Resources Institute – employ anthropologists and ethnobotanists to help guide participatory plant breeding efforts involving both scientists and farmers. (Rhoades 2005: 76–8)

Industrial agriculture is one of the major stresses on indigenous landscapes, and another is the widening global search for minerals and resources. As Alan Rumsey and James Weiner (2001) have shown, mining often heads the list of activities that have major social and ecological impacts on indigenous communities. Stuart Kirsch works on these issues in Papua New Guinea, where mining has been massively destructive, and he draws attention to the role of transnational corporations in this infringement of human rights (Kirsch 2003). A committed advocate, he has written extensively about the indigenous communities' protests against the destruction of their local ecosystems (and thus their livelihoods), and their collaborative use of anthropological methods in trying to explain these realities and communicate their concerns to decision-makers (Kirsch 2006).[2]

HUMAN RIGHTS

Anthropologists have long been active as researchers and advocates in many areas concerned with human rights, including the most fundamental rights to safety, and to sufficient food and water (see Nagengast and Vélez-Ibáñez 2004). Thus John Van Willigen and V. C. Channa have conducted research on violence against women in India, in particular as it relates to the cultural and religious practice of requiring bride's families to provide dowry, which is a source of considerable conflict. Attempts to criminalize and legislate against this practice have been ineffective, and they have argued that 'policies directed against these social evils need to be constructed in terms of an underlying cause rather than of the problem itself' (Van Willigen and Channa 1991: 117). Their in-depth ethnographic work therefore seeks to illuminate the causal factors, in the hope of assisting the development of more effective measures to ensure the safety of Hindu women.

The safety of women and children was also the focus of Penny Van Esterlik's work as an activist in the controversy surrounding corporations selling baby formula as a substitute for breast milk in 'Third World' countries (in Ervin 2005: 151). This controversy flared up in the 1970s and 1980s, when Nestlé found its market share in Western nations diminishing. There were major protests when it tried to open new markets in countries where the lack of clean water and facilities for boiling water sufficiently, as well as a lack of funds, made it a significant health risk (quite apart from the fact that the formula had been rejected in wealthier countries because of growing understandings about the better immunizing effects of breast milk). Penny Van Esterik became a passionate advocate against this exploitation of poorer communities, and she argues that there are compelling reasons to participate in advocacy causes. The breast-or-bottle controversy that she dealt with had a lot at stake: children's health and levels of infant mortality; the relationships between mother and child; processes of social change; people's capacities to adapt; and a critical issue concerned with the power of nation-states and international corporations: 'Scientific knowledge, as provided by anthropologists and others, is valuable for these battles. A series of expert testimonies can be provided, sometimes for court cases, sometimes as part of public relations campaigns through the media or as preparation for public debates' (Ervin 2005: 153).

Controversies about the selling of unsuitable or substandard goods in poorer countries have grown since the Nestlé issue, as have concerns about the commercial exploitation of disempowered groups. In the last decade, there has been growing disquiet about the social and ecological costs of globalization,[3] and anthropologists are interested in it both as analysts of social movements,[4] and as advocates for groups whose cultural and economic security is threatened by changes being wrought at a global level. Many work in the legal arena, bridging the gaps between indigenous or specifically cultural ideas about law and moral order, and the national and international legal frameworks that often override these (see Rodríguez-Piñero 2005, Toussaint 2004).

Counter-development movements are emerging as people resist the appropriation of their resources, and direct protests against globalization are springing up all around the world. As well as turning an anthropological eye on multinational corporations, June Nash (1979) has studied the rise of these resistance movements, occurring most particularly in places that have been marginalized in the reorganization of global capital.

> These are the areas that are becoming the center of dissent in day-to-day protests against the dislocations and environmental contamination caused by global enterprises. At the same time that populations are forced to migrate in search of work, global enterprises are going underground, buried in the underworld of dotcoms and obliterating their tracks with multiple conglomorate identities... Anthropologists are by inclination and profession predisposed to study the peripheral phenomena of everyday life everywhere in the world, and especially in marginal areas. Our hidden bias for Third World perspectives is becoming more explicit as the failure of modernity projects becomes explicit. With the widening gap between rich and poor – countries, regions, and people ... many of these formerly marginalized areas have become frontiers of the latest capitalist advances, where we find indigenous people engaged in a fight for their territories and their way of life. (Nash 2005: 177)

Nash focuses on people 'whose cultivated historical memories and everyday lived practices enable them to attest to ways of life that are alternatives to capitalism'.

> Many continue to practice collective lifeways and to relate to cosmic powers in ways envisioned by their ancestors. These normative practices are not the result of passivity, but rather the product of practiced resistance by those who have experienced the trauma of conquest and colonization. (Nash 2005: 178)

LAND RIGHTS

Globalization is, of course, merely the latest development in a long process of expansion by industrialized societies, which resulted in the colonization of many parts of the world in the 18th and 19th centuries. There was widespread appropriation of land owned by indigenous or less powerful groups, and this appropriation continues in the contemporary world with what many regard as 'economic colonialism'. So, as well as fighting to retain their rights to water and other resources, many groups are now battling to reclaim their land. Their hope is to regain the right to share in its management and use, or at the least to be compensated for its loss. The result is a number of bitter conflicts over land and water rights in which, once again, different cultural perspectives are a critical factor (see Trigger and Griffiths 2003. Toussaint 2004). It is therefore unsurprising that this has become a major area of activity in anthropology. As resources are sought in ever more remote areas of the globe, threatening the land and livelihoods of more and more communities, it is likely that there will be an increasing need for cultural translators who can mediate between groups in conflict, and for advocates who can assist less powerful groups in defining and defending their rights.

> Land is the key to the cultural and often even the physical survival of indigenous peoples... If forced off their land, tribal societies can be physically annihilated. They are in a sense cast adrift with no way to fend for themselves in an alien society – a common trend in the Americas as various nations seek to counteract spiraling international debts by ruthless exploitation of their hinterlands. In these circumstances indigenous populations come under immediate threat because of an inability to maintain their land holdings in the face of vastly more powerful settler populations that are apt to regard indigenous peoples' claim to land as inconclusive at best. (Maybury-Lewis 1985: 137–40)

In Canada, when a major hydroelectric scheme was proposed at James Bay:

> The anthropologists played various roles in aiding the Cree, such as training the people to conduct their own research into land use, the harvesting of results, possible impacts on trap lines, and so on. It was this sort of evidence that became crucial support for the Cree claim that the hydroelectric proposal to dam the northern rivers would have dire and irreparable consequences for their subsistence way of life... The Programme in the Anthropology of Development at McGill University provided a wide range of socio-impact studies of the consequences of the hydroelectric project. These allowed the Cree to prepare their case ... [and] resulted in measures such as the James Bay and Northern Quebec agreement, which set aside certain territories for the exclusive use of the Cree, reserved some twenty-two species of fish and game for the exclusive use of Cree people, and instituted a program for Native game wardens that enabled the Cree to monitor the effects of the white man's incursion into their hunting territories more effectively. (Hedican 1995: 155–6)

Also in Canada, Elizabeth Mackay (2005) looks at how non-indigenous groups resist the reclaiming of land by Native communities, and the difficult issues faced by contemporary settler societies who find several generations of investment in land challenged by recent claims. As David Trigger and Gareth Griffiths (2003) have shown, similar issues confront Australian landholders, most particularly since the Native Title Act of 1993 which (after 200 years of European settlement) acknowledged Aboriginal people's prior ownership of the land. In New Zealand too, although the original Treaty of Waitangi continues to offer some protection to indigenous ownership of land and resources, the control of land and water remains contentious, with particular angst emerging in recent years about the foreshore and seabed, and the ownership of the rivers.

RECONCILING LEGAL PLURALISM

Markus Weilenmann

Office for Conflict Research in Developing Countries, Rüschlikon, Switzerland

I run an independent consulting firm, the 'Office for Conflict Research in Developing Countries' and offer legal anthropological consulting services to development agencies or NGOs, who operate in Africa in the domains of social and legal politics.

The bureaucratic state powers of Africa govern several cultures and states. There are the pre-colonial orders left behind by societies of foragers; simple or complex chieftancies; sacred kingdoms and so on; and there is the bureaucratic state model, imported by the European colonial powers such as France, England, Germany and Belgium, aimed at administering indigenous cultures through Western law. These developments constitute a long-lasting discrepancy between the official state law and diverse socio-cultural ideas about justice.

The Consultancy Office analyses this conflict and suggests ways to mitigate the negative implications of legal pluralism. It has offered legal anthropological advice in Burundi (for Misereor, International Alert, the Center for Humanitarian Dialog and RCN Justice et Démocracie), in Cameroon, Ethiopia, Ghana, Ivory Coast, Malawi and Senegal (all for GTZ), in the Democratic Republic of Congo (GTZ, Misereor and the Evangelical Development Service) and in Rwanda (for the Swiss Development Cooperation). In addition, regular and systematic advice is required by programme officers of various organizations, for the training of staff members.

In many parts of the world aspirations to protect key habitat areas for conservation purposes are creating further pressure on indigenous ownership and use of land. Anthropologists have been central to efforts to persuade conservation organizations that what they fondly imagine as 'uninhabited wilderness' or 'pristine' areas have, in fact, been inhabited by indigenous peoples for millennia, and that they need to take on board the cultural and economic needs of these communities.

An example is provided by Marcus Colchester's work. He made use of his anthropological training in becoming the Director of the Forest Peoples Programme of the World Rainforest Movement and an Associate Editor of *The Ecologist* Magazine. He has helped to design international campaigns to draw attention to indigenous rights in Venezuela, and has received numerous awards for his scholarship and activism.

> There are currently some 100,000 officially recognized protected areas world-wide covering as much as 12 per cent of the land surface of the planet. The great majority of these areas are owned or claimed by indigenous peoples... The emergence of indigenous peoples as a social movement and as a category in international human rights law has contributed to conservation agencies re-thinking their approach... A new model of conservation can now be discerned based on a respect for the rights of indigenous peoples and other bearers of 'traditional knowledge'. (Colchester 2004: 20)

Indigenous communities are not the only groups to find their way of life threat-ened by major conservation schemes. Sometimes local farmers find that common land is seen as 'fair game' for the creation of national parks. For example, Tracey Heatherington (2005) has conducted research in rural Sardinia on the controversies surrounding the proposed creation of Gennargentu National Park. This required local communities to contribute large areas of communal land to the project, and when their protests about doing this were simply dismissed, she was able to help them to build a more powerful case by showing that their 'love for the commons' rested on key cultural precepts that made a defence of the commons, in essence, a defence of their traditional values.

PARTICIPATORY ACTION

Anthropologists have a key role in contributing to a better understanding about local forms of ownership and tenure, and people's relationships with places. This can be communicated in a variety of ways, many of which could be described as 'participatory action research' (PAR), which involves members of the community in a collaborative research process that enables them to achieve their own aims: 'Participatory Action Research (PAR) is a research strategy whereby the community under study defines the problem, analyzes it, and solves it. The people own the information and may contract the services of academic researchers to assist in this process' (Szala-Meneok and Lohfeld 2005: 52).

Such collaboration between local communities and anthropologists is becoming more common, and anthropological training increasingly provides access to the methods entailed. For example, medical anthropologist Patricia Hammer runs an ethnographic methods training centre in the Peruvian Andes, which emphasizes PAR methodologies, and enables students 'to engage in ongoing investigations in local agricultural communities' in relation to local issues around 'health, ecology, biodiversity and community organization' (Hammer 2008: 1).

Participatory action research is well suited to work on land and resource issues. For example, along with many anthropological colleagues in Australia, I have been involved in the compilation of evidence for land claims. The methods used in this context also have wider utility, as a way of recording important cultural knowledge. I have therefore spent much of my time with Aboriginal people in north Queensland doing 'cultural mapping',[5] which involves travelling with the elders around their 'country', much of which lies outside the reserve area held by the community, in neighbouring national park areas and cattle stations. Cultural mapping entails recording, in a variety of media, all of the information about each group's sacred sites and important historic places, and their traditional knowledge about the land and its resources. This collaboration has resulted in a detailed collection of cultural information, which is now archived in the community, and provides a key teaching resource for younger generations, as well as a body of evidence for indigenous claims to the land. These are ongoing, but in the meantime the community has been able to negotiate a joint management agreement with the Queensland Parks and Wildlife Service, and to substantiate their ownership claims sufficiently to persuade local graziers to co-sign Indigenous Land Use Agreements.

However, a fully successful land claim is a faint hope, at best, for most indigenous groups, and many have been displaced. Along with land appropriations, political conflicts, environmental degradation and other pressures have created many refugees and economic migrants, and such groups often need support, most particularly when they are forced to relocate to areas geographically and culturally distant from their own. There is often a useful role for anthropologists in providing advocacy and cultural translation for these communities. For example, Lance Rasbridge worked with Cambodian refugees in Dallas, as a 'refugee outreach anthropologist' for a health organization:

> My search for an applied position was in a large part a response to the profoundly emotional experience of conducting research with refugees ... the situation of refugees demands involvement ... I coordinated both the medical team and the refugee clients and their sponsors and caseworkers, occasionally protecting one from the other and often mediating between them. My role as a coordinator frequently centers on compromise: sensitizing the agencies, medical providers, and refugees to each others expectations and limitations... A common scenario involves sensitizing the medical community to non-Western medical beliefs and practices. (Rasbridge 1998: 28–9)

Jeffery MacDonald notes that there are approximately 20 million war refugees living in the United States. He worked with Iu-Mien people from Laos, who had fled to Oregon:

Like many refugee researchers, I soon became an applied anthropologist, first providing services for the Iu-Mien. Later, I took a position in a refugee resettlement social service agency, where I began to work with other Southeast Asian ethnic communities, providing direct client services and training, doing needs assessment research, and managing and designing culturally specific programs for Southeast Asian refugees... As my reputation has grown in the Southeast Asian community as an expert sympathetic to community needs... I have had to take on the roles of advocate for individuals and of community political activist. (Macdonald 2003: 309)

As these examples show, advocacy can take a variety of forms. At times it becomes very formal, for instance when anthropologists act as 'expert witnesses' in the legal arena. This happens regularly in land claims, where they conduct research, compile evidence, and present this to the land claim court or tribunal. It is also becoming a more frequent role in relation to refugee communities. Thus Stephanie Schwander-Sievers, who had conducted lengthy ethnographic research in Albania and Kosovo, found herself much in demand as a cultural translator and expert witness in legal cases involving asylum seekers – people seeking political refuge – from these areas:

In both types of cases, I was asked to explain various issues involving 'Albanian culture', either in a written report or, on some occasions, as an expert witness in court during trial... I was usually asked to comment on the risks involved if an asylum seeker were to be returned to his or her home country, and how socio-cultural issues at home would affect that risk... Regarding criminal cases I was often approached by police detectives during the criminal investigation process... I was usually asked to explain ... particular aspects of Albanian culture and how these would give cultural sense to a violent deed and help explain its motives... In legal procedures and in court, particularly in asylum cases, individuals from different cultures and legal background come into contact. Here the anthropologist both participates in, and observes, relations of power. (Schwander-Sievers 2006: 209–17)

ME AN EXPERT? ANTHROPOLOGY, THE LAW AND ASYLUM-SEEKERS

Marzia Balzani

Roehampton University London

I never set out to be of any use in the world and made sure that my first degree was completely non-vocational: Latin and French literature to be precise. I spent my time lost in seventeenth-century French drama, formulating imperfect subjunctives, journeying through nineteenth-century *bildungsromans* and perusing the poetry of the Augustan age. Then I stumbled — via the ancient Roman 'Lupercalia' (an odd wolverine ritual that even Cicero found perplexing) — across a discipline that studied the rituals of contemporary peoples. My next few years were sorted: I went off to study social anthropology.

From dead Latin to defunct Sanskrit was a short step, and the prospect of a few years in India 'doing fieldwork' was too good an opportunity to miss. I headed to the desert state of Rajasthan and hid out in dusty archives and palaces talking to old men about the former glories of the Raj. This was fieldwork on kingship, an institution that no longer legally exists in India, and so my study of the past in the present continued. Although focused on rescuing dust-laden manuscripts from the ravages of time and termites, I nonetheless encountered all the usual issues that plague the world. There was the mistreatment of women and children in the form of domestic violence, and even the occasional *sati* (the ritual sacrifice of widows on the funeral pyres of their husbands). And in a country where half the population lives below the poverty line, violence against the poor and untouchable, and the denial of human rights was, inevitably, part and parcel of everyday life.

On my return to the UK I found myself subjecting innocent anthropology students to the intricacies of the caste system, Hindu-Muslim violence, the glories of kinship charts and the wonders of patrilateral parallel-cousin marriage. My world was still mediated by text and the careful evaluation and interpretation of differing versions of the same reality.

Then, one day a colleague asked me to give a paper at a conference on violence against women in multicultural Britain. Despite protesting that I knew nothing worth repeating, I was persuaded to offer an anthropological perspective on domestic violence in British South Asian communities. After my presentation on 'honour crimes', a well-known professor came to talk to me, and my journey into legal anthropology and the writing of expert witness reports in asylum cases in the UK began.

In Britain refugees receive a very bad press. If the newspapers are to be believed all crime, evil and immorality (and no doubt global warming too) stem from this numerically rather small group; the British never commit any evil acts, and if we were to rid ourselves of these 'money-grubbing, welfare-scrounging foreigners', the country would become an idyllic utopia. My work with refugees, however, leads me to think of most asylum seekers as unfortunate people who have managed to survive some appalling experiences.

When individuals seek refuge in Britain they are interviewed, and have to provide evidence to justify their requests to remain here. This evidence has to show that they have been persecuted, and also why they would risk further persecution if were forced to return to their country of origin. Many asylum claims are rejected, and a 'Letter of Refusal' from the Home Office explains why. Asylum seekers can appeal against the decision, and solicitors acting on their behalf ask experts to prepare reports explaining to the Asylum Immigration Tribunals why a case should be reconsidered.

Anthropologists are consulted when it seems that a cultural explanation might be of use. For example, if a woman is widowed and has reason to fear for her life in Pakistan, she might seek leave to remain in the United Kingdom with her naturalized British brother. This was the situation in one of the first legal expert reports I produced, for a woman who had witnessed a serious crime and was at risk from the family of those convicted. Not only was the strong documentary evidence of persecution rejected as 'not accepted' — the Home Office also considered that the 'right to family life' did not mean that adult siblings should be allowed to join each other. It was held that the kinship bond between an adult sister and brother was not a primary one, and that the widow in question should therefore return to Pakistan. If her life was in danger in her own home, then she should simply move to a different city. After all Pakistan is a big country.

My report showed how, from an early age, brothers and sisters in Pakistan are raised to behave in culturally prescribed ways, with the understanding that as they get older the sister will not bring dishonour to the brother, and the brother will undertake to help his sister in later life. This is a close bond, much more pronounced than in the UK. I was able to demonstrate that women in Pakistan do not usually live alone, and that those compelled to do so are vulnerable to exploitation and harm. Armed with cultural knowledge, my report set out why, in this particular case, it was not safe for this woman to return to her home.

Other cases I have worked on include those of persecuted religious minorities such as Christians and Ahmadis in Pakistan, and Muslim women who have married Hindu men in India. Some require knowledge of customary practices, particularly where the violence is gender-based. The Home Office may say that women can return to their country of origin and go to crisis centres, but the reality is that many are killed long before they can ever get to these, and even the centres may not protect them from further abuse. Further, some legal systems punish as a crime behaviour that in the UK would be considered only a moral failing. For example, a married woman who commits adultery in Britain may be considered foolish, may annoy her husband, or may find that her behaviour generates gossip. In Pakistan, however, such a lapse is not simply a private matter: it is a crime that can land a woman in prison and end with a potential death sentence. In such cases, my knowledge of the legal system can make this risk clear to an asylum judge. Then all I can do is to hope that the judge makes the right decision.

One thing I must never do as an 'expert' is to say if I think a case is true or not. All I am expected to do is to assess the plausibility of any particular asylum claim in the context of my knowledge of the country and the position of the individual making the asylum claim. The judges are expected to decide on the truth of the case. My work is to produce an account, a narrative of events, and to interpret these in the light of what I know as an anthropologist. This is where my earlier years of translation, novel reading, and sorting through archives of overlapping but never quite matching accounts of events, has finally turned me into: someone who is, from time to time, of use to others.

Advocacy is thus an expanding part of anthropological activity, which draws directly upon the discipline's strengths: in seeking a deep understanding of other cultural realities; in translating this between groups, and in ensuring that research is underpinned by ethical considerations and a concern for social justice. In the contemporary discipline it is plain that there is a continuing role for 'the scholar as activist', and as the issues change and develop, so too does this role (see Rylko-Bauer *et al.* 2006).

2 ANTHROPOLOGY AND AID

CROSSING BOUNDARIES

The in-depth knowledge about particular groups and societies that ethnographic research provides means that anthropologists are potentially very useful advisers for international organizations, whose work crosses cultural as well as national boundaries. For example, there is growing involvement of anthropologists in government agencies: in ministries of foreign affairs, diplomatic services, and in organizations such as UNESCO or the World Health Organisation. There is especially a need for the skills and insights of anthropology in the governmental and non-governmental organizations (NGOs) that try to assist people suffering from famine, poverty or ill-health, or from human rights abuses, conflicts or persecution. In the latter areas it is sometimes difficult to discern a dividing line between work that might be described as advocacy, and that which is more directly focused on providing aid and assistance.

In areas concerned with food and water provision, or in the alleviation of poverty, there are frequent overlaps between the provision of aid and the encouragement of

development. As the next chapter shows, they share many common issues. However, there is a fundamental difference between 'helping people in trouble' and 'changing the way that they live'. This chapter therefore focuses on humanitarian activities that simply aim to help when things go wrong.

There are many governmental and non-governmental agencies involved in aid: the latter often receive government funding, and the former increasingly contract work out to independent or semi-independent agencies. However, although most governments remain involved in the provision of aid to some extent, in the last few decades there has been a rapid proliferation of non-governmental aid organizations, not just internationally, but also at national, regional and local levels. In many instances these have taken up tasks that were formerly the direct responsibility of governments, creating a set of alternative institutional arrangements.

> There is already a whole NGO culture in the world, with its characteristic symbolism ... behavioural patterns ... and a special type of leadership ... NGOs develop clustered networks within which there are hierarchies and competition, especially for sources of funding. The best known among the biggest global NGO networks are social volunteer, child protectionist, human rights, ethno-cultural and peacemaking ones, although every country and every region has its particularities. (Tishkov 2005: 11)

AID AND AMBIGUITY

The large-scale shift from government agencies to NGOs represents a major social change, which is in itself of interest to anthropologists, raising many questions about whether these new institutions assist or inhibit effective governance and democracy. Some analysts have argued that the sharp increase in the number and scale of NGO organizations is an outcome of people's disillusionment with formal governance and bureaucracy, and an attempt to return democratic power to citizens.

> Nongovernmental organisations are now considered heavyweight actors in the global political arena, as well as in many local and national ones. This reputation has arrived at a time when professional political actors, such as parties and governments, have fallen into disrepute. NGOs are valued because they are viewed as legitimate representatives of civil society ... in a wide variety of issues. (Acosta 2004: 1)

Other anthropologists observe that NGOs are unelected, sometimes circumventing – and thus potentially undermining – democratic processes, empowering elites, or allowing governments to abdicate responsibilities for issues that have traditionally fallen squarely within their remit. Claus Leggewie (2003) has commented that although social movements can provide useful inputs to mainstream politics, their lack of a democratic mandate raises questions about their legitimacy, even when some actively promote democracy, and William De Mars (2005), describing them as 'wild cards', notes that they change the whole context in which governance happens.

Every situation is different. For example, Celayne Shrestha's research shows that there were only 250 NGOs in Nepal in 1989, but then, after a more democratic government was instituted in 1996, NGO numbers jumped to 5,978 within a year, as groups saw an opportunity to break with a state that had long been seen as corrupt and self-serving: 'For the intelligentsia, as well as many frontline NGO workers, NGOs offered an opportunity to break with "corrupt", personalistic modes of appointment and promotion and access to services' (Shrestha 2006: 195).

But Valery Tishkov, whose work is concerned with NGOs in post-Soviet Russia, warns that NGOs cannot be assumed to be an unambiguous reflection of democratic aspirations: 'Some pursue hopelessly separatist agendas. Others perform foreign policy functions a state finds inconvenient to accomplish directly. Others install a "benevolent colonialism" complete with local westernized bourgeoisies' (Tishkov 2005: 1).

As he points out: whatever the agenda of an NGO or its impacts on the people involved, being unelected: 'a voluntary organisation is practically impossible to abolish' (Tishkov 2005: 6). Steve Sampson, who has analysed the recent activities of Western NGOs in the Balkans, is similarly dubious about their effects, suggesting that in this instance they created a new kind of 'project elite' that led to a rejection of Western aid, stirring up local nationalists and weakening the post-Yugoslav states (Sampson 2003).

So there are many complex questions about the aims of international aid organizations: what are their effects on the functions of government? Who actually benefits from their efforts? What are the social and cultural costs of aid-based relationships? What political and ideological values are being promulgated in the process? By addressing these 'under-the-surface' questions, anthropologists have sought to look beyond comfortable everyday assumptions about aid, and to make deeper analyses of relationships between NGOs and the recipients of their efforts. There are often major disparities in power in these relationships, and part of the task of anthropologists and other social scientists is to reveal these dynamics. Thus Alnoor Ebrahim's research focuses on the way that power relations are maintained through public discourses:

> A discourse is a specific and historically produced way of looking at the world
> and is embedded within wider relations of power – power that is manifest, for

example, in the scientific 'expertise' of development economists, professionals, and expatriates that serve as advisers, funders and consultants to Southern Governments and NGOs. (Ebrahim 2003: 13–14)

Whether anthropologists choose to work directly with groups, or to seek funding from the (relative)[1] freedom of a university post, they still have to deal with a slightly tricky reality: that their work is also reflexive and thus potentially critical of their host/funding organization and its activities. Focusing their analytic skills on the dynamics of interactions between groups, anthropologists have therefore tended to have a cautious relationship with government agencies and NGOs alike. In essence, they hope to retain sufficient independence that they can balance a desire to put their skills to good use in helping people with an honest appraisal of the complex political and economic realities of aid/development relationships. Clearly this is an area in which some diplomatic skills are helpful, and of course some organizations welcome and recognize the benefit of reflexive feedback. There is also considerable scope for researchers to define their own roles and activities in projects:

> Not all development projects are 'bad', and … there is some room for applied anthropologists to determine the role they play within them… The applied anthropologist can become one of the few avenues through which poor rural people have their needs and perceptions communicated to the wealthy and powerful designing and implementing projects, both international and national… I do not deny the politics of representation embedded in the development process, nor that by working on a project I am placed within this specific field of power relations. However, some development projects benefit local people regardless of how flawed the epistemological ground from which they have grown. (Grace 1999: 125)

Jocelyn Grace's experience as a consultant in Indonesia showed her that the recipients of aid are rarely passive subjects, and often have considerable agency in directing the process: 'Women in rural Indonesia want nearby and clean water supplies, and do not want their babies to die within a week of being born, or their children to suffer polio or Hepatitis B. They take what they want from such projects, and ignore or reject what they do not want' (Grace 1999: 127–8).

These examples suggest two major roles for anthropologists in relation to international and national governmental and non-governmental aid agencies. One is to 'step back a bit' and examine the social, economic and political realities of the interactions between agencies and the recipients of aid; and the other is to give more direct assistance to organizations that they feel are genuinely trying to help people in need.

ANTHROPOLOGY SHOULD BE APPLIED

Mary-Ellen Chatwin

Minority Community Advisor, USDA

I have applied training in the anthropology of food to research the eating habits of students at a polytechnic university in Switzerland: this was to help the local health office to ensure that students have access to a better diet. I also carried out a study on women and how they try to get back to work after stopping, for the City of Lausanne's Employment office. I have studied organizations for the Institute for Life and Peace (in Sweden), examining their effectiveness in programming for returning displaced persons after conflict. I became involved in this kind of work when I happened to be in the Caucasus during the armed conflicts. Then the Secours Populaire Francais (a French aid organization) asked me to head their food distribution program. That is how I started 'hands-on' development work.

Anthropological input is often appreciated by local populations and communities, as they immediately realize that a 'special kind of understanding' is there, which is not the case in the usual development style of interventions. Anthropology should be applied at a national level to all development programmes that intend to make changes in the lives of countries in need (such as disaster relief, poverty reduction, and programmes for vulnerable communities and the elderly).

NGO-GRAPHY

Exploring the interactions between aid agencies and recipients has a number of potentially useful outcomes. Greater transparency leads to better informed decision making and illuminates the different perspectives of the parties involved, assisting communication between them. Researchers in the Department of Anthropology at Durham University, for example, have a collective research project concerned with NGOs in Ghana and India. Their work explores the different perspectives of the state, the NGOs and the donors, and looks at the impact of their relationships on the poverty eradication programmes that have become the major focus on NGO activity in those areas (Alikhan *et al.* 2007).

In Ifugao, in the Philippines, anthropologist Lynn Kwiatkowski considers similar questions at an international level, examining the interactions between transnational organizations and local communities:

> Some of these global institutions have financially supported, and in some cases directed, local non-governmental organizations (NGOs) that seek to improve the conditions of everyday life in Philippine communities... I discuss some of the cultural issues, political contestations, and contradictions that can arise

for progressive NGOs working in 'cultural communities', or among indigenous cultural groups, as the NGOs operate within a broader context of national and international political and economic processes. (Kwiatkowski 2005: 1)

Sometimes – as well as looking at the bigger picture – an anthropological perspective on the internal dynamics of institutions is useful and anthropologists have begun to do more 'close-up' ethnographic work within NGO organizations. Thus Laëtitia Atlani-Duault spent ten years amongst aid workers, studying them and their state and non-state partners, as they attempted to 'export democracy' to post-soviet countries of Central Asia and the Caucasus. This close ethnographic engagement not only gave her an understanding of the realities of their lives, but also enabled her to step back and consider the wider political implications of their activities (Atlani-Dualt 2007).

This kind of work draws on a well established area of anthropology concerned with organizational analysis, initiated by Elton Mayo's work on 'human relations' in industry in the 1920s (in Roethlisberger and Dickson 1939), Sue Wright's early research on the *Anthropology of Organisations* (Wright 1994) and Mary Douglas's work on *How Institutions Think* (Douglas 1987). Many anthropologists are involved in this kind of work today. Alberto Corsin-Jiménez, for example, has long-term research interests in the anthropology of organizations, in particular the 'moral projects' of capitalist organizations and the way that ethical and moral issues are negotiated in purportedly ethically conscious institutions. As he says, 'the institutionalisation of power has been a central concern of the anthropology of organisations from its earliest days' (Corsin-Jiménez 2007: xiii).

This kind of approach is well suited to the NGO-graphy being undertaken at the International NGO Training and Research Centre (INTRAC). Under INTRAC's aegis, Celayne Shrestha has investigated the everyday 'informal dimensions' of NGO life in Nepal; Janet Townsend has considered the different discourses encountered in state–NGO relationships in south India; and, in the same region, James Staples has used ethnographic examples to show

… how an NGO's official intentions are regularly subverted – wilfully or otherwise – by the competing political and personal interests of various stakeholders, often with unpredictable consequences. Although this disparity between official intention and what actually happens is often blamed for the NGOs' failures … it is only the continued miscommunication between stakeholders – and the co-existence of multiple ideas about what the NGO is for – that allows the organisation to function at all. (INTRAC 2007: 1)

Charlotte Hursey points out that there is still comparatively little analysis of NGOs and a real need for this kind of work: 'Although ethnographic approaches have been applied to the study of the management and structures of private and public organisations, there are still comparatively few detailed accounts of the internal lives of non-governmental and civil society organisations, especially at the local level' (in INTRAC 2007: 3).

However, this is changing rapidly: 'In recent years the subfield of political anthropology, NGO-graphy (i.e., the ethnography of NGOs), has dramatically expanded as anthropologists have begun to examine the work of NGOs' (Iskanian in INTRAC 2007: 3–4).

ASSISTING AID

Many anthropologists are keen to assist aid agencies directly, and their professional associations have often encouraged their members to make use of their skills in this way. Some years ago the Royal Anthropological Institute created the Lucy Mair Medal of Applied Anthropology, which recognizes excellence in using anthropology for 'the relief of poverty or distress, or for the active recognition of human dignity'. An obvious area of application is concerned with the provision of food and medical aid in times of famine or other forms of disruption (such as earthquakes and tsunamis). Anthropologists have sometimes taken the initiative in offering their skills in this regard. For example, in 1984, the American Association of Anthropologists (AAA) set up a Task Force on African Hunger, Famine and Food Security:

> The premise behind providing rosters of anthropologists knowledgeable about Africa and hunger problems, and symposia and publications on their ideas and methods, is that anthropologists offer unique perspectives and capabilities that might improve performance of intergovernment (IGO) and nongovernment organizations (NGOs) that monitor and respond to hunger problems. (Messer 1996: 241)

Even – perhaps especially – in times of famine, a systemic view is useful, and anthropologists think carefully about how food is managed within societies and how this can be assisted and optimized.

> Food systems research addresses potentially all aspects of food procurement and consumption strategies... It is useful for the community and donors offering and delivering food aid programs, or development programs more generally, to have better understandings of the objectives of the aid community. (Messer 1996: 243, 255)

As a member of the AAA Task Force, Art Hansen has stressed the need for research that engages with local complexities:

Our original mandate was to work out better ways to utilize anthropologists and anthropological knowledge to help Africa and Africans during that major famine. Our concern at the time was that the planners and staff of assistance programs often had little appreciation or knowledge of how Africans helped themselves. That ignorance could result in assistance being less effective or, at worst, becoming itself a secondary disaster. (Hansen 2002: 263, 273)

Hansen's work highlights some of the dangers of short-term introduced solutions, and the reality that even apparently 'local' communities and economies are always subject to external pressures. Working with villagers in north-eastern Zambia, he observed that their intense cultivation of cassava had enabled them to absorb a rapid population increase with an influx of refugees, but then an invasion of the cassava mealybug destroyed the cassava and triggered a famine. Some major changes in agriculture and technology followed, and the community became increasingly reliant on maize and the expensive fertilizers needed to grow it. This reliance led to further famine: 'Sustainability and famine are complex conditions, created and influenced by political, economic and ecological factors. Apparent sustainability can be fragile, and locally self-sufficient sustainability is a fragile illusion. Localities are not isolated and self-sufficient; they are incorporated and vulnerable' (Hansen 2002: 261–2).

DEALING WITH DISPLACEMENT

The loss of land – and thus livelihood – to other groups is only one cause of population displacement. Famines and floods can create large numbers of refugees, as can political conflicts, environmental degradation, urban expansion, economic pressures and large-scale infrastructural developments (such as dams). Where refugees arrive without resources – in refugee camps or in other countries – there is a need for humanitarian aid, which, like other forms of assistance, can be delivered most effectively when there is an understanding of the recipients' cultural beliefs and values.

It is also critical to appreciate the effects of displacement and migration. Michael Cernea defines eight basic problems that can arise when people are displaced: 'landlessness, joblessness, homelessness, marginalization, food insecurity, increased morbidity, loss of access to common property resources, and social disarticulation' (Cernea 2000: 19). Resettlement schemes can be very inadequate: for example, Satish Kedia and John Van Willigen (2005) observe that when dams were built on the Amazon, many communities located in its river valleys were left to fend for themselves further upriver and along the trans-Amazon highway, with consequent disease outbreaks (malaria and leishmaniasis) and the breakdown of formerly stable social communities.

An appreciation of the effects of displacement is particularly important when refugees or economic migrants move to countries very different from their own, and many anthropologists work with ethnic minorities located in societies far from their homelands.

For example, drawing on experience as an advisor to the Overseas Development Agency,[2] Katy Gardner (2002) has worked with Bengali elders in East London, exploring their experiences of migration to the UK, and the implications this has for their management of ageing and illness. Margaret Gibson (1988) looked at the experiences of the children of Sikh immigrants in an American high school, and Aihwa Ong has investigated the cultural changes taking place in diasporic Chinese communities around the world: 'Today, overseas Chinese are key players in the booming economies of the Asia Pacific region. In what ways have their border-crossing activities and mobility within the circuits of global capitalism altered their cultural values?' (Ong 2002: 173).

Migrant communities of a very different kind are the focus of Christopher Griffin's (2008) work. He first used his anthropological training in a post as the warden of Westway, a permanent encampment in west London, used by travellers and gypsies. Here, alongside his job as the caretaker of the site, he was able to conduct long-term ethnographic fieldwork, and to write extensively about the history of the gypsies, their lives as nomads, their narratives of migration, and their sometimes difficult experiences of race relations.[3]

UNDERSTANDING RACE AND RACISM

The cultural understandings provided by anthropology are particularly important in understanding issues around race and racism, and a number of practitioners work in agencies devoted to upholding human rights and encouraging cross-cultural tolerance. Ideas about 'race' are often implicit in 'ethnic' or 'religious' conflicts, and there is a widespread need for anthropological skills in resolving the extreme inter-group conflicts that occur across national, cultural, political and religious boundaries (see Wolfe and Yang 1996).

Conflict resolution depends heavily on understanding – and so tolerating – 'the other'. Jane Cowan, for example, works with Bulgarian minorities in Greece and the former Yugoslavia, where she looks at human rights issues, examining the way that international mechanisms such as the League of Nations supervise treaties and deal with minorities' claims for rights to difference and independence (Cowan 2000). She explores the sometimes tense interactions between civic organizations, revolutionaries, minority claimants, international bureaucrats, diplomats, NGOs and the media. Her work facilitates better communication and understanding between these parties, and thus assists in the resolution of conflicts.

In racial and other conflicts anthropologists have an important public role in challenging the essentializing stereotypes that perpetuate conflicts. Religious differences often provide a putative basis for conflicts, and anthropologists have gone to considerable lengths to make visible the more complex social, political and economic factors that sit under the surface of these. Jonathan Benthall (2002), for example, has focused on the politics of aid in the Muslim world, and the emergence of religious NGOs, studying the ideas and practices of charitable work in Muslim cultures, and the political and religious forces that shape it. Hastings Donnan (2002) has also considered how Islamic cultures are represented, as well as conducting extensive research on the long-running 'religious' conflicts in Ireland (Donnan and McFarlane 1989), and his ethnographic insights have been useful in presenting a more subtle view of inter-group relations.

In a contemporary world, ideas about 'terrorism' have come to the fore. Daniele Moretti (2006: 13) suggests that anthropologists can be useful in this area in several ways: by drawing on their fieldwork experience in areas or with groups that appear to be the source of terrorist activities;[4] by considering the ways that terrorism is represented in the political arena, and in the media; and by contributing to analyses of the causes and effects of terrorism. Just such an analysis has been undertaken by Mary Douglas and Gerald Mars (2007), whose collaborative research considers the factors that lead (or enable) dissident minorities to create political enclaves and generate terrorist activities.

Obviously, although there are various places in which terrorism occurs, the major focus in the last decade has been on Muslim cultural groups, both in Islamic regions and as minorities elsewhere. Anthropologists have been called upon to close the 'culture gap' by:

> (1) providing Western audiences with a nuanced picture of the complexity and flexibility of Islam and Muslim culture… (2) exposing the socio-economic and political processes that foster Islamic extremism and terrorism… and (3) demonstrating that Muslim and Western culture are not as radically different as some appear to believe and that either is just as capable of tolerance and extremism as the other. (Moretti 2006: 14)

Moretti does not comment on the potential for Muslim anthropologists to perform similar tasks, but clearly in an international discipline such as anthropology there is scope in all countries for researchers to offer more informed views of other societies. Moretti's own fieldwork has been conducted in Oceania, where many small nations receive US aid, and have expressed support for its 'war on terror'. However, each has its own perspective on the issues. In Papua New Guinea, for example:

> Reports on 'terrorism' and the 'war on terror' were followed and debated with concern. In these discussions, some claimed to be supportive of 'the terrorists', who they regarded as freedom fighters engaged in a just war of liberation. For many more, the Americans and their allies had no business invading Iraq… With a local history of colonialism which included over five decades of exploitation, land alienation and natural resource pillage at the hands of other Western powers, it was not that hard to see why many could sympathise with the Iraqis and Osama, who they saw as Iraq's foremost protector against the West.
>
> Yet, in spite of such apparently widely held sympathy for their struggle, 'the terrorists' were viewed with a degree of ambiguity and anxiety. (Moretti 2006: 14)

Birgit Bräuchler's research on Islamist groups in Indonesia is concerned with the way that fundamentalist ideas are disseminated and promoted through cyberspace:

> The Internet has become an important instrument for the information politics of radical Muslim groups… The Communication Forum of the Followers of the Sunnah and the Community of the Prophet (FKAWJ) … sent its fighters, the so-called Laskar Jihad or Jihad troop/fighters, to Ambon in April 2000 to help their Muslim brothers against the 'Christian attackers' in the Moluccan conflict – a conflict that was also extended into cyberspace by several actors… Through these strategies the cyber actors create an image and construct an identity that is congruent with their offline philosophy but extends its reach. (Bräuchler 2004: 267)

As these examples make plain, the resolution of conflicts around the world, and the alleviation of poverty and disease depends heavily on work that enables cross-cultural understanding. Sadly, there is much that needs to be done in this area, but those who undertake this kind of work can at least feel that what they do is worthwhile, and hope that it makes a difference.

3 ANTHROPOLOGY AND DEVELOPMENT

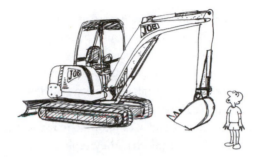

CRITIQUING DEVELOPMENT

The anthropology of development has much in common with the anthropology of aid. It often requires interdisciplinary collaborations, and almost invariably entails interactions between different cultural groups. A consequent need for cross-cultural translation has long made development a major area of interest for anthropologists. As with the provision of aid they are also wont to analyse and critique the process *of* development, as well as providing assistance *in* various parts of that process with international agencies, governments and the recipients of these organizations' developmental efforts. However, although there is a great deal of overlap between these areas, a key difference is that while the provision of aid is not necessarily intended to do more than restore a (presumably) faltering *status quo,* the fundamental principle of development is one of initiating change (see Olivier de Sardan 2005). So although – like aid – development is generally presented as dealing with a problem that needs solving, or a condition that needs to be cured, it is more accurately defined as 'a synonym for more or less planned social and economic change' (Hobart 1993: 1). 'Development has often been linked to, or equated with modernisation; that is the transformation of traditional societies into modern ones, characterised by advanced technology, material prosperity and political stability' (Hobart 1993: 5).

The idea of development therefore rests on an assumption that there are technological, material and political goals to which all societies should aspire, and that wealthier countries should assist others in attaining these. It is hard to fault this principle, on the face of it, particularly when many groups around the world are plainly struggling even to subsist, but there are some important questions to ask. Quite apart from the pragmatic reality that aspirational lifestyles that consume a lot of energy and resources are not sustainable in ecological terms, even for a minority of the world's people (and we have yet to address that problem successfully), there are more complex questions about the values being presented as 'ideals' and the social and cultural costs of transforming 'traditional' ways of life into a more homogenous 'modern' vision reliant on constant economic growth and industrial modes of production.

'Development' is a largely European and American idea which emerged in the post-war era (Arce and Long 1999: 5). Attitudes and policy were based on assumptions about the superiority of nations that had successfully modernized themselves, and 'backward' or 'underdeveloped' countries were described as 'the Third World', representing an earlier stage of technological inferiority and ignorance. Development would help them to 'catch up'. The implication was that local traditions were a bar to 'progress' and should be discarded, and a 'developmentalist' relationship was created with Third World countries, requiring that they replicate European and American models (Escobar 1995).

Because anthropologists work with a variety of cultural groups, they are keenly aware that there are many alternatives to this dominant model, and – as social analysts – they also observe that there are some highly differential power relationships involved in development and, at times, some rather less than altruistic aims.

> Because the prevailing rhetoric is of altruistic concern for the less fortunate, it is useful to remember that development is big business... In one form or another, development is very profitable not just to the western industries involved, but to those parts of governments which receive aid, let alone to development agencies. And the giving of development aid and the extension of markets for manufactured products is more than balanced by the processes ... by which the countries to be developed make up the major source of cheap raw materials and labour. Less obviously, the idea of 'underdevelopment' itself, and the means to alleviate the perceived problem, are formulated in the dominant powers' account of how the world is. (Hobart 1993: 2)

An important aspect of the anthropology *of* development is to:

> do what Laura Nader recommended more than a decade ago, which is to 'study up' and look at larger organizations, processes and policies... Development anthropologists are also challenged to learn the languages of policymakers and macroeconomists, whose economic reform and investment programs are having far-reaching impacts in many areas of the world where we work and study. (Little 2005: 53)

In the early days of anthropological involvement in development, it was more readily assumed that this work assisted an altruistic enterprise, although anthropologists such as David Pitt (1976) provided a 'bottom-up' perspective on what was then a very 'top-down' process. Jocelyn Grace, who has worked with government agencies in Australia and the United States, was an early commentator on the dilemma of participating in what has been described as 'a western imperialist enterprise' (in Escobar 1991: 659):

> A bank-teller recently asked me what I did at university. When I explained that I did research on maternal and infant health in rural Indonesia, she asked: 'Is it any use?'... This is one of the attractions of working in development, as it seems to offer an opportunity to put knowledge to use in effecting some positive change in the 'real' world. However, this is a rosy and naive view of development, and of the anthropologist's role within it. (Grace 1999: 124)

With the rise of more market-driven ideologies, a more analytic view of the development process is emerging and an important part of what anthropologists bring to the field of development – as they do to the area of aid and other fields – is a critical analysis about larger social and political process in which it takes place. This involves examining what is actually going on between the parties involved, deconstructing the rhetoric and the ways that groups are represented, observing what actually happens to resources, and making visible the underlying dynamics. This critique has been immensely useful in engendering a much greater awareness of the complex issues in this area (see Nolan 2002, Mosse 2005, Mosse and Lewis 2005).

DEVELOPING AN UNDERSTANDING

Yongjun Zhao

Adviser, DFID China

I work as the 'institutional and sustainable livelihoods adviser' for the UK Department for International Development (DFID) in Beijing, China. My job is to provide high-quality advice on institutional development and governance issues for key programmes in rural development, rural water supply and sanitation, water resources management, fiscal reform and 'China in transition' policies.

Having trained in anthropology and environmental studies I make use of anthropological theory and practice in my work. Anthropological critiques of development and governance in the development industry have been valuable in enabling my understanding of how institutions and governance can be of crucial importance to the achievement of donor objectives. As an adviser, I try to make an anthropological critique of government policy and development practice, and so assist in building effective partnerships between government, donor agencies, civil society and other organizations.

SUPPORTING A GRASSROOTS APPROACH

Ruth Dearnley

ACTSA

My MA was very specifically focused around a critique of the 'development' industry and the policies associated with it. I was interested in the structural changes that could be made to the ways in which 'development' is approached. There seems to be a wealth of opportunities for anthropology graduates within the NGO/development field. In my opinion, these industries would benefit from a more anthropological perspective: it is easy for ideals to get swept aside in order to benefit organizational/bureaucratic aims. As only a recent graduate, I am still coming to terms with the idea of adjusting my anthropological ethics and principles to those of the workplace!

I recently took up an internship with a not-for-profit organization called ACTSA, which began as the first anti-apartheid movement. Since 1994, however, it has been focused on broader goals for southern Africa: issues such as democracy, wiping out world debt and engaging in free trade. Working closely on campaign coordination in this small organization, this position enables me to introduce an anthropological perspective that supports the grassroots approach that ACTSA delivers.

Anthropology provides the ability to think critically, analytically and objectively and to apply these attributes to everyday problem-solving within a professional environment. Moreover, an anthropological understanding enhances one's ability to act with diplomacy when working with people who have conflicting opinions or outlooks.

IN DEVELOPMENT

Anthropologists are also closely involved in development activities, and making the underlying realities visible is equally vital at a local level. Alberto Arce and Norman Long (1999: 2) suggest that there is 'a desperate need' for empirical, ethnographically informed research inputs, to articulate local realities and communicate these to development agencies. These inputs are critical at each stage: in creating appropriate designs for projects; in ensuring that they are carried out with an appreciation of local cultural beliefs and values; and in evaluating their progress and outcomes.

CULTURE AND DEVELOPMENT ACTIVITIES

Scarlett Epstein

PEGS (Practical Education and Education Support), Kingsway, England

I have been 'retired' now for 20 years, during which period I have worked continuously in the field of development anthropology, directing research projects on problems facing developing societies. My first project was a four-year 'cross-cultural study of population growth and rural poverty' and the second was an 'action-oriented study of the role of rural women in development'. I engaged Third World doctoral students in this research: 20 per cent of my students now hold professorships in their respective home countries; another 20 per cent work in health and education and 60 per cent are involved in development projects in Africa and Asia.

I have focused, as a consultant, on poverty alleviation and rural development in general and in particular on income-generation for some of the poorest women. Conducting micro-society studies in south India and in Papua New Guinea, I acquired an in-depth understanding of the interplay between culture and developmental activities. In my work I emphasize the important part culture plays in response to new development opportunities. My anthropological training has helped me to get economists, who usually base their planning on the 'rational economic man' model, to include cultural variables in their considerations, and this has helped to reduce the high failure rate of projects.

Ideally, anthropologists will be involved at each of these stages. Ted Green, for example, worked in development for many years (see Green 1986). This led to his involvement in the design for a project assisting women's self-help groups or 'zenzele',[1] in Swaziland (Green 1998). In earlier research he had shown that there was a positive correlation between these self-help groups and other development projects. USAID therefore decided to provide development training for *zenzele* group leaders, and asked him to help design the programme. After it had run for several years, Ted was asked to come back and evaluate its progress. His qualitative analysis, based on detailed ethnographic research in the area, was able to show the many – and often subtle – social and economic effects of the training programme, as well as contributing to wider theories about rural development and the political status of women.

IMPACTING GLOBAL PROGRAMMES AND POLICIES

Edward Green

Senior Research Scientist, Harvard Center for Population and Development Studies
In the late 1970s, I was struggling to gain a foothold in the academic world. There had been an over-production of Ph.D.s in fields like anthropology because people like me found ingenious ways to avoid the Vietnam war by lingering in graduate school. More than once during my two-year appointment at West Virginia University, a colleague suggested that I might find applying anthropology to the problems of developing countries more satisfying than cranking out scholarly articles on matrilineal kinship, the subject of my dissertation.

In 1980 I managed to land a three-year job as social scientist on a rural waterborne disease project in Swaziland. I quickly strayed beyond my mandate and began spending time with traditional healers (incorrectly labelled witchdoctors). Then another project needed someone to do a quick study of traditional healers as potential partners in public health ventures, such as the promotion of oral hydration therapy for children with diarrhoeal diseases. I was happy to accept this extra assignment, and so got onto a career track that lasted for about twenty years. We developed an approach that consisted of workshops for the *bi-directional* exchange of medical and healing knowledge (we avoided the term training) about a particular topic such as diarrhoeal disease, and later, contraception, STDs and AIDS. In addition to Swaziland, I initiated programs like this in South Africa, Mozambique, Nigeria and, for a briefer period, was consultant for such a program in Zambia.

A hypothesis that motivated our work was that public health efforts aimed at encouraging behavior change or the adoption of new technologies can and should take advantage of the prestige, credibility, authority, and widespread availability of traditional healers, especially in a country with an extremely weak health infrastructure. The idea was to make *allies* of indigenous healers, rather than ignore or confront them.

Research suggests that traditional healers see and treat many or most STD cases in Africa. Healers also sometimes use knives and razors in administering medicines, potentially facilitating the transmission of HIV. At least 80 per cent of Africans rely on traditional healers for treatment of all conditions, even if many also consult biomedically trained practitioners. In Mozambique, the proportion relying on traditional healers may be even higher. Preliminary census studies by our team suggested a ratio of roughly one traditional healer for every 200 people, while the physician/population ratio in Mozambique was about 1:50,000, with some 52 per cent of doctors concentrated in the capital city.

Once research provided a base of ethnomedical information, we identified common ground between Western medical and indigenous thinking with a view to building upon existing local beliefs and practices. Our assumption was that ethnomedical practices can (by Western public health measures) be considered either promotive of health, damaging to health, or of no direct health consequence but of cultural value. In simplest form, our strategy was to encourage practices that promote health, discourage those that damage health, and respect the remainder while not interfering with them.

Next, we developed a strategy for communication with traditional healers that embodied these elements. Our medically trained staff learned enough about indigenous health knowledge to develop educational strategies that went far beyond simply using local names for diseases; we also incorporated indigenous ideas, symbols, and prevailing practices to the extent that these were feasible.

I have documented my research in ethnomedicine and my applied work with African healers in several books as well as in journal articles, book chapters, and conference presentations. Most importantly, major donor organizations such the UN, the World Bank, USAID, and the WHO, have all come to believe in and support collaboration with traditional healers as a valid approach to achieve public health goals.

I often wish that I had stayed in this popular area of research and applied work, because in 2001, my career took a turn towards work that is *un*popular in the same environments. My research showed that having multiple and concurrent sexual partners drives sexually transmitted HIV epidemics, therefore this behavior should be targeted for change (alongside efforts to promote the use of condoms). Uganda has experienced the greatest decline of HIV infection of any country. Its home-grown prevention program was based largely on behavioral change, specifically on reduction in casual sex, although condoms and delay of sexual debut also played a role. Yet there was great resistance to accepting these simple facts on the part of AIDS experts. It is always tempting to think we can rely on technological fixes to complex behavioral problems that are rooted in diverse cultures. I spent 2001–2 working on a book entitled *Rethinking AIDS Prevention* and speaking out as much as possible (Green 2003). I teamed up with a Ugandan infectious disease specialist at Harvard, and he and I often presented together, including on *Voice of America* TV. I testified four times in Congress, I published op-eds in the *NY Times* and *Washington Post*, and I basically argued in whatever forum I could find that 'primary behaviour change' should be promoted, especially in generalized HIV epidemics.

In December 2003, I was invited to be part of an AIDS-related delegation to four African countries. My *Rethinking* book appeared the month before, and it led to spirited discussions and debates about what works in AIDS prevention. There now seems to be increasing acceptance that *both* behavior-based, primary prevention *and* technology-based risk-reduction interventions are needed.

CONNECTING MULTIPLE REALITIES

Like aid, development has often been imagined (and represented) as an active 'top-down' process of donors dispensing assistance to relatively passive disadvantaged groups, but although this points to the unequal power that often characterizes such relationships, both aid and development are better considered analytically as an interaction between groups. Anthropologists have long been aware that there are 'multiple realities' in development (Grillo and Stirrat 1997), and one of their major contributions has been to conduct ethnographic research that 'sets out explicitly to make connections between local people's understandings and practices and those of outside researchers and development workers' (Sillitoe 1998: 224).

PROMOTING MEANINGFUL PARTICIPATION IN DEVELOPMENT

Paul Sillitoe

Professor of Anthropology, University of Durham

I have worked as a consultant for bilateral and international agencies (DfID, FAO, UNESCO, GTZ) and international oil and mining companies. I have also had research grants to facilitate the incorporation of indigenous knowledge in development programmes (abbreviated to IK in the acronym-littered world of development). This has entailed working with development practitioners and natural resource scientists to inform their work with a local perspective.

Development projects are organized into stages: project identification; planning and preparation; appraisal of proposals; project implementation; monitoring; and final evaluation. Anthropology is well placed to contribute to each of these. Knowing regions and communities intimately through extended periods of research, anthropologists are well qualified to assist with project identification, and are likely to be able to engage local people meaningfully in the process. The success of projects depends on the real participation of the intended 'beneficiaries', but all too often projects are devised by agency experts with little local input. For instance, I recall a meeting with an IFAD team on a project identification mission for the whole of South Asia. They were visiting some half a dozen countries in a month, spending a day or so in each place. It was no way to identify potential projects, let alone involve people. Some use the derogatory term 'development tourists' for such consultants.

Anthropologists can also make valuable contributions to planning and preparation, and the appraisal of project proposals. They have the mindset to promote meaningful participation and not impose a pre-conceived model. The inclusion of anthropology in projects leads to an appreciation of local views and ensures that local voices are heard on their own terms. For example, during an irrigation engineering project in Bangladesh, it became evident that a finely tuned understanding of local land-holding rights and village power structures was necessary to plan a scheme that would be workable. It was not simply a case of engineering deep tube wells and canals, but also of coming up with a way of operating and maintaining the scheme that made sense locally. The importance of local consultation was starkly evident following the multi-billion dollar Flood Action Plan (FAP) programme in which dykes and canals were constructed. I recall a DfID Fisheries Advisor asking in amazement why local farmers had dug through a new embankment, breaching the expensively engineered flood protection arrangements: 'what possessed people to do such a thing?' It turned out that the embankments were not allowing the monsoon flood waters to drain away, and were preventing farmers from planting their next rice crop.

Anthropologists also work on project implementation, and this often involves managing other staff, including local participants. Here again anthropologists have a particular contribution, being familiar with other cultural ways of working and not expecting to impose a 'Western' regime. Anthropologists can also make useful contributions to the monitoring and evaluation of projects, asking questions that do not occur to others.

Most development practitioners and the natural scientists in this area are committed to tackling the poverty that blights many lives, and are sympathetic to our endeavours, realizing that in the past large sums have been wasted on initiatives that ignored local ideas. Nonetheless, they find anthropology puzzling: as one natural scientist colleague put it 'doing research with you is like jumping from an aeroplane without a parachute and hoping that things will work out on the way down.' We therefore have to work hard to make anthropology readily intelligible to others, so that they can see its contribution.

It is always challenging to integrate indigenous knowledge into the development process. We need to meet demands for development to be cost-effective and time-effective, generating anthropological insights that are readily intelligible to non-experts, while not downplaying the complexities. The uniqueness of indigenous knowledge — small-scale, culturally specific and geographically local — hampers its incorporation in development, impeding the formulation of generalisations that might inform wider policy and practice. We need principles that facilitate generalization without transferring ideas that may be inappropriate in other contexts, and my colleagues and I have tried to set out some methodologies that will assist this process (Sillitoe, Dixon and Barr 2005).

An interdisciplinary approach is central to IK research, combining the cultural empathy of social scientists with the technical know-how of other specialists. An integrated perspective requires learning from other disciplines, as well as from local people. There must be a genuine flow of ideas and information between all parties. For example it is increasingly realised that rainforests in Papua New Guinea are not 'pristine' environments but have been subject to human interference for millennia, so the idea of creating conservation areas from which people are excluded does not make ecological sense (even if it was practicable politically), as they have long been part of local ecosystems. To meet conservation interests it is therefore necessary for biologists to work closely with anthropologists to understand local forest use practices. Success depends on fostering consensus, joint ownership and open debate. It is necessary to promote a collaborative atmosphere in which neither scientific nor local interests feel threatened, all parties having a role in negotiations, and contributing vital skills and knowledge.

In working in the development field, it can be useful for anthropologists to specialize in fields such as health, demography, governance, natural resources, engineering and education. My own interests encompass natural resources management, appropriate technology, and development, with a particular focus on sustainability and changing social and political relations.

At first sight IK work may seem straightforward: we just have to ask local culture bearers about their views. But we soon encounter cross-cultural issues that challenge what we think we know. Knowledge is diffuse, and it is not homogenous; there is often little local consensus. Much information is transferred through practical experience, and people are unfamiliar with expressing all that they know in words. Knowledge may be passed between generations using alien idioms: symbols, myths, rites and so on. Translating it into foreign words and concepts may misconstrue other's views and actions. The dynamism of IK also presents difficulties: it cannot be documented once-and-for-all. We therefore need an iterative strategy, closely linking ongoing IK research with development interventions.

It can take several years (not months or weeks) to achieve meaningful insights into local knowledge and practices, and from this perspective to provide 'cultural translation' for development agencies. This is often problematic in contexts with politically driven short-term demands for quick results. And it is not just a question of the time it takes to learn language, cultural repertoire, social scenario and so on, but also the investment of time and energy needed to win the trust and confidence of local communities who frequently have good reason to be suspicious of foreigners and their intentions.

We cannot understand cultures by looking at individual parts of them in isolation: we have to consider the whole picture. For example, in oil field developments in Papua New Guinea, it would seem unlikely that religious beliefs could be an issue, but this is exactly what happened with people talking about the oil coming from the body of an enormous multi-headed subterranean snake that the oil drill had speared. The idea originated in their belief that spirits sometimes manifest themselves in the form of frightening snakes. They consequently became increasingly anxious at the cosmological implications of oil and gas developments and their potential to lead to disasters. Such views may seem bizarre to people in the petroleum industry, but they clearly need to be aware of them to understand the reactions and demands of the landowners whose agreement is necessary for production.

We also need to beware of accumulating ethnographic information not directly related to development issues, and of potentially disempowering people by representing their knowledge in ways beyond their control, maybe infringing their intellectual property rights. These are issues that anthropologists are trained to be aware of, and where they are well placed to make significant contributions to development endeavours. It is an exciting and challenging time to be involved in this area.

'Multiple realities' are formed, in part, by different bodies of knowledge, which are often highly localized and specific. They contain their own areas of expertise, which, as well as being integrally important to the cultural group concerned, can also be invaluable in creating successful outcomes to development projects. Local knowledges have much to offer in other areas too, for example in medicine and environmental conservation, and anthropologists have often been influential in ensuring their preservation and valorization. Darrell Posey spent many years recording the ethnobotany of indigenous groups in South America, and highlighting the relevance of this expertise for contemporary ecological management (Posey 2002);[2] Rajiv Sinha and Shweta Sinha (2001) have recorded local knowledge about therapeutic plants in India, and Michelle Hegmon and her colleagues provide accounts of Native American ethnobotany from prehistoric times to the present, pointing to some of its lessons in relation to current farming and conservation practices (Hegmon *et al.* 2005).

A key way of ensuring that local knowledges are brought to bear on development projects is through the participatory approaches that are integral to anthropological research.

> Today, many anthropological research methods are immensely popular in international development ... The Participatory Research Appraisal (PRA) movement, which hit international development in the 1980s and 1990s, and was even being adopted by mainstream organizations like the World Bank or USAID, draws its basic methodology from anthropology ... Participatory methods aim to involve the local population in an engaged, self-interested manner instead of making people an object of research in which the outcome is only of interest to scientists. (Rhoades 2005: 72)

Robert Rhoades (whom we met in Chapter 1, discussing advocacy) points to the efforts of agricultural anthropologists working at the International Potato Center. The Center has 5 main objectives: increasing potato production, protecting the environment, saving biodiversity, improving policies, and strengthening national research. Anthropologists have worked with the CIP's interdisciplinary research teams in all of these areas, and have had a critical role in bringing local perspectives into the equation.

> Anthropologists helped a team of post-harvest technology scientists generate a new system of storing potatoes that was subsequently adopted by thousands of farmers in over 20 countries. Serving the team as cultural brokers, the anthropologists demonstrated that the scientific preconceptions of farmer conditions were incorrect and then pointed to common ground upon which both scientist and farmer could communicate. (Rhoades 2005: 72–4)

The anthropologists succeeded in highlighting the farmers' real concerns and demonstrating the advantages of using methods of storage that, as well as being practical, fitted into local social and cultural traditions. By 'translating' the farmers' experience and demonstrating its utility, they were able to convince the scientific community that there were major gains to be made from more collaborative approaches. The CIP adapted its development policy to engage with local cultural realities, the interdisciplinary team developed new methods accordingly, and the model helped to establish the Participatory Research movement.

> Anthropology's advantage in this kind of research was in its comparative methodology and ability to analyze whole systems, not just component parts. Other scientists in the center, such as breeders or agronomists, had a very precise but reductionist view of their subject crop. The anthropologist, on the other hand, was interested in how the farmer system was adapted to the environment and the role of human culture in this adaptation. (Rhoades 2005: 75)

The anthropologists went on to gather information on potato production in 132 different countries, and the team's ethnographically informed model has since been applied to research on many other crops around the world.

As a central human activity, farming remains a major area of interest for development anthropologists. James Fairhead (1990, 1993) has focused on local knowledge in farming communities in Zaire; Elisabeth Croll and David Parkin (1992) brought together a number of researchers to consider the relationship between anthropology, the environment and development; Patrick Herman and Richard Kuper's (2003) work is concerned with the effects of international trade negotiations on farmers in Europe; and Miranda Irving's research focuses on the issues raised around farming and irrigation in Oman (see her autobiography in the concluding section). Farming is not merely an economic and practical activity though: it is also a way of life and, working with high country sheep farmers in New Zealand, Michele Dominy (2001) considers how, in a settler society, they construct their identity and attachment to the land.

Farming is a precarious way of life at the best of times and not all development projects are successful. Sometimes anthropologists are asked to find out why they failed: for example, in Lake Titicaca, on the high Andean border of Peru and Bolivia, Benjamin Orlove and Dominique LeVieil (1989) compared private fish canneries; state and private trout farms; and a trout cage project assisted by international NGOs. All were established to increase fish production and, over a period of 20 years, all of them failed. The ethnographic analysis pointed to a need to 'ground' development projects more carefully, suggesting that the failure was largely due to the lack of accountability of distant state bureaucrats, who were unable to control overfishing in the lake, or to provide regular professional assistance. In this case the NGOs involved were also able to establish projects without being accountable for the outcomes, reflecting what Carol Smith (1996: 41) calls 'the lack of popular responsibility held by development agents in much of the Third World'.

It is certainly a challenge to chart the linkages between efforts to provide developmental aid and the realities of what happens when it arrives; and to identify the factors that decide whether or not projects succeed. Janine Wedel spent a decade studying the impacts of Western aid to Eastern Europe following the collapse of communism, and she highlights the need to follow the process through:

> I followed the aid story from the policies, prescriptions, rhetoric and mode of organisation of the donors ... through to the recipients so dramatically affected by those policies ... I concluded that the way in which donors actually connected with recipients could play a pivotal role in aid outcomes. The individuals involved, the means by which the connections were established, and the circumstances in which they connected were of key importance. Yet this was precisely the element of this process that was so often overlooked ... Many people discussed the need for aid and the specific problems it would address ... Yet how aid is delivered, by whom and to whom, their goals, and the circumstances that surround these individuals and their activities, is critical. It determines what recipients actually get, how they respond to it, and whether aid succeeds or fails. (Wedel 2004: 14–15)

Many development projects involve the provision of loans to boost economic activity. This support has major potential to create not just economic change but also to rearrange social, cultural and political relationships. There are key questions: who is enriched or empowered by loan schemes? Who loses out? How do such schemes affect cultural beliefs, values and practices? Such questions have formed the focus of Raymond Ocasio's work with communities taking loans for urban sanitation in the Honduras (Ocasio *et al.* 1995). Conducting research in Bangladesh, Sidney Ruth Schuler and Syed Hashemi observe that in loan schemes, as in other development projects, there are some major issues around gender and equality. Their research looked at the relationship between women's participation in rural credit schemes, the empowering effects of self-employment on women's status and autonomy, and control over their own fertility: 'Participation in credit programs appears to empower women ... strengthening women's economic roles gives them more autonomy and more control over important decisions affecting them and their families, as well as contributing to their self-confidence, and their ability to plan for the future' (Schuler and Hashemi 2002: 278, 292).

Feminist approaches in anthropology have paid particular attention to gender relations, and have often been linked to aid and development activities hoping to assist women and children. For example, Soheir Sukkary-Stolba has worked in nineteen different countries in Africa, Asia and especially the Middle East, in projects designed to assist poor rural women, especially single mothers and widows. She has helped to design family planning training sessions for midwives, interviewed rural women about water issues, and collaborated in research investigating childhood diseases (in Gwynne 2003a: 123).

Health-related development, like other forms of development activity, benefits from a holistic approach. Thus Elliot Fratkin and Eric Roth (Fratkin and Roth 2005), in working with formerly more nomadic cattle herders in northern Kenya, considered the wide range of social, economic and health effects created by their recent settlement. Michael Trisolini, in his research in public hospitals in St Lucia (Trisolini *et al.* 1992), similarly located the research in its social context, and thus demonstrated the need for community involvement in health management. This research recalls a message well established by Demetri Shimkin's earlier work (in the 1960s), which focused on the role of community health workers in rural Mississippi, and pointed to a need for

> ...a thorough understanding of the social, economic, political, and health systems operative in a community... Any health behavior changes ... could only be made if culturally sensitive and appropriate models were employed... The social institutions of the extended family and the church were used as the settings in which modifications of high-risk health behaviors were to occur... By understanding the community, real changes in measurable health outcomes occurred. (Shimkin 1996: 287, 292)

Shimkin went on to work on health issues in Africa, and commented that:

> The pattern of foreign aid has been far from optimal. A major difficulty is that each donor is concerned with his or her own priorities and ways of doing business... Cooperation between foreign donors and between external and domestic projects is generally poor. In consequence, there is often little feedback, and the long-term improvement of health facilities and capacities is often slight... In this context the social and behavioral sciences are of exceptional importance. Their proper use is indispensable for sound epidemiology and the design of effective health services. (Shimkin 1996: 285–6)

CONSERVING CULTURAL DIVERSITY

An important external pressure on local communities is the growing worldwide support for wildlife and habitat conservation. While conservation efforts are undoubtedly vital for the maintenance of biodiversity, they have tended, sometimes, to neglect the needs of local people who may rely on access to the same land and economic use of its resources for their food and livelihood. Attempts to replace local modes of production with a transnational model combining conservation and the development of a tourism industry have led to major conflicts in some areas.

In addition to highlighting the issues of social justice that these conflicts raise, anthropologists have argued that cultural diversity is as important as biodiversity,

not just for the well-being of human populations, but also because it may be more effective in maintaining other species. They have shown that, in maintaining biodiversity, the low-key environmental management of small-scale societies can be as effective as – and sometimes more effective than – a mixture of 'national parks' and more intensive surrounding development. Peter Little provides an example, drawing on his research with Maasai herders in Kenya:

> I was invited by the Kenya Wildlife Services (KWS) to help establish a socioeconomic monitoring unit to look at project impacts and to gather ongoing data in a community-based conservation project.
>
> The role that pastoral livelihoods in East Africa play in shaping the savanna landscapes and their rich biodiversity cannot be understated. East Africa possesses a rich historical and archaeological record documenting the significant influences of pastoral land on savanna habitats and the wildlife herds that inhabit them... This evidence strongly suggests that the savanna ecosystems of East Africa, which support the richest variety and density of large mammals in the world, were shaped by human activity and were not the 'wilderness' areas so often considered by early explorers and naturalists...
>
> Current communities of herders, who played such important roles, are increasingly impoverished by the expansion of national parks and game reserves, as they have lost access to valuable rangelands and critical water points. At least 20 percent of critical Maasai grazing lands have been taken over by wildlife reserves and parks since the 1940s. (Little 2005: 48)

Fortunately, the KWS was headed by the well-known anthropologist, Richard Leakey, who pointed out that the Maasai pastoralists are 'par excellence conservationists ... if the Maasai had not been so tolerant, we wouldn't have any wildlife in the Maasai Mara today.'

The involvement of anthropologists in these debates has helped to persuade international conservation groups to think more carefully about the role of local

communities, and to work with them in trying to protect wildlife and wider ecosystems.

> Recent events in Kenya have resulted in some healthy – if not contradictory – rethinking of pastoral land use and its effects on savanna landscapes... Confronted with the prospects of large-scale subdivision and capital-intensive agriculture near some of Kenya's most important wildlife areas, international conservation groups and the government now embrace pastoral land use ... for its positive benefits to wildlife conservation. (Little 2005: 48–9)

Similar progress has been made in Australia, where conservation organizations are increasingly keen to work with Aboriginal people. With input from anthropologists such as Bob Layton, Uluru (Ayers Rock) and Kakadu National Park are now managed jointly by National Parks rangers and local indigenous communities (Layton 1989), and in Far North Queensland, where I have conducted research for many years, a local Aboriginal community established one of Australia's first river catchment management groups, bringing together different groups of water users and initiating more collaborative management in the Mitchell River watershed areas (Strang 2001a).

Conservation organizations and indigenous communities sometimes find themselves on the same side when confronted with large-scale infrastructural development schemes. Major dams and hydro-electric projects are among the most controversial of these, and as in other forms of development, an understanding of the different perspectives of the various groups involved is vital, as is some anticipation of the potential social impacts of such schemes, which often displace whole communities. These kinds of developments benefit from 'social impact analysis', which is a way of systematically considering the kinds of impacts that they will have on local groups (Goldman 2000). Thus in Canada, when a large hydro-electricity development was proposed in James Bay, a team of anthropologists conducted research with the Cree tribe:

The Programme in the Anthropology of Development at McGill University provided a wide range of socio-impact studies of the consequences of the hydroelectric project. These allowed the Cree to prepare their case so as to emphasize the threats to their subsistence base. This resulted in measures such as the James Bay and Northern Quebec agreement, which set aside certain territories for the exclusive use of the Cree, reserved some twenty-two species of fish and game for the exclusive use of Cree people, and instituted a program for Native game wardens that enabled the Cree to monitor the effects of the white man's incursion into their hunting territories more effectively. The Cree are also taking over outfitting operations in the region, and they jointly control decisions concerning sport-hunting quotas. The agreement established the right of the Cree to the yield of meat, and the Income Security Programme for Cree hunters and trappers proved an economic safety net that evens out fluctuations in the hunting yield. (Hedican 1995: 155–6)

But dam building around the world continues: Sanjeev Khagram (2004) and Ranjit Dwivedi (1999) have highlighted the social and cultural issues raised by the building of the controversial Narmada Dam in India, Jun Jing (1999) has written about the dispossession created by the Three Gorges Dam in China, and other ethnographers have noted the particularly disempowering effects that this displacement has had on rural women (Tan *et al.* 2001). My own recent work has been concerned with conflicts over dams and water resources in Australia (Strang 2009). With an intensive developmental agenda, competition for the control and use freshwater resources has become a major issue. 'The story of water is all too often a story of conflict and struggle between the forces of self-interest and opportunities associated with "progress" and the community-based values and needs of traditional ways of life' (Donahue and Johnston 1998: 3).

GLOBALIZATION

Clearly one of the major pressures for development is the process of globalization itself. In the new millennium, the global picture retains many of its previous wealth and power divides, but it is greatly complicated by new information-based technologies, rapid transport and communications, and flows of capital and commodities. Anthropologists have therefore also turned their analyses to considering how development activities function within these wider processes. As well as creating expanding markets and new demands for resources, globalization has required the formation of many new cross-cultural relationships: between transnational corporate networks and local communities; between large and small societies; and between materially rich and poor countries. In this intensifying global interaction, there is both a need for effective cross-cultural 'translation', and for a thoughtful analysis of its social and cultural effects.

Anthropologists such as Angela Cheater (1995) and Marc Edelman and Angelique Haugerud (2005) have tried to set out some new ways to analyse the linkages between local and global dynamics. More specifically, Akhil Gupta and Aradhana Sharma have considered how globalization changes ideas about the state, nationhood and identity. Studying call centres in India, and the issues created by the 'outsourcing' of jobs to countries with cheaper labour, they observe that:

> Outsourcing is seen as both a sign of state 'openness' modernity, and good macroeconomic liberalization by the defenders of transnational capitalisms, *and* as a charged symbol of decreasing state sovereignty and control by economic nationalists... As a symbol of economic globalization, call centers have come to occupy a central place in debates on the 'outsourcing' of jobs from the North. Corporations, and increasingly state bureaucracies in the North, are farming out customer service and processing-related jobs to the South as part of their cost-cutting measures... One of the most important fears fuelling the backlash against outsourcing is that high-end, white-collar workers in the North are now in danger of being displaced by cheaper labor in the South (and especially in the Indian subcontinent). Some of those who cheered the 'efficiency' of global competition in hastening the decline of the heavily unionized 'smokestack' industries in the North have now become economic nationalists, as they find themselves in danger of being displaced by the same capitalist forces. The emergent transnational economic order is transforming the relationship between citizenship, national identity and the state. (Gupta and Sharma 2006: 2, 4)

Transnational trade takes many forms, sometimes with widely dispersed effects. One of the world's fastest growing industries, for example, is international tourism. Bringing different cultural groups into contact and exerting a range of developmental pressures, this is an area of major interest to anthropologists. Thus James Carrier (2004) looks at how 'local' and 'global' understandings of the environment meet in debates about marine parks in Jamaica; Don Macleod (2004) charts the way that tourism in the Dominican Republic has led to the wholescale appropriation of the local environment and its resources; and Kenneth Macdonald's (2004) research on tourism in the mountains of Pakistan shows how a view of conservation as a form of 'alternative development' repositions local fauna as 'global property' and indigenous hunting as 'poaching', to be replaced by putatively more sustainable trophy hunting for wealthy foreigners.

However, tourism is a double-edged sword which can also assist local groups in maintaining a way of life: 'The cultural survival of indigenous groups ... and the survival of the environment and wildlife are closely interlinked and, according to

some, can result in new types of tourist activities (including ecotourism) that benefit local development' (Little 2005: 50).

In making wealthy societies more aware of the realities of others, international tourism has also assisted less advantaged groups in demanding 'Fair Trade'. Peter Luetchford's work examines the way that ethically motivated trade operates. He has conducted ethnographic research on the relationships between cooperatives of coffee producers and the various NGOs and other agencies in Costa Rica who negotiate with Fair Trade counterparts and commodity markets in the north.

> Although I have shown that as policy fair trade does not operate as envisaged, it is at least implementable. Fair trade opens up moral, economic, and political possibilities in development ... from ethnography we can begin to see how policies take shape in practice. (Luetchford 2005: 144)

There are other, more problematic aspects of globalized markets. For example, Nancy Scheper-Hughes was asked to assist an international Task Force looking at the issues raised by global traffic in human organs for transplants. She carried out ethnographic research in Brazil, South Africa and India,

> ...examining the ethical, social, and medical effects of the commercialization of human organs, and accusations of human rights abuses regarding the procurement and distribution of organs to supply a growing global market.
>
> [This involved] ... forays into alien and at times hostile and dangerous territory to explore the practice of tissue and organ harvesting and organ transplantation in the morgues, laboratories, prisons, hospitals, and discreet operating theaters where bodies, body parts, and technologies are exchanged across local, regional and national boundaries. Virtually every site of transplant surgery is in some

> sense part of a global network. At the same time, the social world of transplant
> surgery is small and personalistic; in its upper echelons it could almost be
> described as a face-to-face community. (Scheper-Hughes 2002: 270–1)

Investigations of a practice regarded by some as 'neo-cannibalism' raises many
ethical and social issues. Scheper-Hughes notes Veena Das's comment that 'a market
price on body parts – even a fair one – exploits the desperation of the poor, turning
their suffering into an opportunity' (in Scheper-Hughes 2002: 280) and reflects
that:

> The social scientists and human rights activists serving on the task force remain
> profoundly critical of bioethical arguments based on Euro-American notions
> of contract and individual choice. They are mindful of the social and economic
> contexts that make the choice to sell a kidney in an urban slum in Calcutta or
> in a Brazilian *favela* anything but a free and autonomous one. (Scheper-Hughes
> 2002: 280)

Globalization is an outcome of widespread economic growth and expansion.
Whether in the form of tourism or trade, it inevitably places greater pressure on
resources, and creates more competition for these. A major consequence has been a
general intensification in efforts to privatize and exploit, in particular, vital resources
such as water and land (Goldman 1998, Cohen 2002). This has had important social,
political and environmental implications in every cultural context, and has often led
to bitter contests between groups even in affluent Western nations: as demonstrated,
for example, by the widespread protests against Margaret Thatcher's 1989 water
privatization in the United Kingdom (Strang 2004), and current conflicts over water
allocations in Australia (Strang 2009).

While there are no easy solutions to these kinds of problems, anthropological
research can assist groups in communicating different perspectives, potentially defusing and enabling some resolution of conflicts. A key contribution lies in understanding the particular local context and why pressures on resources and conflicts
over ownership arise in the first place. For example, Matthew Gutmann looked at
local perspectives on the North American Free Trade Agreement (NAFTA), which
led to a popular uprising in Mexico:

> Thousands of Tzotzil, Tzeltal, Chol and other indigenous peoples made clear
> their very different interpretation and expectation for NAFTA: they launched
> an armed uprising in the southern Mexican state of Chiapas to denounce the
> Agreement and demand democracy, liberty, and justice for *indigenas* and all
> people in Mexico. (Gutmann 2006: 170)

In Central and South America there have been many conflicts about land and
resources. In the 1980s, attempts to privatize water in Mexico led to angry protests by

women in low-income urban areas, who organized mass rallies and street blockades. Vivienne Bennett's work looks at the political dynamics underlying these protests:

> Poor urban women are often the protagonists in these protests because infra-structure problems, especially inadequate water services, have an immediate impact on the difficulty of their housekeeping work. At the same time, women's needs are inadequately represented or addressed by formal political institutions such as political parties. As a result, protest has become the public voice of poor urban women... At least part of the objective of women's actions becomes the transformation of gender relations. (Bennett 1995: 108)

Violent protests also resulted from more recent attempts to privatize water in Bolivia. Robert Albro (2005) investigated the violent civil revolt that followed, exploring the relationship between regional and global activist networks. This work is part of an important and expanding body of anthropological research concerned with understanding the new transnational social movements, which are often the source of 'counter-development' – resistance to globalizing forces and imposed development schemes (see Hobart 1993, Arce and Long 1999).

'Counter-development' is evident at a local level too. James Fairhead and Melissa Leach's (1996) work shows how groups in Africa devise alternative narratives to challenge 'expert' knowledge, and Ralph Grillo and Andrew Stirrat (1997) similarly point to a need not only to articulate the multiple perspectives involved in development activities, but also to consider how groups resist the imposition of others' visions of desirable 'modernity'. Thus as members of interdisciplinary teams, or as individual researchers, anthropologists are closely involved in every aspect of development, working with communities and networks around the world as they, in various ways, welcome or resist social and economic changes and negotiate their relationships with others.

4 ANTHROPOLOGY AND THE ENVIRONMENT

'ENVIRONMENTAL' PROBLEMS

As environmental problems around the world become increasingly pressing, it is plain that although most of the challenges we face are framed terms of 'climate' or 'ecology', their causes are anthropogenic – they are caused by human activities. This points to an urgent need to understand 'why people do what they do' in relation to the environment. Why do societies develop economic practices that degrade land, over-use resources, and threaten the wellbeing of other species and indeed entire

ecosystems? Why don't they rein in population growth and resource use to sustainable levels? What enables some groups to have much smaller ecological footprints than others? These questions are not ecological: they are social and cultural, and involve particular beliefs, values and practices that lead to different ways of interacting with the material world.

WATERWAYS AND LIFEWAYS

Veronica Strang

Professor of Anthropology, University of Auckland

The question about 'why people do what they do' in relation to the environment is what brought me to anthropology in the first place. After working as a freelance writer for a number of years in the United Kingdom, South America, the Caribbean and Australia, I found myself in Canada, focusing mainly on environmental and health issues: acid rain, water pollution and so forth. All the emphasis was on the ecological problems: the prematurely autumnal forests; the 'elephant snot' algae in the lakes. No-one seemed to be asking what made people develop different environmental values and decide to conserve or exploit natural resources. Not long afterwards, I spent a year in the Australian outback, working with a stock team composed of Aboriginal and non-Aboriginal people. It was plain that although they were doing the same job in the same place, they had very different relationships with that environment, and very different values about how land and resources should be used and managed. How did that happen?

On returning to England, I thought — naively — that I might get an answer to that question by spending a year or two studying anthropology. I did get some idea, but the experience mainly served to make me realize that the question was much larger than I had imagined. Further study was clearly in order, and by then I was hooked anyway because, after a dozen years of travelling the world, living in other cultural spaces, I finally had a way of making sense of the things that I had observed. My doctoral research took me back to Queensland to compare different groups' relations to land along the Mitchell River, and it did make visible some of the factors which lead to the development of different environmental values (see Strang 1997). That work led to a couple of part-time jobs in Oxford, one teaching anthropology at the Pitt Rivers Museum (magic place — seize any opportunity to go there), and another at the University's Environmental Change Unit, with a research team looking into domestic energy use. My task there was to consider why people would (or wouldn't) make efforts to conserve energy, and to add this to the policy advice that the team was giving to the Minister of the Environment.

An opportunity to help start a new anthropology department tempted me to the University of Wales for a few years, where I returned to my earlier research interest in water (as one might well do in Wales). I persuaded a number of UK water companies to fund some research in Dorset, on the River Stour. As in Queensland, this involved interviewing the various groups of water users along the river, so that the ethnographic data could be considered alongside the ecological issues. But in this case I was more interested in the cultural meanings encoded in water. I chose the River Stour in order to work with an arts and environment group, *Common Ground*, who were composing music and poetry about the river with local community groups. Water has very powerful and emotive meanings. The research looked at how people interacted with it, why they wouldn't conserve it, and why (more than a decade after the water industry was privatized) they were still mad as hell about losing public ownership of it (see Strang 2004).

A year or two later I was back on the other side of the planet, with a Royal Anthropological Institute Fellowship in 'Urgent Anthropology'.[1] Returning to the Mitchell River, I did some more work with the Aboriginal community in Kowanyama, looking at the way they presented their relations to land in the political arena, and doing a lot of 'cultural mapping' with the elders, recording data about their sacred sites and 'story places'.

I had barely unpacked again in the United Kingdom when I accepted a university post in New Zealand. In theory, that is where I live now, although in the last few years I have spent a lot of time back in Queensland, investigating the wider social and cultural aspects of water issues along the Brisbane and Mitchell Rivers. With the harsh water shortages that Australia has been experiencing, there is increasing conflict over access to resources, so this research continues to keep me busy.

My ongoing 'water works' also led to an invitation to join the Scientific Advisory Committee for UNESCO's International Ecohydrology Programme. As its name suggests, this brings together researchers in ecology and hydrology from many different countries. However, until recently the group had paid little attention to the social and cultural aspects of human engagements with water. My task is to assist the programme in encompassing these dimensions. Being a tiny cog in the wheel of one of the world's largest NGOs is a new and intriguing experience.

With water resources coming under increasing pressure, most countries are introducing new systems for governing and managing water, and trying to find new technical solutions to water shortages. Often this is very 'top down', and my concern, as an environmental anthropologist, is to ensure that the views of the people most affected by these changes are clearly represented, and that reforms are developed with an understanding of the social and cultural beliefs and values that direct water use and management at a local level.

There are many other strands of research that I would like to investigate further: for example thinking about the design of water features in gardens and public parks; the use of horses in stock work and the human-animal relations that this entails; concepts of ownership and property in relation to water. And ... and ... and... And that's the trouble: inside or outside the academe, anthropology can take you anywhere, into whatever area of research seizes your imagination and enables you to feel that you are doing something worthwhile.

'Environmental anthropology' has therefore come to the fore in recent years, but this is not really a new focus for the discipline. The localized 'grassroots' approach that generally characterizes anthropology has always involved paying close attention to the relationships between human groups and the places that they inhabit, and to the ways that people think about, make use of and manage resources. Environmental anthropologists are interested in how populations interact with ecological opportunities and constraints; what makes human–environmental relationships change over time; and why, sometimes, societies make unsustainable choices (see Haenn and Wilk 2006). There is ample opportunity to learn from the past; for example, writers such as Alfred Crosby (2004) have charted the long-term social and environmental effects of movements of seeds, plants, animals and germs around the world; Jared Diamond's (2005) popular work examines societies that have 'collapsed'; and anthropologists such as Geoff Harrison and Howard Morphy (Harrison and Morphy 1998 [1993]) have considered how cultural adaptations fit into larger evolutionary processes. Anthropologists work with all kinds of societies: hunter-gatherers, pastoralists, agriculturalists, and the larger industrial societies that now dominate most parts of the world. In terms of environmental issues, there are some key questions: how do particular groups understand the relationship between human beings and the material world? How do they arrange the ownership and management of land and resources? What are their ideologies and values? One of the advantages of a highly comparative discipline is that it shows very readily that different cultural groups have quite specific ways of understanding and directing human-environmental relationships, and that this is intricately bound up with their systems of knowledge and their social, economic and political arrangements.

For example, research with hunter-gatherer communities in Africa, Australia and South America, and in colder parts of the world, such as Alaska, reveals cosmological beliefs[2] in which ancestral beings inhabit the land and water, often appearing as non-human species. Human relationships with the environment therefore tend to be based on ideas about partnership with these beings and a responsibility for mutual support. In such societies, 'traditional'[3] wealth and power lie in ecological knowledge, as hunter-gatherers depend on knowing every detail about the surrounding landscape and its resources. Similarly intimate knowledge about local ecosystems is often held by small-scale communities that rely on shifting horticulture or forest 'gardening'. This in-depth local ecological knowledge allows for the maintenance of small-scale economies, which archaeological evidence suggests have been sustainable for many thousands of years.

Today, many of these small groups are under pressure: their lands and resources have frequently been appropriated, and their way of life is being subsumed by large-scale societies and their industrial economies. Anthropologists have often directed their energies towards recording the extraordinary cultural diversity of indigenous societies, partly to assist them in preserving traditional ideas and knowledges, and also to chart the various processes of change and adaptation through which such communities try to 'hold their own' in larger societies and a globalizing world. In relation to environmental issues, there are useful questions about the values and characteristics that enabled them to maintain sustainable ways of life for so long – and to consider whether there is scope for larger contemporary societies to learn from this experience. For example, Darrell Posey's (1989) research with indigenous communities in the Amazon led him to consider the lessons that other groups could draw from their ecologically sensitive methods of forest management,[4] and working with communities who do not see 'nature' as something completely separate from themselves encouraged Philippe Descola and Gisli Palsson (1996) to think critically about the way that Western societies treat 'nature' and 'culture' as separate categories, which allows for 'nature' to be objectified in ways that many environmentalists regard as exploitative. Explorations of alternative perspectives and values are illuminating, and this work highlights one of the major gains of a comparative social science: that by offering insights into different ways of understanding the world, it enables people to step back and consider their own in a new light. This reflexive view is essential, of course, if we are to understand – and potentially change – the factors that create socially and ecologically unsustainable relationships with the environment.

INDIGENOUS KNOWLEDGES

One of the most important things that anthropology brings to the environmental arena is an appreciation that resource management emerges not just from specific cultural ideas about 'what resources are for' but from whole belief systems and the structural arrangements of a society, which includes its forms of governance and decision-making, its economic practices, its social and spatial organization, and its laws concerning the ownership of resources and access to them. 'Governance' is not just a matter of political parties: in many societies, religious beliefs play an equally important role. For example, Stephen Lansing's (1991) research with a community of rice growers in Bali showed that the hydrological management of water flowing from a mountain lake through weirs and channels into farmers' rice paddies was actually conducted by the priests responsible for a series of 'water temples' placed at key points in the streams.[5] Lansing's major challenge was to translate this reality for the 'development experts' who wanted to come in and tell the farmers how to manage their resources better. As it turned out, the priests' local hydrological experience, and the farmers' knowledge about planting, pest management and so on, assisted by a social and religious framework that maintained fair access to water for all, was shown to be considerably more in tune with the realities of local ecosystems, and with local social needs, than the ideas promoted by external agencies. 'The anthropological contribution has been to bring people back into the discussion by highlighting their perspectives, as well as the gap between local knowledge and that of the planners and "experts"' (McDonald 2002: 298).

Anthropologists have therefore devoted considerable energy to recording local systems for classifying and understanding ecology, and there is now a large body of literature on 'traditional ecological knowledge' that not only provides a rich lexicon of information about habitats and species but also describes some very diverse ways of thinking about these, producing localized expertise which has sometimes been described as 'ethnobotany', 'ethnobiology' or 'ethnoscience' (see Bicker, Sillitoe and Pottier 2004).

Stephen Lansing's role in 'explaining' local knowledge to development experts is one that is frequently carried out by environmental anthropologists. In conducting ethnographic research, many of us find ourselves acting as 'cultural translators', not just for indigenous groups or local farmers, but also for the various groups involved in resource management, which often include mining and manufacturing industries, government and non-government agencies, natural scientists, catchment management groups, recreational land and water users, conservation groups and suchlike. Each of these groups will have its own perspective on resource management issues; its own ways of understanding local ecology; its own forms of knowledge and expertise; and its own aims and values. Some cross-cultural translation can therefore help to ensure that each group has a 'voice' in the proceedings, and each can gain an understanding of the other perspectives involved. This is pretty essential if they are to reach any kind of amiable agreement.

Local knowledge is often enlightening: for example, James Fairhead's (1993) work on environmental change in Africa, shows that quite often the 'received wisdom' on problems such as land degradation and deforestation is contradicted by the experiences of local groups. And, working in South America, Ronald Nigh found that while deforestation for cattle farming was framed (and often demonized) by environmentalists as a core problem, a closer ethnographic analysis of local issues showed that better outcomes could be achieved by working directly with cattle farmers to understand and improve their managerial practices. This 'allowed us to reduce the area of a ranch devoted to pasture to one-third or even one-tenth of the area, while at the same time increasing bioeconomic production in absolute terms. The project has also allowed some reforestation to occur, as well as generating income to support changes' (Nigh 2002: 314).

POLITICAL ECOLOGY

Failing to engage with local communities can carry a high social and ecological price tag. Susan Stonich's research in Honduras examined what happened when the government attempted to boost the economy and pay off foreign debt by expanding shrimp farming along the coast, without considering the traditional land owners. Coastal land was given to investors – often government officials, military leaders and urban elites. There was a massive leap in shrimp production (1,611 per cent in ten years), but also major social and environmental consequences. The previous small landholders lost their access to newly privatized ponds and wetlands that they had relied on for fishing, harvesting and firewood. There were few jobs to replace these local economic practices. The shrimp farms devastated the habitats essential to other species and, in effect, the government's decision created the conditions for 'a permanent human and ecological crisis in the region' (Stonich, in McGuire 2005: 94).

Implicit in each of these examples is the reality that ecological crises affect not only plants and animals but also the people who are not powerful enough to pass the costs on to others. There are many such groups: not just indigenous communities whose land is appropriated by larger societies for national parks or commercial activities, but also – as in the Honduras example – people displaced by developments that remove their ability to make a living. Examples include local fishing communities whose resources vanish when over-fished by industrial trawlers from elsewhere; small farmers pushed out by industrial agriculture and urban expansion; whole populations forced to migrate when intensified farming in fragile environments leads to desertification. Eric Wolf pointed out several decades ago that

> People were not simply engaged in the 'work process' of applying technology to nature ... they were people caught up in struggles to obtain and retain access to resources, to resist or manipulate the 'penetration of capital' into the countryside, to fight peasant wars when the opportunities arose – real people enmeshed in relations of power. (Wolf, in McGuire 2005: 92–3)

Anthropologists such as Thomas Hylland Eriksen (2001, 2003) and James Carrier (2004) have highlighted the importance of understanding the interface between local perspectives and larger processes of globalization. Writing about the social causes of environmental destruction, Michael Painter and William Durham point out that we also need to consider the policies and 'the ideology that orients resource use – for example, the position that rapid economic growth is the best way to address social and environmental problems – and what groups benefit from that ideology' (Painter and Durham 1995: 8). There is also a question about who *doesn't* benefit. As Barbara Johnston's (1994) work underlines, environmental injustices can be understood as a kind of unequal exchange in which the less powerful pay the price for the enrichment and comfort of more powerful groups.

As human populations expand and cycles of production and consumption intensify, the ownership of natural resources is increasingly contested. Most countries around the world are witnessing growing competition for water, land and other key resources, with major debates about the extent to which these should be held in common, or privatized, with dominant groups seeking – sometimes aggressively – to ensure that their access to resources and their economic advantages are secure.

Approaching these issues through what has been called 'political ecology'[6] goes under the surface and makes these power relations visible. This can involve analysing and at times critiquing the activities of powerful elites. For example, anthropologists such as Kim Fortun have examined corporate environmentalism and the ways in which it frames ideas about institutional responsibilities and environmental management:

> Corporate environmentalism promises to help us clean up the past and manage future risks, while continuing to provide 'better living through chemistry' ... a commitment to both continuity and change, to be realised through initiatives that transfigure but sustain our ways of desiring, responding, and understanding. (Fortun 1999: 203)[7]

Examining the discourses of different interest groups, and how they represent and promulgate particular beliefs and values, is an important part of anthropological research. Anthropologists also consider how different groups evaluate and present risk and, here too, the translation of local knowledges and the context encapsulated by ethnographic research can be helpful. Edward Liebow, for example, worked with rural landowners in America's Washington State, analysing their responses to a proposal to build a major hazardous waste incineration plant nearby. He observed that local groups are often excluded from decision making, leading to deep conflicts:

> In practical terms, the issue here is deciding who gets seats at the table when these choices get made; in other words, what qualifies as applicable knowledge and insight... One specific aim of the practice of anthropology in environmental planning is to give voice to the knowledge and insights of non-specialists, whose experience ... lends authority to lay judgements about environmental dangers and the public agencies responsible for managing those dangers. (Liebow 2002: 300)

Current debates on climate change also benefit from what is commonly called 'discourse analysis',[8] which examines how groups present ideas in ways that substantiate their views and support their own interests. Plainly climate change is an area that is becoming increasingly important analytically: Kay Milton and other anthropologists are investigating public understandings of the issues (Milton 2008), and researchers such as Michael Glantz (2001, 2003) are considering the social effects of climate change on communities, and the implications of these effects for policy development. Some anthropologists are directly employed in climate change research institutes, for example, Annette Henning works at the Solar Energy Research Center (SERC) at Dalarna University in Sweden, and believes that energy use and its impacts are urgently in need of social analysis:

> The issues of climate change call for in-depth research by social scientists in collaboration with technical researchers and professionals outside the academic world... Anthropological theories, methods and research are needed, not only for the study of how humans around the world adapt to climate change, but for studies that might actually contribute to climate change mitigation. (Henning 2005: 8)

UNPACKING GARBAGE

Climate change is not the only waste-related issue with potentially major social and ecological effects. Social analysis is also illuminating in considering other kinds of waste, and in recent years popular interest has been raised by what Americans have called 'garbology' (see Buchli *et al.* 2001). William Rathje's work in Tucson Arizona hit the headlines by applying archaeological thinking to household waste. As he says:

> All archaeologists study garbage ... our data is just fresher than most... What we do not have and what we need are specialists to study the crucial relationship between people and things, especially now, as the need to manage resources efficiently becomes essential. The Garbage Project studies household garbage because, whether dealing with ancient Maya or modern America, the household is society's most commonplace and basic socioeconomic unit. (Rathje, in Podolefsky and Brown 2003: 98–9)

Rathje's (2001) work on garbage, supported by the Environment Agency and the Solid Waste Council of the Paper Industry, has obvious relevance for planning in waste management, as does his research on food waste, both at a household level and in larger cycles of production, consumption and distribution.

Each stage in the larger cycles that create waste is critical, and many environmental anthropologists work with groups who produce food and goods. There is an entire sub-field of 'agricultural anthropology'. For example, Yunita Winarto (1999) has examined debates between local farmers and scientists on pest management in Indonesia; research by Carolyn Sachs (1996) considers the ways that gender roles are constructed in farming; and Ben Wallace (2006) is involved in a project attempting to understand the social pressures that have led to deforestation in the Philippines. Such research is generally conducted with a view to assisting the development of better agricultural strategies, and in each instance, researchers bring the social and cultural aspects of farming to the fore. Thus, conducting research on a strawberry farming cooperative in California, Miriam Wells highlighted the differences between a 'top down' purely economic assessment of its success, and the local perspectives of the participants, which pointed to the cooperative's importance in providing disadvantaged Mexican farmers with social status, security, and more stable family and community lives, as well as better access to education and other social services (Wells, in Ervin 2005).

HUMAN–ANIMAL RELATIONS

Environmental anthropologists also go to sea, as fisheries management is critical in terms of food supply. There are major issues about the ecological sustainability of fish populations, as well as the social sustainability of the many communities who depend on fishing for their livelihoods.

> Fisheries anthropologists have worked long and hard to find, document, and recommend solutions to the problem of a resource that has no owners... Most significantly they have placed notions of co-management – the call for local communities to share in the management of their own resources – firmly on the agendas of state and international resource management. (Van Willigen 2005: 98)

A 'resource that has no owners' raises complex questions about who should have rights of access, and as anthropologists have shown, this is very much an arena in which power and politics are critical, both at an international level, in negotiations over quotas, and locally, between different groups of resource users and managers. Thus Bonnie McCay (2000, 2001), who works on fisheries policy issues, seeks ways for fishers and policy makers to collaborate in finding workable solutions for fishing communities. There are some useful ethnographies of diverse local management schemes, and these are not always conventional: for example, James Acheson (1987) produced an ethnography about the 'lobster gangs' who protect communal access to resources in Maine, ensuring a greater density – and so more effective conservation – of lobsters in 'their' territories.

Environmental anthropologists are also keenly interested in broader conservation issues, and there is a fast-growing area of research concerned with human–animal relations and 'animal rites' (as well as animal rights). Classically, this has involved research exploring the various ways that cultural groups categorize and relate to animals (for example, as totemic beings, or as spiritual creatures) or examining how societies have made use of animals in systems of production, either hunting them as prey, or domesticating them to varying degrees.

Gregory Forth's (2003) research in Indonesia, for instance, considers how the Nage people incorporate birds into religious ideas, myths and poetry, and regard them as having prophetic abilities. Paul Sillitoe's (2003) ethnographic work with New Guinea Highlanders considers how animals – in particular pigs – are classified and dealt with in consequence. Understanding how particular societies relate to animals is useful in a variety of ways. It provides insights into their cosmological beliefs and understandings of the world; their interactions with 'nature'; the ways in which they organize themselves socially; and their ideas about identity and personhood. It also helps us to understand why people think some species are – or are not – worth conserving and protecting.

Anthropologists have often worked with communities whose way of life is bound up with particular animal species. For example, Gideon Kressel's (2003) research on shepherding in the Middle East and Israel considers how groups are struggling to preserve a traditional form of pastoralism that they see as their cultural legacy, while also encompassing the political realities of the region. Such lifeways are integral to the preservation of cultural diversity, and many anthropologists believe that it is important to record and publicize ethnographic accounts of them in the hope of broadening the wider political reality to encompass and valorize these groups and their cultural traditions.

From a very different perspective, James Serpell's (1996) research takes a look at how many societies have created the idea of 'pets', and incorporated animals into their domestic lives. This work shows how cultural groups think about animals as semi-persons, or as fellow members of the family, and how their worldviews use animals creatively as categories of characteristics (feline or foxy) or behaviour (being boorish, bullish, bovine ... or chicken). These understandings help to explain how people interact with the particular range of species in their environments, as well as revealing the way that they organize social relationships and evaluate behaviour.

The social and cultural meanings of hunting, even in urbanized industrial societies, have been considered by anthropologists such as Matt Cartmill (1993) and, more recently, Garry Marvin (2006), whose research with English foxhunting groups informed highly contentious debates on whether this activity should be banned. Rather than taking sides in the conflict, Marvin sought to articulate the deeper meanings and ideas located in hunting:

> What I wanted to do was something different – I wanted to understand what foxhunting is *per se*. I sought to understand the social and cultural processes that constituted foxhunting. As an anthropologist I have a particular interest in human-animal relations, and it seemed to me that at the heart of hunting were some complex configurations of such relations... I regularly heard those who participated in foxhunting defend it against attacks from the outside but that defence never seemed to tally exactly with how they spoke about hunting, the experiences they had of it and the meanings it had for them when they were talking amongst themselves. (Marvin 2006: 193, 194)

Marvin was asked to act as an anthropological consultant in the Home Secretary's enquiry into 'hunting with dogs', and to produce a neutral account interpretatively describing a 'typical' hunting day with comments on its cultural meanings. This was considered by the enquiry alongside material from both pro- and anti-hunting groups. He was then hired by the Countryside Alliance to help with a legal challenge to the banning of foxhunting by producing a report on the potential social and cultural impacts of the proposed ban on rural communities. Thus several of the parties involved in the debate made use of his ethnographic research, and the deeper understandings that it provided.

As species extinctions have reached unprecedented levels, research on human–animal relations has become more focused on the social and economic practices that result in the loss or degradation of plant and animal habitats, and in the pressures on endangered species. Quite often there are clashes between environmental groups and local communities whose view of animal (or other) species may be less protective. Such conflicts have been analysed by Dimitri Theodossopoulos, who investigated 'troubles with turtles' on a Greek island (2002), and by Adrian Peace (2001, 2002), whose research – which includes 'an ethnography of whale watching' – considers diverse cultural perspectives on dingoes, whales and sharks in Australia.

ANTHROPOLOGY AND ENVIRONMENTALISM

Concern about wildlife is one of the major drivers for conservation organizations, and the 'green' movement as a whole has proved to be one of the most influential social movements of the last 50 years. It is therefore an important area of study. A broad perspective is offered by Stephen Yearley's (2005) analysis of social movements, while leading environmental anthropologists such as Kay Milton (1993), Eeva Berglund and David Anderson (2003) have written more specifically about conservation organizations, protest groups and environmental activists, providing insights into their internal cultural dynamics and their contributions to public discourses.

CHANGING THE WORLD

Kay Milton

Professor of Social Anthropology, Queen's University Belfast

How did I get into anthropology? Well, I went to a very traditional English grammar school in the 1960s with a snobbish headmaster who was obsessed with league tables and how many students he could get into university. When I expressed a wish to be a cartographer (I have always loved maps), which didn't require a university education (although it probably does now), he gave me a 'don't be silly' look and told me to think about what I wanted to study at Cambridge or, if not Cambridge, at least Durham (his *alma mater*). One thing I was certain of was that I didn't want to study any of the subjects I was already doing at school — I wanted a change. Anthropology was something new, and meant I could apply to Durham, keep my headmaster happy, and avoid sitting the Cambridge entrance exam!

There were two other important influences. My father collected African sculpture, so from an early age I was surrounded by strange wooden figures from foreign lands. I often thought about these figures and the people who made them, and wondered what sort of lives they led. And I was crazy about animals. I read Gerald Durrell's books about his animal-collecting expeditions, watched every wildlife documentary I could, and became determined to visit Africa and see lions and elephants in their natural habitat. At school, I had loved biology, but avoided it at advanced level because it meant having to kill and dissect poor innocent mice, so there was no hope of a biological career. Anthropology, I thought, would get me to Africa. I would study people who are, in any case, the most complex and interesting animals of all, and you don't have to kill them or abuse them in order to study them — in fact it is strongly discouraged.

I had no ambition, at that stage, to be a professional anthropologist. Even when I had finished my degree, I didn't know what I wanted to do. So I became a research student, and when, two years later, a lectureship in social anthropology came up at Queen's University in Belfast, I applied and was offered the job, probably because there was absolutely no competition. If you know anything about the history of Ireland you will appreciate that no-one wanted to go to live in Belfast in the early 1970s. So there I was, an accidental anthropologist, being paid, amazingly, to teach the most interesting subject imaginable — and, yes, it did get me to Africa, a few years later. I spent a fascinating fifteen months living in an African village and managed to see plenty of elephants and lions, and many other spectacular animals.

That experience gave me a nudge, a bit later in my career, towards environmental anthropology. I was thoroughly ashamed and angry at what my species, and especially my society was doing to our beautiful planet and the non-human beings that share it with us — I still am. So I did what many fledgling environmentalists do: I joined local wildlife and conservation groups, volunteered for work parties, went to conferences and meetings, and generally got involved.

In the mid-1980s the pressure was on for us to do research and write books and articles. Since my voluntary environmental activities were occupying much of my spare time, I started researching and writing about them. That is how I came to focus on environmentalism, spending much of the following twenty years or so trying to understand what makes environmentalists tick, why they care about the natural world, how they think about it, how they seek to influence the lives of others, what drives their commitment.

But, you might ask, isn't that rather a strange thing to do? Aren't anthropologists supposed to go to exotic places and study other cultures? And how did I manage to remain 'objective' while studying people whose commitment I shared? The first question is easily answered. Anthropologists, as you will realize reading this book, can study anything and everything that people do in any cultural setting, and many analyse the societies in which they grew up, as well as and in comparison with other cultures.

The second question, about objectivity, is more difficult, but there is a clear answer. Anthropologists are human beings like anyone else, and have commitments, views and political allegiances. Being objective doesn't mean abandoning these, it just means suspending them, stepping back and examining them in order to understand them better. Anthropology gives you the training to do this. When I study environmentalists, and question the values and assumptions on which they base their arguments and actions, I know that I am also reflecting on my own values and assumptions. In a similar way, many anthropologists have been drawn into areas of research because of their personal commitments to a particular cause — feminism, development, social justice, world peace — motivated by a desire to understand that cause and make it more effective.

As an anthropologist who was also an active environmentalist, I did much of my fieldwork in committee meetings. This may sound dull, but it wasn't at all, because the meetings were about what interested me most — how people manage and interact with the natural world. At one stage I was on fifteen different committees, covering everything from local park management to the national council of Europe's largest conservation organization. I was also on a government advisory committee, commenting on proposals for oil exploration in the Irish Sea, wind farms, new housing developments, changes in environmental legislation — pretty well anything that affected the landscape and wildlife of Northern Ireland. All the time I was doing this, I was applying my anthropological knowledge as well as collecting material for my research. And when my time on the committees came to an end, I was told that I would be difficult to replace because I understood the human, cultural side of nature conservation as well as the biological side.

I didn't get paid directly for any of this work: I remained a professional academic, and the research was part of my job. I got the distinct impression, though, that had I wanted to move out of academia and into a non-governmental organization, or even into the environmental branch of the civil service, it would not have been difficult. It was clear to me that an anthropologist's skills are not only useful, but also recognized and valued, something that does not always happen. So I would advise anyone who wants to change the world to go for anthropology. The better we understand ourselves, the better our chances of making changes that lead to a better future.

Concerns about conservation are not only confined to wildlife and habitats: there are many groups equally concerned to preserve cultural heritage in its various forms although, as Barbara Bender's work on Stonehenge demonstrates (1998), they often have very different ideas about how this should be done. Her research with the various groups arguing over Stonehenge – English Heritage, druids, New Age groups and so forth – shows how each imagined, evaluated and represented the site, and served to explain the sometimes extreme conflicts over its management and use.

A BRIEF HISTORY OF WHY I CHOSE ARCHAEOLOGY

Danny Dybowski

Field Archaeologist, University of Wisconsin

Approximately ten years ago, when I was in the US Navy, I visited Greece and Italy. The port visits there were short and sweet, and did not provide nearly enough time to see all of the archaeological sites. However, in Naples, I decided to go on the group tour visit to Pompeii and Mount Vesuvius: this was a life-changing experience for me. I did not know that I had an interest in anthropology then. I did not even know that anthropology was connected with archaeology, which had been passion for me ever since it had been glorified in movies like *Indiana Jones*. I had no idea what course of study I was going to pursue at college when I got out of the navy. At that point in my life, I didn't realize that I was different from the other crew members on the ship, because they tended to go to bars and drink heavily when they were at a port visit, and I tended to go to museums and experience the local culture.

I began to read more and more about archaeology, and I also became very interested in the culture on the ship. I liked learning about different people and about the psychological aspects of how we all did or did not get along in such a cramped environment. Over 6,000 people were living and working together creating a socially cohesive unit functioning as one complete whole, and this fascinated me, sparking a life-long interest in human behaviour.

My visit to Pompeii made me realize that archaeology was not just something in the movies, but was an actual discipline that could be studied in college. I signed up to study anthropology at a community college near my home town north of Detroit, Michigan, and quickly realized that archaeology was a sub-discipline of anthropology. After that, I knew that I was going to become an archaeologist: I went on to do a Master's degree at the University of Wisconsin, Milwaukee, and to work on a large stone tool collection from southwestern France, at the Milwaukee Public Museum.

Anthropology to me is the study of people, at all times and all places, and if you can think of anything else about human behaviour in between, you are probably right. It is a discipline that prepares students to understand human beings of all ethnicities, all cultures, and all time periods, ultimately refining our perspectives and objective worldviews while simultaneously respecting others. In what may seem to be a time of disorder in our world today, an understanding of anthropology provides hope and optimism: it enables us to open up dialogue with other cultural groups while respecting their particular worldviews.

Although conflict between groups – over land and resources, animals, habitats and important cultural sites – is a common theme in environmental anthropology, I don't wish to give the impression that this subdisciplinary area is all about conflict. There are many strands of research that are simply concerned to gain a deeper understanding about how human beings interact with their environments. For example, analyses by Barbara Bender (1993), Chris Tilley (1994), Jeff Malpas (1999) and Rodney Giblett (1996) illuminate the processes through which people make cultural landscapes and locate meaning in them.[9] Kay Milton's research with environmental groups led her to consider closely how humans develop emotional attachments to places, or to 'nature' (2002, and Milton and Svašek 2005). This has fostered a lot of work in this area, such as that by Tracey Heatherington, whose research on communal territory in Sardinia showed how '…attachment to the land is perceived as inherent to cultural identity, economic futures and the persistence of community … belonging to the town commons is felt in the body and in the family. It is an object of ongoing 'love', nostalgia, passion, worry, grief and jealousy' (Heatherington 2005: 152–3).

Human engagement with the environment is mental, emotional and physical, and the 'anthropology of the senses' has proved to be a rich area of investigation, in which researchers such as David Howes (2005), Stephen Feld and Keith Basso (Feld and Basso 1996) have shown how even sensory experience is heavily mediated by culture. There are close intellectual ties between this kind of work and the anthropology of art (see Chapter 8), which considers how aesthetic experiences, like the senses, are culturally formulated to create and appreciate particular forms of artistic expression (Coote and Shelton 1992, Morphy and Perkins 2006).

The way that people interact with the material world, cognitively and physically, is an intriguing area of research. Alfred Gell (1998) wrote about how artefacts and tools become 'prosthetic extensions' of the self and Janet Carsten and Stephen Hugh-Jones (1995) have examined the way that houses create extensions of individual and family identities. I became interested in this theme in my own work on water and cultural landscapes, looking at how people express creative agency and identity through domestic homes and gardens (Strang 2004) and through wider productive endeavours such as agriculture and manufacturing (Strang 2009).

This kind of research also connects with areas such as architecture and urban planning, in which it is vital to have an understanding of how people relate to their surroundings, both in creating successful urban spaces, and in helping to move towards more sustainable ways of living. For example, David Casagrande and his fellow environmental anthropologists are involved in an interdisciplinary project in Arizona, working with biologists and ecologists to bring urban landscaping, human behaviour and water conservation together in experimental research aimed at contributing to water management policy (Casagrande *et al.* 2007).

Environmental and architectural themes also come together in Marcel Villenga's work, which considers vernacular (local) traditions in architecture, and considers what can be learned from these. He notes

> ... the strength of the need, desire and capacity of human beings all around the world to be in control of their own built environment, to create buildings that

are intimately related to their own sense of identity... Buildings can be culturally responsive and environmentally sustainable, if creative use is made of resources and vernacular methods are used in combination with modern and sometimes innovative technologies ... anthropology has the potential to contribute much to these attempts. (Villenga 2005: 7)

Communities need to be socially as well as ecologically sustainable. Gretchen Herrmann's research is concerned with the community-building potential of neighbourhood garage sales in suburban developments and cities.

Under the auspices of attracting more shoppers and making some extra money by cleaning out unneeded goods, neighborhood sales get residents out of their dwellings and mingling among themselves, sometimes for the first time. Some neighborhood sales have been organized expressly for the purpose of getting the neighbors to know one another in areas undergoing transition. They provide a positive means to combat a perceived 'decline of community' in the United States today... Neighborhood sales also define the neighborhood to the larger community, as well as promote internal solidarity. (Herrmann 2006: 181)

Environmental anthropology therefore examines many different aspects of human-environmental relationships, bringing the social and cultural aspects of these to the surface, and providing insights into the diverse ways that cultural and sub-cultural groups engage with the equally varied social and material environments in which we live.

5 ANTHROPOLOGY AND GOVERNANCE

THE BIG PICTURE

Anthropologists are increasingly providing advice to government agencies, becoming involved in policy development and planning, and assisting decision-making processes. Some work at a 'big picture' macro level, in government 'think tanks' and senior administrative bodies. Many do more specialized work with the agencies responsible for urban planning, environmental management, housing, health and welfare, education and child care, or engaged in dealing with pressing social issues, such as poverty, homelessness and crime. Some of these areas are considered in more detail in other chapters, but here we are more specifically concerned with the use of anthropology in relation to governance and policy.

Why are anthropologists useful to governments and their agencies? In essence, this kind of work draws on core skills in anthropology: a commitment to examining the social context in depth, and to understanding the different perspectives and relationships of the people in it. Although often done at a local, community level, this can also be applied on a smaller scale, within a single institution, or on a much larger scale, to consider regional or national concerns.

At the national 'big-picture' level, Mils Hills was the first social anthropologist to be employed by the Ministry of Defence in the UK, and went on to achieve another first in working for the UK Cabinet Office. In his career, he says, he has 'consciously and consistently drawn on social anthropological concepts and principles' and he issues 'a sort of manifesto or call to arms for those who may consider the options for career development outside those seeming established "tracks" for anthropologists':

> This is a real case of anthropology in action… My anthropological training has, rather than stymieing my deployment potential, provided me with an arguably unique springboard into areas of work that few – including me – could have anticipated… For the past six years I have been required to bring swift understanding of complex issues, many of them technological or, increasingly related to policy. The aim of this understanding is to assist those in specialist areas who may, for example, have become stove-piped in their approach and hence lost sight of any wider strategic picture. In other cases, the absence of a concept-drive approach … has meant that managers have no means of progressing their work because they have lost sight of what it is that they seek to achieve. The freshness and innovation that anthropologists can bring – working in concert with others – means that such impasses can be passed. (Hills 2006: 131–2)

Hills points to several key contributions from anthropology to policy and decision making: its use of 'grassroots'-level evidence to inform analysis; its strengths in being able to consider events in relation to a wider context; its ability to understand and empathize with diverse views on issues; and its commitment to communicating this understanding across cultural boundaries. He also makes an important point in observing that anthropological *theory* is readily applicable, and can make a critical difference in how events are analysed. It is not enough, he says, to list facts or sign petitions:

> The real strength of academics … should not be merely making a mark on a page; it should be making a mark on a problem by evolving, and applying, what we do best, i.e., generating concepts to better understand… Given that all wars and conflicts are essentially wars about *meaning* – of identity, ownership of natural resources, of control, of purity, of profit, of greed, and grievance … surely anthropologists concerned with the comprehension and generation of meanings should be claiming a role. (Hills 2006: 130–1)

Honggang Yang is similarly passionate about the potential for anthropology to analyse social dynamics at local and national levels. He began by using his anthropological training to resolve conflicts about the management of the local commons between homeowners in Florida, and then moved up to a larger scale, to assist the Carter Presidential Center in Atlanta in its efforts to resolve conflicts between nations, at times working directly with the former President: 'I was thrilled when I was hired as a research associate in the conflict resolution program there. Later I learned that it was my cross-cultural knowledge and applied anthropological training in the fields of peacemaking and conflict resolution that had attracted their interest in me' (Yang 1998: 201).

Yang's role at the Center was to provide 'cross-cultural translation' in areas such as mediation, election monitoring/observing and convening negotiations. In this role he made extensive use of ethnographic accounts to inform developments and to suggest avenues for communication and conflict resolution.

Anthropologists and other social scientists are also involved increasingly in government 'think tanks' analysing social, political and economic issues on a broad scale. For example, Saffron James works for The Future Foundation, an independent social think tank based in the London, which focuses on social policy development.

ANTHROPOLOGY IN THE FUTURE

Saffron James

The Future Foundation

I work as an applied anthropologist at The Future Foundation, an independent social think tank in London that produces a range of qualitative and quantitative research monitoring two main areas: changes in the family and family life, and consumption and consumer behaviour. I am the only anthropologist in the company, and my role is to incorporate anthropological theories, concepts and methods into the work that we produce. The firm is especially interested in new ways of thinking about social change and using ethnography.

I have worked on a number of projects for UK government departments, exploring the social and cultural changes that are likely to impact on public policy-making in the next ten to twenty years. This has included issues such as crime in the community, education and its relationship with entry into the workforce and, more recently, consumption and emotion.

I think there is huge potential for anthropology to be applied to public-sector thinking, especially where public policy-making and social life intersect. I have been surprised at the lack of understanding of how cultural and social factors might impact on the success of government policy, and at some of the assumptions that underpin policy – such as uniform ideas of community and citizenship.

I am currently developing ideas for an ethnographic study about the meaning of ageing – looking at the terms used to refer to Britain's ageing population (such as 'grey voters' or 'silver surfers'). These descriptors are quite often derogatory but are widely adopted by institutions and marketers when referring to different groups of elderly consumers. The aim of the research is to build on the Future Foundation's existing work (which is primarily quantitative) looking at the changing structure of Britain's ageing population and the implications of this for future public/private sector planning. However, there is very little insight into what it means to be healthy, wealthy and 'elderly'. I want to explore what these terms mean to people who are over sixty-five, and look at how they construct their identity in relation to popular descriptions and stereotypes. The aim will be to incorporate the work into the research the firm uses, which feeds into public and private sector thinking.

The Future Foundation tends to focus very heavily on what is going on (quantitative trends and forecasts), rather than why things are happening and what they mean. A lot of its work is also about consumer behaviour and tends to take a rational, economic perspective. I emphasize the rich, deep insights into behaviour that ethnography can provide, and I try to describe the benefits of anthropology's holistic approach in giving behaviour a cultural and social context. Feedback from my colleagues is good: they are interested in how anthropology can bring different approaches to their core areas of research.

With an understanding that 'knowledge is power' anthropologists have turned an analytic eye on partnerships between national think tanks and international organizations such as the World Bank, for example considering how a 'knowledge economy' has emerged in relation to reform and development around the world (Stone 2000).

Similarly, observing widespread changes in the formation of nation states and in the roles and responsibilities of governments, anthropologists have become very interested in governance itself. Cris Shore has led the way in focusing on political elites (Shore and Nugent 2002) and corruption (Haller and Shore 2005), and he has done extensive fieldwork at the European Parliament in Brussels, examining the organizational culture of the 'Eurocrats' who administer the European Union (Shore 2000, see also Shore and Wright 1997). John Gledhill (2000) has turned a critical eye on the subtle ways in which power is acquired in political life. Other researchers have focused on government bureaucracies themselves: there is, for example, Michael Herzfeld's (1992) classic work on how these become detached from people's needs through 'the social production of indifference'; Robert Jackall's (1983) research into how bureaucracy shapes the moral choices that managers make, and Josiah Heyman's analyses of the power of bureaucratic institutions in which he comments that: 'A crucial step in inferring the marks of power is the ethnographic study of ordinary practices within organisations ... we cannot and should not avoid bureaucratic phenomena, tiresome and unromantic as they often seem' (Heyman 2004: 487).

UNDERSTANDING OTHER PEOPLE'S WORLDS — AND YOUR OWN

Cris Shore

Professor of Social Anthropology, University of Auckland

Class was probably the main reason why I became an anthropologist. Or rather, it was the awareness of class differences that first awakened in me a sensitivity towards cultural 'otherness'. Britain is well known for being a 'class society', yet few people appreciate the extent to which class differences reflect cultural differences. My parents belonged to what used to be called the 'middle-class intelligentsia': both Cambridge University educated; both high-achieving professionals (my mum was a doctor who joined the National Health Service, my dad a Labour MP and government minister during the 1960s and 1970s); both deeply committed to an ethos of public service. Our house had books from floor to ceiling: my best friend, who came from a single-parent working-class family, didn't have a single book in his house. Being opposed to educational elitism, my parents sent all four of their children to local comprehensive (state) schools. With 2,000 boys from across south London, my school was rough, even by contemporary standards. Most of the boys were being educated for working-class jobs and probably less than 15 per cent went on to take university entrance exams. To survive fighting, gang warfare and playground abuse you had to adapt, become 'street-wise', and play by a set of local rules. Long before I'd ever heard of Basil Bernstein, I developed two ways of speaking: a 'restrictive code' of slang and expletives at school, and at home, an 'elaborated code' with a more extensive vocabulary that included words with more than four syllables.

Coming from a political background, it was not surprising that I developed an interest in politics, or at least in the questions of power relations and government that are the bedrock of political science. My first attempt at university failed. I went to Birmingham to study politics and modern history but, bored by the sterile manner in which these subjects were taught, dropped out and spent a year doing manual jobs, which, I discovered, were more boring than even the dullest lecture. When I returned to university — this time Oxford Polytechnic — I was far more motivated. I chose anthropology and geography as my majors, and never looked back. A course on peoples and cultures of the Mediterranean got me really hooked — that and spending the summer of my final undergraduate year living on a small island in the lagoon of Venice, and studying community tensions for my end-or-year dissertation.

Encouraged by my teachers, I applied to do graduate research on the relationship between communism and Catholicism, and was accepted into the Ph.D. programme at Sussex University. Poland seemed like an obvious research site, but my plans changed when a revolt that started in the Gdansk shipyard that year led to the mobilization of Russian tanks on the border and the declaration of martial law. Italy seemed a good alternative, so instead of focusing on Catholicism in a communist country, I decided to study the role of communism in a Catholic country. For eighteen months I lived in the Central Italian city of Perugia, where I became engrossed in Italian politics and society and completed one of the first ethnographic studies of a major Western political party.

Returning to Britain in the 1983, I was eager to finish my Ph.D. and 'get on with life' and find a 'proper job'. I was offered a job with a major British trade union but turned it down to return to Italy, this time to teach English to political science undergraduates. George Orwell wrote that nothing teaches you more about a country than having to earn a living there. Working in an Italian university, I experienced a dimension of Italian life that I had not really appreciated before: the corruption, clientelism, feudal-like hierarchies and nepotistic employment practices were fascinating and appalling in equal measure.

The following year I took up a short-term research internship at the European Parliament in Brussels, which sparked a life-long interest in the EU. I had the option of staying on in Brussels to work as a journalist, or applying to become an EU official, but despite the high salaries, the life of a Eurocrat never appealed to me. Instead, my partner got a job in a London, so I went back with her, and ended up with a fixed-term job at Oxford Brookes University, which left me with a passion for teaching and writing. Few new lectureships in anthropology were available at that time, but I eventually obtained one at Goldsmiths College in London.

During my thirteen years at Goldsmiths I published several books and helped establish a new journal (*Anthropology in Action*). I was also awarded a large grant to study the organizational culture of the EU civil service, which brought me back to Brussels as a professional observer. Europe is still a major research interest, although my family and I moved to New Zealand in 2003. The first three years here, as Head of Department at Auckland University, have left little time for writing, but have rekindled my interest in bureaucracy, and I recently embarked on new research studying university reform.

Confucius once remarked: 'find a job that you love doing and you will never work a day in your life'. He was, of course, quite wrong. My granny, while less prophetic, used to say: 'No job that was ever worth doing is without moments of grind.' For me, anthropology has been — and remains — an inspiration. It has taught me about the world we live in and, perhaps more significantly, about the hidden structures that shape societies. It teaches you how individuals, ideas, institutions and events connect (both at local and global levels). For those who are interested in otherness, or for those who want to understand the conditions of their own existence, I would say anthropology is a must.

THE NOT SO BIG PICTURE

At an institutional level, Dennis Wiedman sees a useful role for anthropologists in assisting strategic planning in organizations, making use of their training in depicting the dynamics of situations holistically and working with all of the participants. He has done some institutional level work himself with Florida International University, using strategic planning 'to guide a rapidly changing university to fulfill its evolving mandate for 30,000 students' (cited in Ervin 2005: 109). And some anthropologists, such as Marilyn Strathern (2000), have stepped back from their university institutions to consider how the academy has changed with the introduction of managerialism and an 'audit culture'.

There are other levels of engagement, for example working in human service areas (see Richard and Emener 2003). In Canada, Alexander Ervin was asked by United Way to do a 'needs assessment' for the whole city of Saskatoon:

> Officials hoped that the study would provide some simple formula for helping
> them to make their hard financial decisions, but they also wanted a general
> study of community conditions that could be used by other government and
> nongovernment agencies. For nongovernment charitable organisations, pressures
> were becoming overwhelming. Because of government cutbacks in direct services
> and funding to human service agencies, more and more was being expected of
> the non-profit sector. The United Way had to sort out these difficulties in its
> planning. (Ervin 2005: 109)

The research project identified needs in seventeen 'human service' areas, including
employment, housing, poverty, a range of health issues, recreation, substance abuse,
ageing and Native issues, and showed that 'about 25% of the population was
potentially in need of the sort of services that were provided by United Way or
parallel agencies' (Ervin 2005: 88). It also illustrated the cultural and sub-cultural
diversities within the city, and the way that these intersected with particular social
needs.

> The case study documents anthropology's potential for conducting mainstream
> community policy analysis and formulation... We needed to identify insiders'
> perspectives and the significant issues in each area. We also had to find out what
> was common to them all and establish the level of priority for each need...
> Anthropologists are especially well attuned and preadapted to conduct formal
> needs assessments because of their focus on cultural and social awareness. After
> all, they have been doing these assessments implicitly for decades as ethnog-
> raphers. (Ervin 2005: 89–90)

The concern for social justice that characterizes anthropology leads many practitioners to work with disadvantaged groups. Frank Munger (2002), for example,
has promoted the value of ethnography in revealing the various aspects of poverty
and economic survival strategies in a globalizing economy. Survival strategies are
culturally specific, and an understanding of these and their ethnographic context
can greatly assist aid agencies in tailoring their activities to fit local needs.

The way that local and national governments deal with problems also benefits
from ethnographic insights. For example, Kim Hopper's (1991) research on the
realities of life and the mental health issues for homeless people in New York has
enabled the authorities charged with rehousing or providing assistance to people
on the streets to do so in ways that accommodate these realities and deal more sens-
itively with the mental health issues involved. Patricia Marquez's (1999) work with
homeless youths in Caracas was directed towards similar improvements, with the
ethnographic approach to their experiences as a sub-cultural community yielding a
useful understanding of their particular social rules and moral universe.

Poverty and crime do not necessarily go together, but there is often a relationship between social disadvantage, poor education, and levels of criminal involvement. Gaining an in-depth understanding of the experiences that people have and the social contexts they inhabit provides important insights into the causes of crime. For example, Mark Totten and Katherine Kelly used 'life course analysis' with young offenders who have been convicted of murder or manslaughter:

> We wanted to uncover the participant's world from his or her own viewpoint... The research explored the intentions, meanings and motives young people ascribe to their actions within the context of having them recount their life experiences. Our theoretical position suggests that involvement in the criminal justice system and in high-risk activities was the result of a lifetime of events that, in turn, contributed to the risk of committing homicide. (Totten and Kelly 2005: 77)

The importance of understanding the context is also highlighted by Scott Kenney's work with the families of homicide victims. He found that it was vital to consider broader issues, such as how people interacted with the criminal justice system, and their communities' cultural responses to crime: 'My research project dealt with murder... While my initial goal was to examine gender differences in active coping among homicide survivors, it quickly became apparent that this was a group troubled by far more than the crime itself' (Kenney 2005: 116).

James Vigil worked with Chicano schoolchildren in America, and observed that their poor educational performance was persistently explained in terms of racial or cultural deficits, creating barriers for the children:

> ...culturally biased performance tests, political opposition to bilingual education, and teachers and administrators unfamiliar with (or even hostile towards) Chicano culture. Meanwhile ... the urbanization of the United States in combination with the transformation of the economy to a high-tech service orientation, has made the acquisition of a sound education more important than ever before. (Vigil 2002: 263)

His research focused on how these conditions, and the marginalization that comes with them, contributed to the growth of a street-gang subculture and crime in urban areas. By doing in-depth ethnography within the 'sub-culture' of gang membership, his research pointed to ways that problems could be addressed at an educational level, through special programmes and through more effective home–school linkages.

Clearly insights into all of these factors are helpful to social service agencies and those concerned with maintaining law and order. In investigating the underlying causes of crime, anthropologists have therefore encouraged government agencies to look beyond simple cultural or racial stereotypes, and to consider – and address – the real causes of social dysfunction.

HOME WORK

Having a home is a basic human need, and anthropologists' skills are useful for agencies involved in housing and urban planning. There is a wide range of ethnography examining how different societies think about, design and use domestic and public spaces, and the culturally diverse ideas and values that come into play in this process. The economics of having a home are also a key issue for many people, particularly in urbanized societies, and there is useful anthropological research being done in this area too. For example, Erve Chambers was involved in a project evaluating a programme designed by the United States Department of Housing and Urban Development. The programme was meant to give financial assistance to low-income families and allow them more choice in rental housing, as well as inducing builders (with inspections) to provide better quality facilities. Located in Boston, his research evaluated the effects of government policy on families, looking at how it affected their choices and their costs of living (in Ervin 2005: 106).

As people become more mobile and cities expand, social tensions can rise. At the other end of the housing market, Brett Williams' (2006) work is concerned with the clashes of culture and class that can arise when urban neighbourhoods become 'gentrified', bringing together people from different backgrounds, with very different ideas about who 'belongs' in the community, what constitutes neighbourly behaviour, and how public space should be used. Even in small, everyday conflicts, an understanding of cultural differences is helpful in resolving disputes, which (as the number of 'neighbours at war' on reality TV illustrates) can escalate rapidly.

Access to housing can also be determined by cultural perceptions. For example, Kathryn Forbes' research showed how stereotypical images of Mexican farmworkers created a barrier for them in California's housing policy:

> Despite the desperate need for affordable housing in the rural areas of Fresno County, local policy makers either have failed to aid or have actively discouraged attempts to increase the stock of affordable housing... Public officials make policy decisions based on both a land use ideology that rationalizes governmental failure to serve Mexicans working in the agriculture industry and portraits of farmworkers and farmworker families that reflect stereotypes... This ideology and these stereotypical profiles operate to render invisible portions of the Mexican farmworker population who have been working in the area for decades. (Forbes 2007: 196)

PRESCRIPTION AND PERSUASION

Another basic human need is for health and wellbeing. The involvement of anthropologists in medical issues and in health care is examined more closely in Chapter 7, but the general health and welfare of the population is also a major issue for any government, and a number of anthropologists are employed in assisting policy development and implementation in this area. Health care can be intensely political, most particularly when access to resources is uneven. Cori Hayden's (2007) work, for example, is concerned with the ethical and political issues around access to medical resources. Her research has focused on the debates in Mexico when the government, frustrated by the soaring costs of imported pharmaceutical products, enabled the legal creation and use of generic 'similar' drugs with the argument that this was in the public interest.

In practical terms, there are two key ways of enacting government policies: legislatively, through laws and regulations; and through persuasion – communicating and promoting ideas and information, encouraging some kinds of behaviour, and discouraging others.

One of the major prerequisites for public health is a healthy environment. As well as researching environmental issues directly (Chapter 4.), anthropologists work with the regulatory agencies responsible for protecting public health in a variety of ways: for example, by ensuring that food providers practise good hygiene; that industries do not release pollution into the communities where they are located; and that individuals do not impinge on the health of their neighbours.

Thus Roberta Hammond (1998) made use of her anthropological training in understanding the people and the cultural dynamics surrounding her work as an environmental health specialist in Florida, in Franklin County's Department of Community Affairs. Using research methods such as open-ended interviewing and participant observation, she was able to 'elicit as complete a contextual framework as possible for the problem or situation at hand':

> I incorporated various features of ethnographic field work in the performance of my duties as a public health official... By participating in community life, I was able to increase my sensitivity to residents' concerns and gain a more balanced view of the issues important to them versus those important to the state. On the other hand, in the observation mode, impersonal detachment as an outsider allowed me the use of authority in enforcement and other unpopular actions necessary for a public health official. In all cases, good listening skills facilitated better community relations.
>
> While I am sure that differences of gender, socialization, and personality also affected the outcome of my work, my background in anthropology helped me

> to adjust to a difficult field situation. This involved regulating an isolated, rural community with cultural values far removed from those of the lawmakers in the state capital and even from my own... Anthropologists and anthropology can provide skills and tools for work in many jobs not normally considered anthropological... My experience underlines what practicing anthropologists already know: anthropologists need not limit themselves to traditional academic and research positions; their skills can be applied in a variety of field circumstances. (Hammon 1998: 197, 199)

Sometimes government policies combine both regulation and persuasion. For example, in trying to ensure a healthy physical environment, governments regulate waste disposal and enforce building codes, while simultaneously trying to persuade populations to adopt 'green' behaviours such as recycling rubbish and using energy efficiently. Anthropologists such as Hal Wilhite and his colleagues have therefore turned their attention to examining household energy use in America and Japan (Wilhite 2001), examining the social and cultural factors that encourage conservation. Such research, focused on why people do (or don't do) certain things, enables government agencies to make judgements about where behaviour might be amenable to persuasion or incentives, and where regulation or technical solutions may be the only way to achieve change.

Ensuring a healthy environment is only half of the equation. Another major responsibility of government agencies, along with delivering direct health care, is in guiding social practices in relation to health. How people think about and take care of their own health is a direct reflection of their cultural beliefs and values, and an understanding of these is helpful not just in designing appropriate health services, but in actively encouraging populations to maintain or adopt healthy practices. There are many potential areas of research here: nutrition, exercise, work-life balance, sexual behaviour, alcohol and drug use, mental health and so on. Governments' abilities to regulate health-related behaviour are limited: they can define a legal drinking age and pub opening hours, or criminalize drugs, but the governance of health is more generally directed towards education and persuasion.

For this, governments require 'social marketing' – methods for encouraging positive social behaviours – which arose in part from anthropology's development of 'cultural models'. Social marketing campaigns are often health related, focusing, for example on family planning and contraceptive use, or safe sex practices.

> Cultural anthropologists have contributed a great deal to such efforts. For example, the brand name given to contraceptives, and they way they are packaged, is crucial to their acceptance... Over the last fifteen years a number of very concerted social marketing efforts have been directed at the prevention of HIV/ AIDs. (Gwynne 2003a: 241)

Another example of the use of anthropology in social marketing is offered by Christopher Brown's (2002) work with a nonprofit social marketing firm in Tampa, Florida. Brown was employed to assist a public health programme – an early childhood intervention scheme that provided social services to families with children whose development was delayed. The staff observed that although their programme could benefit children, many families were not taking advantage of it. Brown's task was to find out why people were not enrolling their children and to design a social marketing programme to encourage them to do so. He found two key issues: the ideas that people had about whether children needed regular visits to pediatricians (who were the major point of referral to the programme), and the cultural model of health care to which parents subscribed.

The ability to look below the surface and discern the underlying factors is also vital in a different area of health and welfare: the problem of domestic violence and abuse. Like other aspects of health and well-being, this requires considerable sensitivity to cultural beliefs and values, and a careful balance between respect for personal and domestic privacy and the protection of people's basic rights. A good example is provided by Anannya Bhattacharjee's research in New York (2006), which is concerned with domestic violence in immigrant communities from South Asia. Bhattacharjee observed that American immigration processes (in which legal immigration status is often spouse based) make women highly dependent upon their husbands, and thus very vulnerable to isolation and abuse. Her work also revealed that immigrant domestic workers, whose visas are often sponsored by their employers, are similarly isolated and disadvantaged:

> The employer may deny her sponsorship or hold the power to do so over her. She is extremely vulnerable to all forms of abuse, often works around the clock, and may be denied basic subsistence. She, too, can face complete isolation as her employer can control her movements much like a husband controls those of a battered wife. (Bhattacharjee, 2006: 343)

Bhattacharjee's research shows how respect for the 'privacy' of domestic space makes it difficult to tackle these problems, and she has used anthropological analyses to rethink ideas about private and public spaces, and to suggest some new directions in tackling domestic violence and abuse.

Cultural insights are equally important in one of the most fundamental of responsibilities that societies have: caring for children and ensuring their healthy development. Anthropologists are involved in many kinds of research relating to children: for example Pat Caplan (2006) conducts research on the social and cultural issues surrounding adoption. Cross-cultural adoptions raise many complex issues and are highly controversial, as illustrated by the public debates surrounding adoptions by 'celebrities' such as Madonna and Angelina Jolie. This is therefore an area that is particularly in need of careful social analysis and cultural sensitivity. The process of raising children in general is another major area of interest for anthropologists. Jonathan Green has worked in the area of child care for a number of years, and observes that

> ... while I became involved ... largely by chance, I have found numerous intersections between my work in child care and early childhood education and my study and research in anthropology... Anthropology has much to add to the field... A key contribution is awareness of the importance of culture in defining interpersonal interactions and discourse... Additionally, applied anthropological concepts of intercultural negotiation and collaborative and cooperative efforts towards change can contribute to improving the quality of day care... How and what we can teach children in the early years of life has immense repercussions for the future of the children and our society as a whole ... it is an area in need of qualitative and quantitative anthropology research and anthropologically informed practice. (Green 1998: 161–5)

EDUCATION

Many people think that education is simply a matter of going to school and acquiring knowledge and skills. However, it is more than that: it is also an important part of how nation-states construct themselves, ensuring that schooling also teaches students allegiance to the state – hence American rituals such as flag raising in schools, and the recent introduction of 'citizenship' in the UK curriculum. However, globalization and commoditization have had a major effect on this process. Anthropologists have been critical of the reframing of education as a commodity (Cooper 2004) and of the effects of selling it internationally.

> Public education remains the nation-state's foremost instrument of forging citizens. But the emergence of 'international education', a system explicitly based on the ideology of globality and outside the purview of national curricula, provides a way to circumvent the citizen-making machine. This [research], based on fieldwork among Chinese secondary school students in Hungary, considers the interaction between 'international education' and transnational migrants in a nation-state whose public education, as the state itself, has little interest in the 'integration' of non-natives. (Nyíri 2006: 32)

In a contemporary multicultural educational domain, there are many new questions to answer, and a major need for cross-cultural understandings. And there are more fundamental aspects of education to consider. Anthropology has long been concerned with understanding human processes of cognition and development.

How do people learn? How do societies transmit information between generations? How are cultural ideas communicated – and contested – between groups? How (and why) are different kinds of knowledges valorized or set aside?

Educational anthropology is therefore a distinct subfield within the discipline. It emerged in Western nations in the post-war era, when there was an influx of diverse veterans (with equally diverse educational needs) into higher education institutions. In America, another important step was the creation of a Council on Anthropology and Education (CAE) in the 1960s. Ideas at the time, about how a 'culture of poverty' could be alleviated by education, tended to assume that this meant a white, middle-class kind of education. The CAE challenged this view and 'advocated for equity, diversity and amelioration of problems affecting education' (Kedia and Van Willigen 2005: 273).

The need to address different cultural perspectives has grown steadily as many societies have become more multicultural, and educational services have had to encompass much greater diversity. As societies have changed, anthropologists have charted the changing social and cultural pressures on their educational systems (Hargreaves *et al.* 2000). These changes have made education an area in which the cross-cultural translatory skills of anthropologists are particularly helpful and, as in other areas of knowledge, anthropologists have been key to debates about the need for pluralism and acknowledging cultural specificities.

> In my observations and analysis, I pondered what might be authentic as education for the Oglala… As I looked at the reservation schools, I saw them as preaching a single, mythical and homogenized version of America, whereas the Sioux had every right to ask that their children be socialized into their own unique ethos. (Wax in Kedia and Van Willigen 2005: 269)

Studies of pre-schools in different cultures have shown wide variations on ideas about individualism, conformity, critical thinking and giftedness. Rosemary Henze worked with teachers directly, as well as educational administrators, to assist them in encompassing diversity in schools (Henze and Davis 1999), and Nancy Greenman observes that:

> Educational anthropologists know that beliefs about what is best for 'the good society' and what is envisioned as 'the good society' vary between and within cultures… One cannot live in these times without realizing that notions of good or effective education are disparate. The choices for educational policy usually reflect the assumptions and perceptions of the powerful and do not necessarily benefit all. (Greenman, in Kedia and Van Willigen 2005: 271)

Some anthropologists have conducted research on specific educational institutions. For example, one of the early researchers in this area, Gerry Rosenfeld (1971), conducted detailed ethnographic research in inner city schools, and his classic text was seminal in defining racial issues in the educational system.

Other anthropologists have looked at the wider educational context: thus Yvonne De Gaetano (2007) has considered the importance of involving parents in the schooling process and ensuring that it has a culturally relevant approach. A careful consideration of the social and cultural context of education is important, in order that the interests of all children – including those from minority or disadvantaged groups – are upheld: 'Most educational anthropologists, some of whom are also teachers, believe that their specialized knowledge makes them potentially more effective advocates for children – and for amelioration of the issues having an impact on their success within their micro- and macro-sociocultural contexts' (Kedia and Van Willigen 2005: 272).

Concha Delgado-Gaitan describes her work as a combination of advocacy and facilitation: 'Through my role as a participant-observer, I have become actively engaged with the community where I research to act as a 'facilitator'. By doing so I am able to act as an advocate for the families, using research data to inform and develop agency for the people as they shape policies and practices in the schools and the community at large' (Delgado-Gaitan, in Kedia and van Willigen 2005: 272).

In multicultural societies, language is also an educational issue both in terms of assisting the children of new immigrants in acquiring sufficient language to participate in the educational process, and in maintaining indigenous languages. Thus Lotty Elderling, working with immigrant families in the Netherlands, highlighted the need for immigration policy to address language acquisition among immigrants, to improve their children's performance in school and their overall social mobility (Elderling, in Kedia and van Willigen 2005: 283).

There is also a role for anthropologists in 'nurturing native languages' (see Reyhner *et al.* 2003). Many indigenous communities, inhabiting larger societies and economies, struggle to uphold their own cultural traditions. Keeping languages alive is central to these efforts, and linguistic anthropologists have often focused their research on understanding and documenting languages not previously written down, in order to explore the diverse worldviews that they express, and to assist contemporary indigenous communities in their educational endeavours. There is also a broader role in assisting the integration of these languages into educational systems. Anthropologists have been closely involved in this, and countries such as Canada, America, Australia and New Zealand have now made major efforts to introduce indigenous educational material to their curricula, along with indigenous languages and pedagogies.

In Australia, for example, there are now multiple efforts to make use of Aboriginal languages and culture in the Australian educational system. Thus, in the Aboriginal community where I work in northern Australia, elders from each of the local language groups participate in the school as advisors and educators, focusing on traditional knowledge, which is also incorporated into the school's literacy material. Working for the Australian Council for Educational Research in the Learning Process, Nola Purdie notes that a recent National Plan for education affirmed the need to value indigenous languages:

> Such recognition must be heartening for indigenous people. Their languages have a unique place in Australia's heritage and in its cultural and educational life. For indigenous learners they are fundamental to strengthening identity and self-esteem. For non-indigenous learners they provide a focus for the development of cultural understanding and reconciliation. (Purdie 2008: 1)

In New Zealand too, schools and universities have attempted to incorporate Maori and Pasifika languages and pedagogies, as well as European educational methodologies, and similar work is being done in North America. Teresa McCarty, for example, works with Lucille Watahomigie under the wing of the American Indian Language Development Institute at the University of Arizona, conducting a range of projects designed to reverse the ongoing language loss in Native communities.

> If new generations are not to 'forget' the heritage language and the collective memory it holds, then traditional language learning environments must be reconfigured and restored, and new ones created... Collaborations between school personnel and community members, and between the school community and educational and linguistic anthropologists, have been central... Our goal is to illustrate the possibilities not just for bringing the language 'back' but ... moving it *forward* into new social contexts as well. (McCarty and Watahomigie 2002: 354)

Anthropology has been influential in encouraging this more diverse approach and Donna Deyhle notes that in a Dine/Navajo school district, 'One issue that has changed, and is very exciting, is that the district seems to be coming full circle – moving from a racially based decision – no Navajo language or culture – to using Navajo language and culture in the school curriculum to enhance student success. Rather than ignoring the ethnographic research, they are trying to "come back on board"' (in Kedia and Van Willigen 2005: 290).

Anthropologists' commitment to upholding cultural diversity has therefore had an impact on policies relating to curriculum development, most particularly in encouraging efforts to create culturally relevant approaches. There is a related need to help students understand the influence of culture on what happens in schools. In Chicago, for example, the Chicago Field Museum runs a 'Cultural Connections' programme, which uses anthropological concepts to help teachers, parents and children to engage with cultural diversity in local neighbourhoods:

The Center for Cultural Understanding and Change (CCUC) at The Field Museum uses problem-solving anthropological research to identify and catalyze strengths and assets of communities in Chicago and beyond. In doing so, CCUC helps communities identify new solutions to critical challenges such as education, housing, health care, environmental conservation, and leadership development. Through research, programs, and access to collections, CCUC reveals the power of cultural difference to transform social life and promote social change. (Chicago Field Museum 2008)

Anthropological research in education is not confined to schools: in Australia, for example, they have been involved in the design of special educational programmes aimed at public servants, in particular the police, to introduce them to Aboriginal concepts of justice and law, before they go to work in indigenous communities.

As well as helping to develop educational policies, anthropologists are also employed in evaluating them.

Traditional ethnographic concepts and techniques applied to evaluation enable the insider's voice to be heard and have an impact on policy decision-making ... an ethnographic approach to evaluation allows for a more meaningful and fair evaluation of a situation, classroom or event... This approach has stirred the imaginations and emotions of many evaluators. It is designed to help people learn how to evaluate their own program. It is built on the premise that the insider's view or emic perspective matters. (Fetterman, in Kedia and Van Willigen 2005: 299)

There are thus many areas of human services in which it is useful to have anthropological training – indeed, as each deals with humans, and their complex ideas and values, it is reasonable to say that there is no area of human service in which such training would NOT be useful. Anthropology can therefore make a contribution to many – potentially all – areas of governance: to the design of new policies; to their implementation, and to evaluations of their efficacy in providing for human needs.

6 ANTHROPOLOGY, BUSINESS AND INDUSTRY

MONEY MATTERS

> Anthropologists understand that work is not just about process, it's about people. If you lose sight of that, you lose.
>
> Anita Ward, Senior Vice President, Texas Commerce Bank

Economic activity, in whatever form, is central to human societies, so it has always been a key area of study for anthropologists. Most societies now rely heavily on a diverse range of businesses and industries, and all, to varying degrees, participate in a globalizing economic market (see Fisher and Downey 2006). The anthropology of economic life has changed accordingly, and today researchers are involved in examining a host of different aspects of 'how people make a living': thus they work with resource industries; a range of service and manufacturing industries; designers and architects; communications and media industries; and market research and advertising companies.

As in other areas, anthropologists think about the internal dynamics of human groups, and also about the wider, external issues that shape these. So when it comes to working with industries, they consider their organizational cultures, and also the larger social and economic context in which production takes place. The most compelling external reality for contemporary businesses and industries is the process of globalization and its vast and volatile international markets. As observed in previous chapters, globalization is of considerable interest to social scientists, and many anthropologists have focused on it directly, considering how it affects different communities, demanding new economic practices and disseminating a range of cultural ideas and values.

> Globalization is a pattern of economic and cultural change involving mutual influence of previously separate and distinct societies. This is not a new phenomenon, because the entire period of colonization was one of unequal transnational economic and cultural exchange. In the postcolonial world, the processes of globalization are made possible by the advent of world capitalism. Multinational corporations are now world powers operating in a world market. On the local level, the flow of investment, profit and consumer goods across borders can provide access to cash for the producers of some luxury goods. In the long run, however, the evidence indicates that peripheral peoples become less well-off because of globalization, while wealth becomes more and more concentrated in the hands of a small elite. (Bestor 2003: 367)

Theodore Bestor looked at globalization in the fishing industry, examining how sushi came to be eaten internationally, and how the creation of a wider market affected bluefin tuna fishers, whose catch is now auctioned for vast sums and flown across the world. He underlines the dynamism of the process as well as its capacity for creating new transnational, inter-cultural relationships and internationalizing previously particular cultural tastes:

> Bluefin tuna may seem at first an unlikely case study in globalization. But as the world rearranges itself – around silicon chips, Starbucks coffee, or sashimi-grade tuna – new channels for global flows of capital and commodities link far-flung individuals and communities in unexpected new relationships. The tuna trade is a prime example of the globalization of a regional industry, with intense international competition and thorny environmental regulations; centuries-old

practices combined with high technology; realignments of labor and capital in response to international regulation; shifting markets; and the diffusion of culinary culture as tastes for sushi, and bluefin tuna, spread worldwide. (Bestor 2003: 368)

Caren Kaplan (1995) was an early analyst of globalization. She has considered the way that 'ethical' corporations such as the Body Shop and Ben and Jerry's promulgate notions of a world 'without boundaries' in which, through multinational corporations, European traders deal directly with producers rather than 'middlemen'. The Body Shop proposed that 'free trade without middlemen means liberation' (Kaplan 1995: 430). Kaplan's critique of the way that this advertising represents a multinational enterprise is an important one, highlighting the language that is used and the values about globalization and capitalism that it carries. She looks at how 'the world' is represented in these discourses, as a place where there is a flow of culture and capital between the West and communities that are celebrated as 'native', 'authentic' or 'tribal'. As an illustration of this rosy view, she examines a joint advertisement by American Express and The Body Shop:

'Trade Not Aid' is a way of trading honorably with indigenous communities in disadvantaged areas – not changing the environment or the culture. Instead we listen to what these people need and try to help them with it. What we bring back with us are stories – how they do things, the connections; the essential wisdom of indigenous groups... Customers come into the Body Shop to buy hair conditioner and find a story about the Xingu reserve and the Kayapo Indians who collect Brazil nuts for us. We showed them a simple process for extracting oil from the nut, which consequently raises the value of the raw ingredient we use. The result is we pay them more for it, and that gives them an alternative to their logging income, which in turn protects the rain forest. (Anita Roddick. Advertisement in Kaplan 1995)

Kaplan carefully picked apart the messages in this material, which, she says, 'can be read as the celebrity marriage of entrepreneurial capitalism to bourgeois feminist travel-and-adventure motifs':

First, the ad copy refers to a site of consumption that can only be in a metropolitan location where information about the Xingu reserve and the Kayapo Indians will be pleasingly novel. It assumes that the customer in the metropole will enter a store to buy a mundane item such as hair conditioner only to procure simultaneously something 'different'. Secondly, it is implied that consumption leads not only to the pleasure of owning something but to the acquisition of a moral object lesson in Roddick's entrepreneurial philosophy, a set of practices she calls 'Trade not Aid'. Trade not Aid emits bits of 1980s-style Thatcher–Reagan injunctions in the 1990s, displaying a savvy, neoconservative message all wrapped up in environmentally sensitive packaging. Finally, Roddick mystifies the conditions of production through primitivism. The Kayapo, a tribe that is well-known in anthropological and environmentalist circles for resisting both national and corporate domination by utilizing sophisticated media, are depicted as simple 'story tellers' who convey an 'essential wisdom'. (Kaplan, 1995: 435–6)

As Kaplan points out, the discourse gives a simple, polarized view of 'developed' and 'underdeveloped' 'First' and 'Third' world people, and a vision of

vanishing natives who require managed altruism from a concerned source of capital development ... the benevolent capitalism of The Body Shop... What is particularly chilling to me is The Body Shop's *representation* of a corporate *replacement* of the nation-state. It appears to be The Body Shop that funds and manages development projects, just as it appears to be The Body Shop that addresses health care, financing, and environmental concerns in its global reach... Both the written text and the images in these ads glamorize and seek to legitimate unequal transnational economic relations... The myth of a 'world without boundaries' leaves our material differences intact and even exacerbates the asymmetries of power that stratify our lived experiences. (Kaplan 1995: 437–9)

Although Kaplan uses the 'ethical' Body Shop as an example, her major point is not to have a go at this particular company: her aim is rather to show *how* representations create imaginary communities and 'mask' the real economic workings of business and commerce and the inequalities that are created and maintained by global capitalism. There is an underlying issue – a vital one for human societies – about the weakening of democratic processes as the functions and services of elected governments are taken over by multinational corporations accountable only to their shareholders.[1]

Global business is concerned, fundamentally, with the use and distribution of resources. This is particularly evident in resource-based industries, such as mining, oil exploration and – as noted earlier – materials such as timber, and food production. Because global economies are reaching further and further into what were until recently remote areas, many anthropologists who work with indigenous communities and peasant societies are now considering how these deal with the incursion of enthusiastic developers and greater involvement in expanding global markets.

This expansion has major social and environmental implications, as demonstrated, for example, by Stuart Kirsch's (2001) research with communities in Papua New Guinea, where mining has become a major part of the country's economy. Kirsch's work, which I mentioned in Chapter 1, points to the massive ecological

damage caused by mining in the headwaters of the Ok Tedi river, and its economic and social effects on the communities in the area. Observing the dominance of transnational corporations in the equation, he points to the local communities' relative powerlessness and inability to demand environmental protection, in an area vital to their social and economic well-being (Kirsch 2003).

FIELDWORK ON THE FLY

Stuart Kirsch

Consultant and Visiting Assistant Professor, University of Michigan

When I first went to work among the Yonggom people of Papua New Guinea, I had to hitch a ride on the *Motuan Chief*, a ship carrying supplies from Port Moresby to Kiunga on the Fly River. We crossed the Gulf of Papua, following the route of the annual *hiri* expeditions in which villagers sailed in huge canoes to exchange clay pots and shells for sago flour and canoe hulls. After a day and a night, the *Motuan Chief* reached the mouth of the Fly. Kiwai people approached in outrigger canoes, offering to trade bananas and fresh fish. As we travelled upriver, the boat stopped to provide supplies to people in tiny, isolated villages. Thick rainforest crowded the river, but subsequently opened up into the patchwork of lagoons and islands where the Gogodala people live. Their enormous longhouses, canoe races, and celebrated wood carvings are combined with a brand of evangelical Christianity that impinges on many of their traditional practices. Midway through our journey we entered the savannah grasslands that the Boazi people call home. Later I learned that they used to prey on the Yonggom in their headhunting raids. Nearer our destination, the rainforest surrounded the river again.

Flocks of hornbills flew overhead and the raucous cries of cockatoos disturbed the quiet afternoon. Finally, after five days, we reached the town of Kiunga.

It took another day's travel by motor-canoe to the village on the Ok Tedi River where I lived for two years. The purpose of my research was to learn about the myth, magic, and rituals of the Yonggom people. During my first week, a group of men took me into the rainforest to tell me the secret myths associated with their male initiation ceremony. From that moment, I was hooked: despite the heat, humidity, and malaria of the lowland rainforest, this was clearly the place for me! Eventually my new friends would call upon me to reciprocate their generosity in welcoming me into their lives.

Upstream from Kiunga is the Ok Tedi copper and gold mine, which began production in the mid-1980s. Plans for a dam to protect the river from pollution were never fully implemented. The mine discharged 80,000 metric tons of tailings — the particles that remain after the ore is extracted — into the river every day. To date, one billion metric tons of tailings and other mine wastes have been dumped into the river system, and more than 1,500 square kilometres of rainforest have been affected, destroying the habitat of the fish, birds, and other animals which used to live there. The mine wastes — and their impacts — will slowly move downstream towards the Gulf of Papua over the next two centuries. The savannah grasslands where the Boazi live will be flooded for eight months of the year; the Gogodala's lagoons will fill with silt from the mine; and the mangrove forests of the Kiwai will be substantially reduced. It remains to be seen whether new problems with acid mine drainage, which releases poisonous heavy metals into the food chain, can be brought under control.

After living with the Yonggom for two years, I began my journey home. There had been a rebellion on the island of Bougainville, which shut down Papua New Guinea's largest copper mine. Bougainvilleans objected to the mine's environmental impacts and the government's failure to distribute its economic benefits. The resulting civil war lasted more than a decade. Boarding a ship in Kiunga for Port Moresby one morning, I reached up to climb over the side of the boat, clutching a souvenir bow and arrows in one hand. When the crew saw these, they called out in fear, imagining that they were under attack by opponents of the Ok Tedi mine!

I assumed that my time in Papua New Guinea was almost over, but soon realized that no one in the capital was aware of the magnitude of the impacts of the Ok Tedi mine. At a lecture at the national university, in a newspaper editorial, and as a guest on a national talk radio program, I warned Papua New Guineans that the fate of the entire Fly River was at risk.

These events launched me on a path of activist anthropology. After years of unsuccessful petitions and protests, the people living downstream from the mine sued Broken Hill Proprietary, Ltd (BHP), its majority shareholder and managing partner. The case was settled out of court for an estimated US$500 million in compensation and commitments to implement tailings containment. Subsequently, when BHP continued to dump tailings into the river, the landowners returned to the courts but were unsuccessful in gaining legal redress. However, BHP decided that the Ok Tedi mine was no longer 'compatible with our environmental values' and transferred its share of the project to a trust fund that will support economic development in Papua New Guinea. Given the current high prices for gold and copper, this fund may eventually be worth US$1 billion.

Throughout their political struggle, I have continued to work with the Yonggom and their neighbours. I advised their lawyers, wrote about the social impact of the mine, and collaborated with environmental NGOs and human rights organizations in Papua New Guinea, Australia, and the United States. I spoke about these issues at the United Nations, advised the World Bank on its support of the mining industry, and published a book about the experiences of the Yonggom (Kirsch 2006). Recently I tried to convince my own university that it erred in inviting BHP Billiton to advise a campus initiative on sustainability.

When I first visited Papua New Guinea, the village on the Ok Tedi River seemed like an archetypal 'out of the way' place. Since then, the mine has become one of the most infamous environmental disasters in the world. I never expected to become involved in the struggle of indigenous peoples against threats to their environment and way of life. Studying anthropology is the beginning of a long and exciting journey, and what happens along the way is filled with surprises!

Work that reveals the deeper effects of a globalizing economy underlines the fact that anthropology is not just about applying qualitative methods: it requires theory and analysis that enables practitioners to look 'under the surface' and make social action more transparent. It also implies a level of intellectual independence, derived from scientific training, and upheld by the ethical codes that guide the discipline. In reflecting on globalization, anthropologists have tended to unsettle comfortable assumptions popularly made about the benefits of economic growth, and the utility of the market as a force for positive change. As in other applications of anthropology, researchers therefore find themselves both 'standing back' to reflect critically on issues and, with a more internal role, trying to conduct research in a way that properly incorporates ethical principles.

ANTHROPOLOGISTS IN BUSINESS

Business and industrial companies are, ultimately, social communities. They share a common purpose, often have common training (for example through business schools, or vocational institutions), and develop their own internal cultures. They are therefore very amenable to the kind of 'organizational research' discussed earlier in this volume: research that specializes in gaining an understanding of institutional cultures, how these work internally and how they interact with larger social and economic networks (Corsin-Jiménez 2007).

In multicultural societies and globalizing economies, businesses and industries increasingly contain people from diverse cultural groups. They have to manage this diversity. Many also have international networks of relationships that bring further – and sometimes even more diverse – cultural perspectives into the equation. The 'cultural translation' skills of anthropology, and its ability to provide in-depth under-standings of social behaviour are therefore an important part of the work that anthropologists do in this sphere.

> Anthropologist Elizabeth Briody earned her Ph.D. studying communities of Mexican-American farm workers and Catholic nuns. For the past 11 years, though, she's been studying a different community – the men and women of General Motors. As GM's 'industrial anthropologist', Briody explores the intricacies of life at the company. It's not all that different from her previous work. 'Anthropologists help elicit the cultural patterns of an organization' she says. 'What rules do people have about appropriate and inappropriate behaviour? How do they learn those rules and pass them on to others?'
>
> Briody is a pioneer in a growing and influential field – corporate anthropology. What began as an experiment in a handful of companies such as GM has become an explosion. In recent years, some of the biggest names in business have recruited highly trained anthropologists to understand their workers and customers better, and to help design products that better reflect emerging cultural trends. (Kane 1996: 60)

Kate Kane presents a range of other examples: Sue Squire's work with Andersen Worldwide, instructing accountants in different ways of doing business around the world; Patricia Sachs' research with telecommunications design engineers at Nynex; Tony Salvador's work as an 'engineering ethnographer' at Intel (Kane 1996: 60). Kane suggests that this new popularity is due to anthropology's holistic approach which is well suited to tackling the complexities of contemporary business activities.

Anthropologists therefore bring to business and industry a unique intellectual perspective from which to consider events analytically. As John Seely Brown, the head of the Xerox corporation's research and development section observed: anthropology and anthropologists 'let you view behaviour through a new set of glasses' (in Roberts 2006: 73). Having discovered the benefits of doing so, Xerox now regularly employs anthropologists. And they are not alone: the number of anthropologists working as employees for businesses, or assisting them as consultants, is growing rapidly (see Morris and Bastin 2004). As Jennifer Laabs observes: 'the corporate jungle is full of cultural anomalies. Business anthropologists are helping to solve some of them':

> Chances are, an anthropologist wouldn't be the first business expert you'd call if you wanted a better mouse-trap – or a better HR program... But maybe they should be ... many companies have found that anthropologists' expertise as cultural scientists is quite useful in gaining insight into human behaviour... Anthropologists study many different areas of business, but essentially they are all people watchers of one sort or another. Business anthropologists have been studying the corporate world for years. (Laabs 1998: 61)

SEEING ALTERNATIVE SOLUTIONS

Ralph Bishop

Global Manager, Qualitative Research, ISR, Chicago

I am currently manager of qualitative research for an international human resources and organization development consulting firm. This entails design and analysis of structured interviews, open-ended survey questions, and analysis of the results. I became involved in this kind of work purely by chance. I signed on as a freelance editor and everybody I reported to quit, so I had the opportunity to take over the department!

The most important thing anthropology does is to help people see alternate solutions to problems, largely because it sees more information as relevant than more constrained methodologies. Statistics tell you what; qualitative input tells you why. You need both.

Laabs (1998) notes that over 200 anthropologists were employed in corporate America, advising businesses on a range of issues, how to encourage creativity; how to manage human resource issues; and how to resolve conflicts and encourage collaboration. As in other ethnographic contexts, anthropologists in business try to understand what is going on under the surface. In an organization, this may mean approaching even mundane things like meetings as analytic opportunities to see what is really going and how decisions actually get made. Helen Schwartzman, for example, took a close look at meetings in an American mental health centre, and suggested that they provide a useful context for understanding events within organizations: 'Meetings are a basic and pervasive part of this life, and yet because they are so prevalent in American society, so ordinary and frequently so boring, their significance as a social form has not been recognized or examined' (Schwartzman 1987: 271).

Anthropologists in the corporate world also consider cultural differences in ideas about what a job is, and what it is meant to achieve. For example, Lorna McDougall works as a staff anthropologist at Arthur Andersen's Center for Professional Education in Illinois, studying why some people learn better from lectures while others do so interactively, and thinking about how to integrate multicultural learning into training. This helped companies to develop better training programmes, and led managing director Pete Pesce to comment that 'an anthropologist brings a lot of value to an organization' (in Laabs 1998: 61).

Businesses and industries all seek to define and represent a particular identity. With his colleague Anthony Giannini, Roger McConochie helps organizations to 'rethink' their corporate history and mythology: 'Companies need a clear "ego sense": a continual sense of organizational self over time… From my experience in corporations, the people on the shop floor have as much need for meaning in their lives as the people in the boardroom' (in Laabs 1998: 61–3).

Good management depends on a clear understanding of what is going on in a company and anthropology can help to reveal this. A classic example is provided by Julian Orr's work with Xerox. He did ethnographic research with a group of the technicians who service Xerox's machines, and he found that their training never kept pace with the new technology that was being introduced. To cope with this they developed an important sub-cultural set of 'war stories' about past machine failures and heroic saves, which served to communicate ideas about what might work to get them out of a jam. Orr showed Xerox how this was functioning:

> Once Xerox found out how technicians solved difficult machine problems, it decided to facilitate and develop this grassroots approach by equipping technicians with mobile radio phones that would enable them to call each other in the field or to contact a roving 'tiger team' comprised of highly skilled troubleshooters… Orr's discovery of the economic power of storytelling within an occupational community provides an unforgettable illustration of the power of culture in an organization. (Kedia and Van Willigen 2005: 247)

There are many such 'sub-cultures' in the workplace: groups of people united by common knowledge and expertise, professional training, a particular language and of course by the particular kind of work that they do. 'Members of occupational or professional groups often have characteristics that parallel those found in small-scale societies, such as a unique system of meanings, practices, and a language that distinguishes them from other work groups' (Baba 2005: 230).

Sometimes the members of particular groups form their own sub-cultural blocs in a company. Marietta Baba points to a wide range of anthropological studies of these: Herbert Applebaum's study of construction crews; Elizabeth Lawrence's ethnography on rodeo participants; and other anthropological research on accountants, locomotive engineers, longshoremen, medical school students, nightclub strippers, police, professional dance musicians, social workers, timber loggers, underground miners, waiters (Baba 2005: 230). Nancy Rosenberger comments that

> Anthropological research goes beyond the official corporate culture into the experiences and perceptions that make up the culture of work ... Anthropologists also illuminate subcultures of work – behaviors and values unique to a particular group of workers – by talking with and observing workers who vary by age, gender, education, socioeconomic status, ethnic background, or by level and job within the organization. (Rosenberger 2002: 403–4)

Rosenberger's own research examined a subculture of young, single women in Japan and Korea, looking at their different experiences of professional work. Most were employed in quite lowly positions, in tasks supportive of men's activities in the workplace. The research considered how they managed this role, and highlighted the 'glass ceiling' that prevented them from advancing up the corporate ladder (Rosenberger 2002).

Anthropologists also consider how 'local' work cultures are formed by wider cultural contexts. For example, Thomas Rohlen's classic research on daily life in a Japanese bank, Uedagin, examined the training of young people in preparation for a lifelong career of service. As Baba says, 'from this vantage point we can see how the national culture of Japan shapes the subculture of the banking occupation in a Japanese setting' (Baba 2005: 242).

MULTINATIONAL AND MULTICULTURAL COMMUNICATION

As noted at the beginning of this chapter, as well as having internal cultures and sometimes sub-cultures, businesses and industries also have a set of external relationships with other groups at national and international levels. These require careful management, and depend, more than anything else, on effective communication. At the most basic level, this means being able to speak the language. English is the mother tongue of only 5 per cent of the world's population, yet Gary Ferraro notes that many Westerners enter the international business arena without studying languages at all. A study of US firms reveals that only 31 per cent considered foreign languages necessary, and only 20 per cent of them required their employees overseas to know the local language:

> International business firms require effective communication at a number of levels. A company must communicate with its work force, customers, suppliers, and host government officials. Effective communication among people from

the same culture is difficult enough. But when attempting to communicate with people who do not speak English and who have different attitudes, ideas, assumptions, perceptions, and ways of doing things, one's chances for mis-communication increase enormously. (Ferraro 1998: 98)

Ferraro offers several well-known instances of mis-translation:

- In Flemish, General Motors 'body by Fisher' became 'Corpse By Fisher'.
- In Chinese, Pepsi-Cola's slogan 'Come Alive With Pepsi' became 'Pepsi will bring your ancestors back from the grave'.
- In Brazil, a US Airline promised plush 'rendezvous lounges' in its first class sections without realizing that, in Portuguese, this implies a room for making love.
- When an American chicken entrepreneur translated a slogan into Spanish, 'It takes a tough man to make a tender chicken' became 'It takes a virile man to make a chicken affectionate'.

The list continues: cigarettes with low tar have been advertised as having 'asphalt'; computers have acquired 'underwear' instead of 'software'; and a hydraulic ram has been listed in an engineering manual as a 'wet sheep' (Ferraro 1998)

While entertaining, these mis-translations also serve to underline Ferraro's point that language is the doorway to understanding culture, beliefs and values – to getting to grips with a different worldview:

> If international business people are to be successful, there is no substitute for an intimate acquaintance with both the language and the culture of those with whom they are conducting business. Because of the close relationship between language and culture, it is almost impossible not to learn about one while studying the other. (Ferraro 1998: 98)

Language is of course not just a matter of words. It reveals basic cultural dynamics, showing, for example, how cultural groups think about the importance of the individual versus the importance of groups; how they value (or don't value) open disagreement; how formal or informal, hierarchical or non-hierarchical they are. There are different ways of saying 'no'; different uses and meanings of silence. Much communication is non-verbal, and what can seem friendly and open in one culture may be seen as aggressive and disrespectful in another.

When I was preparing to go and do my doctoral fieldwork with an Australian Aboriginal community, I read a short text by John Von Sturmer, called 'Talking With Aborigines' (1981) which outlined some of the cultural conventions that I would meet in the field: the need not to march up to people or their camps directly, but to approach them elliptically; the need to use kin terms rather than personal names; the convention that when people die their names are not spoken for some time. There are also more subtle issues about how different adoptive kin require different relationships: some involve 'joking' relationships, some are more formal; some require strict avoidance; some involve social and economic responsibilities. The use of silence in Aboriginal communities is complex, and cannot be taken to mean agreement at all. Such preparation, and lengthy fieldwork, is essential to an understanding of local beliefs and values and ways of understanding the world.

In order to work effectively all anthropologists have to do this kind of thing and, as a result, they are well equipped to assist others in coming at least part of the way down the same road. Although people 'doing business' may not need the depth of cultural understanding and engagement that ethnographic fieldwork requires, it is certainly helpful for them to have some idea about the cultural norms that prevail in the communities with whom they are involved. There is thus a very useful role for anthropologists in assisting them in this regard. As Richard Reeves-Ellington (2003: 247) says: 'Business people who are more culturally aware are also more successful.' He designed and implemented a cross-cultural training programme for an American company that was doing business in Japan. About 50 employees participated in this and the long-term results were impressive. 'Project managers who took the cultural training program were able to cut project completion time nearly in half and increase the financial returns from the projects threefold' (Reeves-Ellington 2003).

In essence, Reeves-Ellington teaches business-people to use the basic methods developed by anthropologists to describe and analyse cultural settings. He enables them to think about the way that things are classified in a particular cultural space; to discern local principles for behaviour; and to consider the values that drive these. He encourages them to think about the 'cultural logic' that they encounter – how do people engage with their environment? What do they consider to be truth and reality? What is their view of human nature? How do they approach relationships and define the purpose of activities? How do they use their time?

He gives his trainees a lot of information about the values and behavioural rituals implicit in business interactions in Japan, for example explaining the formal rituals and ideas that surround business card exchange; the seating arrangements of tables for meetings; the kinds of conference practices that are expected, and the importance of reciprocity in ritual exchanges.

Cultural translation is equally helpful in enabling different groups to communicate across global networks. Thus Emily Martin's (1996) work examines how scientists create a 'global system' of professional knowledge, and how non-scientists interpret this work and respond to it. Working in immunology research laboratories and clinical settings, Martin considered, in particular, how people make sense of medical images, using them to 'imagine' and respond to medical issues. Public understandings of science have major implications for many science and technology industries, defining how their products will be received and used, so these ethnographic insights have considerable potential to assist the design and presentation of information.

ANTHROPOLOGY AND COMMUNICATIONS MEDIA

A lot of public information about science and technology, and indeed about most ideas and products, is gained through a range of media: newspapers, radio, television, billboards and so on. Businesses and industries rely almost entirely on these to communicate with their target audiences, and in this representational arena, as in more direct interpersonal forms of communication, cross-cultural translation and an analytic eye are useful.

Elizabeth Colson and Conrad Kottak make the point that in a globalizing world it is vital for us to consider the way that communications media create multiple linkages between local, regional, national and international spheres of activity, exposing people to external institutions and alternative ways of life (Colson and Kottak 1996). Kottak's own research is concerned with how the introduction of television has changed local life in Brazil. He did a longitudinal study with four communities, looking at their engagement with TV over time (Kottak 1996).

Kottak's research revealed several stages: an initial period in which the novelty of the technology meant that the medium was more of a focus than the message; then a stage at which people were highly receptive to its messages. Things would then settle down into a more subtle and pervasive mode, in which its influence was revealed in changes in behaviour and cultural choices. He makes the point that electronic media instantaneously transmit information and images within and across national boundaries, and that in doing so it is a major socializing agent, competing with family, school, peers, community and church. It directs attention towards some things and away from others, casting television directors as knowledge gatekeepers and regulating public access to information. 'The mass media play an increasingly prominent role in national and international culture. They propel a globally spreading culture of consumption, stimulating participation in the cash economy. Particularly for non-literate people, the most significant mass medium is television' (Kottak 1996: 135).

The research also showed that this is not simple matter of globalization and homogenization: local cultural variations make a major difference to how TV is engaged with and received: 'As print has done for centuries ... the electronic mass media can also spread, and even create, national and ethnic identities. Like print,

television and radio can diffuse the cultures of different countries within their own boundaries, thus enhancing national cultural identity (Kottak 1996: 135).

The issue of how media contribute to the way that people imagine their own and others' identities is also the focus of Daniel Lefkowitz's (2001) research on the Israeli newspaper business. He notes Teun Van Djik's observation that the way news is portrayed often perpetuates racism and prejudice, for example by linking minority ethnic groups and crime, and reproducing ideologically dominant representations of identity. Obviously this has major social and political implications, and there are connections with the kind of work discussed in Chapter 1, in which anthropologists involved in advocacy and conflict resolution try to combat stereotypical representations by providing in-depth ethnographic accounts of cultural groups and their worldviews.

The way that people perceive and represent their own identity also has a major impact on how they engage with 'the market', for example influencing what they choose to buy; what they want to eat; what they want to read; and what they want to see on television. In working with business and industry, a number of anthropologists are involved in this area of research. For example, Simon Roberts' consultancy firm specializes in examining people's responses to media:

> [It is] a small research company called Ideas Bazaar that currently employs four people full time, and a host of freelance researchers, many graduates or postgraduates of anthropology. Our work to date has focused on three principal areas, some by design, some by accident: Print and Broadcast Media, Technology and Communications, and Organisations and Change. (Roberts 2006: 76)

The consultancy's research has covered a variety of areas: conducting audience research and getting involved in programme ideas development for the BBC; making investigations of mobile phone use; studying people's late-night television viewing and their readership of local and regional newspapers.

> Additionally, I and other Ideas Bazaar associates are involved with the iSociety research project at the London-based not-for-profit think-tank and consultancy, The Work Foundation [which] investigates the impact of information and communications technologies in the UK... Most iSociety projects use ethnographic research as a first choice methodology... Broadly speaking we help our clients understand the worlds in which they operate, from their audiences' perspectives, and then we assist them in acting upon this understanding. Our job, as we see it, is to give them a new understanding of a familiar environment. (Roberts 2006: 76–7)

Anthropological experience is also useful in ensuring that communications are culturally sensitive. A few years ago, the Royal Anthropological Institute responded to a request from the UK's Advertising Standards Board to review advertisements in terms of their cultural meanings, and advise the Board accordingly. The panel, composed of anthropologists working in different parts of the world, was able to put forward a range of perspectives on the meanings that might be ascribed to the ads by diverse cultural groups.

As writers such as Sean Nixon (2003) and Liz McFall (2004) have observed, advertising is of course intimately concerned with cultural beliefs and values, hoping to present products in a way that accords with what is considered culturally desirable. Advertising content and how people respond to it is therefore fertile ground for anthropological analysis, as is the 'advertising culture' of the companies who produce this particular product.[2] There are many ways to approach the analysis of advertising: for example, in his work with Japanese advertising agencies, Brian Moeran, who is based at the Copenhagen Business School, thinks of it classically as 'storytelling':

> An advertising agency may be seen as a dedicated storytelling organization... Participant observation in the agency has impressed upon me that making ads is mainly a matter of talk. There is talk about accounts, rival agencies, and all the people and institutions (corporate clients, publishing houses, television networks, production shops, celebrities, and so on) that constitute the field of Japanese advertising. There is talk about ad campaigns themselves – about how one marketing analysis successfully repositioned a luxury item as an everyday commodity, or another creative idea enabled a product to 'speak' to an elusive consumer group, and so on. (Moeran 2007: 160)

Robert Morais conducts research on advertising organizations in America. Seeking to 'unpack' the client-agency relationship he follows Helen Schwartzman's (1987) example in studying meetings, focusing on those

> ... between the manufacturer (client) and the advertising agency, where advertising ideas are presented, discussed, and selected. Although the participants enter

these meetings with the common goal of reaching agreement on the ideas that will be advanced to the next step in the creative development process, the attendees have additional, sometimes conflicting, professional and personal objectives. To achieve their objectives, meeting participants must have a command of unwritten rules, understand subtle verbal and nonverbal behavior, comprehend and navigate the delicate client-agency balance of power, demonstrate the craft of negotiation, and impress their superiors. American advertising creative meetings contain the defining attitudes, behaviors, and symbols of the client-agency relationship. (Morais 2007: 150)

MARKETING ANTHROPOLOGY

A natural extension of investigating communications between manufacturers and customers is in the area of marketing. Market Research is often considered as a separate disciplinary field, but it draws heavily on the data collection methods of the social sciences. In recent years it has enlarged its appreciation of in-depth qualitative approaches such as ethnography, and is also beginning to recognize that analytic approaches applying anthropological theory to elucidate human behaviour can be useful (Mariampolski 2006). As Patricia Sunderland and Rita Denny (2008) have shown, there are now major opportunities in consumer research for anthropologists.

Anthropologists themselves have a range of views about involvement in this field. For Adam Drazin, anthropological skills have considerable utility in a wider 'research industry', and vice versa:

> In between my first anthropology degree and my Ph.D., I worked for several years in this industry of market research and opinion polling. During this experience, I was struck by how the idea of 'research' is at the heart of what it means to be a 'market researcher', and is often more important than the 'market' part of the appellation. Many market researchers I know often identify with academic anthropologists in the sense that both are interested in research first. There are dissenters of course, but it is well known that the best market researchers are people who are simply dying to get onto the next piece of research and find something out. (Drazin 2006: 91–2)

He found that experience as a market researcher helped him considerably when he trained as an anthropologist, and went to conduct ethnographic research in Romania: 'Hundreds of market research projects, chains of focus groups, and training involving tramping the streets of Essex towns knocking on doors with a clipboard had equipped me fairly well for participant observation and data collection' (Drazin 2006: 91–2)

There are times when involvement in market research does create ethical dilemmas for anthropologists. It is widely accepted, for instance, that in focus groups and surveys people very rarely report their behaviour honestly, and that more accurate information may be gleaned by simply observing what they actually do. However, the ethical codes that guide anthropology strictly forbid practitioners to do research covertly, and this led Carrie McLaren to express concern about 'shopping spies': market researchers who covertly spy on customers in shopping malls, fast-food halls and so on, sometimes striking up conversations with them while pretending to be fellow shoppers and sometimes videoing their behaviour. Apparently some market researchers regard this study of what they call 'naked behaviour' as 'ethnography' or 'anthropological studies'. McLaren (2002: 421) is highly critical of this misrepresentation of anthropology, and of the approach itself: 'since focus groups aren't the real world, they're working damn hard to make the real world a focus group'.

Still, there is no doubt that consumer behaviour is an important area of activity, defining, in effect, how societies use and manage their resources. It could be argued that in a public place, such as a shopping mall, security cameras and store staff are already recording and observing behaviour, and it is not practical to ask everyone's permission, or tell them that a research project is underway. However, some techniques clearly go beyond the bounds of simple observation and stray into deception. So, once again, there are some interesting ethical issues to consider.

In general, market research is conducted openly, and represents a straightforward attempt to find out what people think, or what they want, and to produce and advertise goods accordingly. Anthropology can bring greater depth to such data collection, as well as the ability to consider diverse cultural responses.

> With these demographic changes has come a growing awareness of and attention to various ethnic groups by the media, the public at large, politicians and private industry. In market research jargon, these groups are called 'market segments', and efforts to reach them have become more refined. This is part of a longer-term move from mass marketing to target marketing – first toward young people and women and now toward ethnic groups.

> Equipped with this knowledge and trained in sociocultural anthropology, I recently decided to open a research and consulting firm, which I call Surveys Unlimited ... a 'cultural research and consulting company' applying anthropological techniques and analysis to market research. As I met with potential clients, I promoted ethnographic fieldwork as central to the services I offered and advocated using the approach in research on targeted 'market segments'. (Waterston 1998: 106)

Waterston makes the point that, to really appreciate what people want, there is a need to explore their views without preconceptions, and to observe them on 'their own home turf'. As she says: 'exploring issues from the bottom up tunes us into consumers' conceptual systems' (Waterston 1998). Like McLaren, she pays attention to ethical concerns – in this instance questioning the idea of targeting people (and in particular less well-off minority groups) to induce them to buy consumer goods. But, as she points out, there are some erroneous preconceptions to be considered in this regard:

> In my discussions with members of minority groups, many people express resentment at being passed over by marketers. They view attention paid to minority markets as empowering to members of those groups and as providing new work and career opportunities for them... Clearly the phenomenon of ethnic marketing reflects political processes of ethnic identity formation. It should come as no surprise that exploitation and empowerment are two sides of the coin. The anthropological advantage in market research also involves keeping these issues in sight. (Waterston 1998: 109)

As well as dealing with the political and economic aspects of marketing, anthropologists have recently begun to consider the more subtle aspects of how people respond to consumer goods. In Chapter 4 we considered the 'anthropology of the senses' in understanding how people interact with their environments. The kind of work can also inform the commercial sphere. For instance, Virginia Postrel's (2003) research observes how people respond in aesthetic and sensory terms to objects and images, and Dan Hill has charted the rise of experiential products and services and the ways that they are marketed. His work focuses on consumers' sensory-emotive reactions to particular 'brands', and he suggests that considering people's sensory reactions to them provides a much more truthful response than can be gleaned from either surveys or focus groups (Hill 2003).

Making use of the in-depth 'insider' perspective provided by anthropology is therefore useful at each stage in business and industry – in designing communications about products, in observing people's responses to these efforts, and in assessing how products are actually used. John Sherry's (1995) work deals with the latter issue. His career began with research about Navajo activists, and involved looking at how they were using new technologies to interact with outsiders. He now applies that experience in a different context:

> I'm an anthropologist for Intel Corporation, the company that makes microprocessors. Most people think that sounds a little strange – an anthropologist working for a microprocessor manufacturer – but it's not as strange as you might think... I feel very lucky to have a job like this. Sometimes anthropologists wind

up in jobs they never even dreamed of. That wasn't true in my case – I'd been hoping that a technology company would be interested in getting a detailed understanding of how people actually use their products… At Intel, in the Intel Architecture Labs, I work with a small group of social scientists… Our collective goal is to identify new uses for computing power by understanding the needs of real people. We call it 'design ethnography'. It's a great job, and the good news is, there seems to be a growing market for applied cultural anthropologists in this field. (Sherry, in Gwynne 2003a: 214–15)

Following John Sherry's contribution to Intel, the company set up a 'Peoples and Practices Group': a special team of ten anthropologists and psychologists, to research how people use computers and come up with better products: 'In the past, marketing teams might have been given the task of making a product cross-culturally palatable. Increasingly, however, culture is taken into account earlier, at the design stage: for example, the embedded compass in mobile phones to allow Muslims to locate the direction of Mecca' (*Anthropology Today*, 2004: 29)

Other companies have followed suit:

Social scientists, and in particular anthropologists, are precious commodities. Back in December 2002, IBM decided to set up a world class human sciences group. One result is the appointment of Steve Barnett, an anthropologist by training and generally recognized as a 'pioneering business anthropologist' (*Economist Magazine*, 11 March 2004). In 2003, IBM research claimed to be 'adding linguists, anthropologists, ethnographers, and similarly non-technical specialists to its staff in order to provide new insights into clients' businesses (*San Francisco Chronicle*, 21 October 2003).

DESIGNING ANTHROPOLOGY

Adding an anthropologist to a research team is like moving from black-and-white TV to color.

Cathleen Crain, LTG Associates

Anthropologists are increasingly being employed to assist in product design, with this work sometimes leading to the creation of new products. Thus Sue Squires conducted ethnographic research into American breakfast behaviour (Squires and Byrne 2002). As ethnographic research does, this involved observing actual practices instead of merely asking people about what they had for breakfast. It quickly revealed a wide gap between parents' desire to give kids an 'ideal' and socially acceptable 'healthy breakfast' and their lack of time for preparation. Squires was able to consider this analytically, as part of a larger conflict between the pressure that women felt about being good mothers, and the economic pressures on them to work outside the home. The articulation of the need to reconcile these pressures led to the development of a new product called Go-Gurt: a yogurt-based snack that could be eaten on the go. The new breakfast food achieved US$37 million in sales in the first year.

EMBEDDING INNOVATION

Patricia Sachs

CEO, Social Solutions Inc., Arizona

I had a job the whole time I was in graduate school, as I needed to support my kids. I found myself continually making connections between my studies and my work settings. After a five-year research project in developmental and cognitive psychology, it became obvious to me that there was an abundance of opportunities for practical anthropology that could make a difference.

In a nutshell, I founded and am the CEO of an anthropology consulting firm. The area I work in is innovation — we 'embed innovation' in companies by connecting 'customer-centered insight' with 'work-centered intelligence'. We collaborate with organizations to help them develop new innovation practices. We describe ourselves as a business anthropology firm that, like a 'corporate Margaret Mead', has the capacity to understand the world beyond the organizational chart.

I have always maintained that our work is meaningful and useful if it is tied to strategic initiatives for our clients, so that the perspective it offers expands, shapes, and influences how they go about their business. For example: we led the redesign of a leading R&D organization, which took it from a strict 'engineering culture' (meaning a techno-centric, cubicle-centric way of making things) to a contextually embedded understanding of 'what people really do in their real lives'. In other words, we apprenticed engineers in Anthro 101, as it were, teaching them how to 'see' the people for whom they were inventing things, and how to develop insight for innovation from that understanding.

'Design anthropology' is a term which is becoming increasingly common, particularly in hi-tech firms. Think of a company in Silicon Valley and it is likely that nowadays they employ perhaps one or two anthropologists... In some instances a company has the resources to employ people exclusively as ethnographers, rather than have product designers do ethnography themselves... The exploration and interrogation of a context, or of broad themes and concepts, seems to have an affinity with the anthropological project, although it is not an academic one. (Drazin 2006: 99–100)

Greg Guest observes that although many people still imagine that anthropologists invariably disappear off into remote areas:

> Many anthropologists work closer to home. Twenty-first century anthropology encompasses an exceptionally broad range of topics and research settings. Anthropologists are applying the theories and research methods honed in the Australian outback or the Kalahari desert to modern settings, lending new and innovative insights and creating novel solutions. (Guest 2003: 259)

He sees the skills he learned in training as an anthropologist as directly transferable to other fields. 'What anthropologists do in the technology industry is really not that different from what we do in more traditional engagements' (Guest 2003: 259). In his work as an 'Experience Modeler' at a consulting group called Sapient Corporation, he draws on earlier research that he did with shrimp fishers in Ecuador, making a direct comparison between understanding the fishers' relations with top-down regulations and people's difficulties in dealing with incomprehensible technology systems. His task in the technology industry is to help create good technological solutions, and he approaches this on the basis that the design of 'user-friendly' systems requires companies to understand the beliefs and behaviours of their consumers.

> What do anthropologists do in the technology industry? In brief, we use ethnography to better understand users and inform design. Our tradition of *in situ* participant-observation and our holistic perspective can be used to gain a deeper understanding of the complex interaction between individuals, socio-cultural factors, activities and design. Ethnography has an advantage over other forms of research – surveys and focus groups, to name two common examples – because it can reveal user needs in the context of the activity a given design is intended to support. (Guest 2003: 259)

Such work is also more broadly useful to firms who design things for people. Thus Heath Combs has been charting the work of ethnographers paid by furniture companies to study people at home, and consider how they actually use their furniture and their living spaces. 'In the furniture industry, their findings will drive anything from retail store and product design to brand management... Ethnography focuses on closely studying a relatively small number of people to get a detailed understanding of consumer needs' (Combs 2006: 1).

Adam Drazin makes the point that commercial clients are not seeking anthropology *per se* – they are seeking answers to questions and solutions to problems: 'In most cases, a commercial client does not buy anthropology. They buy research in order to address problems. Much commercial research begins with a problem. This is true of all kinds of clients – not only companies and manufacturers, but charities, public bodies and policymakers. Clients go first to research companies in order to solve these' (Drazin 2006: 94).

This view also highlights the reality that anthropology itself – and scientific research more generally – can also be seen as a product: a service that trained researchers provide. It is certainly framed in this way in business and industry, reflecting the economic focus that pertains in this sphere. There is thus a wide range of ways that anthropologists can approach commercial activities: as analysts of globalization, and as critics of its social and environmental effects; as cultural translators; and as experts who can offer commercially useful insights into human behaviour. The opportunities for anthropologists to find employment in business and industry are constantly expanding, as are the potential areas in which they can act as consultants.

7 ANTHROPOLOGY AND HEALTH

HEALTH IN A CULTURAL CONTEXT

Nothing is more fundamental to human life than health; there are major cultural variations in how people think and act on health issues, and all aspects of health – from the cradle to the grave – have an important social dimension. This is, in consequence, one of the major areas in which anthropology is applied.

Anthropological interests in health span both time and space: they focus on temporal change with studies of evolutionary biology; ideas about human genetic development; and analyses of the effects of historical changes on health and well being. For example, Chapter 4 noted some of the health issues that arise when people shift from nomadic patterns of movement to settlement (Green and Iseley 2002). Boyd Eaton and Melvin Konner's (2003) work looks back even further, to consider the mismatch between the diet and lifestyle of prehistoric humans (adapted genetically over millennia), and modern diets and lifestyles, which are the result of very recent and rapid changes. We need to understand ancestral lifestyles, they say, to see why modern humans suffer from chronic illnesses:

> We have been investigating the proposition that the major chronic illnesses which afflict human beings living in affluent industrialized Western nations

are promoted by a mismatch between our genetic constitution and a variety of lifestyle factors ... diet, exercise patterns, and exposure to abusive substances... The genetic constitution of humanity, which controls our physiology, biochemistry and metabolism, has not been altered in any fundamental way since *Homo sapiens sapiens* first became widespread. In contrast, cultural evolution during the relatively brief period since the appearance of agriculture has been breathtakingly rapid, so that genes selected over the preceding geologic eras must now function in a foreign and, in many ways, hostile Atomic Age. (Eaton and Konner 2003: 52)

Other lessons can be learned from the past, too. Payson Sheets notes that archaeologists have found prehistoric crops, agricultural technologies and even medical remedies that can help to cure illnesses. For example, an archaeological analysis of ancient Mayan stone tools in El Salvador revealed that obsidian knives were 100–500 times sharper than the modern surgical razor blades and scalpels, creating cleaner incisions and causing less tissue damage. Archaeological knowledge about ancient Mayan production skills has therefore been drawn upon to make obsidian blades for delicate eye surgery (Sheets 2003: 108).

The application of anthropology in health is also spatial, with specialized research areas such as epidemiology, which considers how diseases spread through populations, and more generally, with the cross-cultural comparisons that are central to the discipline. There is much useful knowledge about health and medicine that can be shared cross-culturally. Although health care in the twenty-first century is heavily dominated by Western sciences, there are many other cultural models about what constitutes good health and how this can be achieved and maintained. Anthropology is therefore useful in translating and communicating different ideas about health between cultural groups, in a variety of contexts. For instance, Andrea Kielich and Leslie Miller work in the area of immigrant health care in America (where 800,000 immigrants arrive each year), and note the importance of understanding diversity in ideas about sickness and health. America absorbs over 800 thousand immigrants each year: 'Each group of new immigrants brings a unique set of cultural beliefs about sickness and health, a vocabulary of medical terms, and, often, a medicine cabinetful of folk remedies, challenging American physicians to use skills not typically taught in medical school' (Kielich and Miller 1998: 32).

In the course of their work they run into Asian ideas about health as an equilibrium between yin and yang; African and Native American ideas about wellbeing as a form of harmony with nature; and, among immigrants from Spanish-speaking countries, ideas about good health as a correct balance of hot and cold. And, returning to the point that Eaton and Konner made about contemporary 'modern' lifestyles, they also find that 'contrary to popular belief, most immigrants arrive here in better health than their US-born counterparts – but their health deteriorates in direct proportion to their length of stay' (Kielich and Miller 1998: 38).

FROM THE CRADLE TO THE GRAVE

Anthropologists are involved in studying health at every stage of human life, even before it begins. A fast-growing area of research is concerned with human reproduction, in particular where this is technologically assisted, for example by *in vitro* fertilization. This practice raises a number of complex social issues, as do reproductive controls, such as contraception and abortion. In such areas, sensitivity to diverse cultural beliefs and values is very helpful – one might say vital. For example, Catherine Chiapetta-Swanson conducts research with nurses in clinics specializing in genetic termination (an abortion that is carried out when genetic abnormalities are found in a foetus). As she points out: 'GT nursing is intense. It is one-to-one care across a range of extremely sensitive procedures, which are emotionally and morally charged for both patient and nurse' (Chiapetta-Swanson 2005: 166). Her research helped hospitals to improve their structuring and management of the process, and to assist the people involved with more effective coping strategies. Human reproduction raises other complex issues too, particularly when it is assisted, thus Charis Thompson's work in fertility clinics in California examines some of the tricky questions raised about kinship and 'chains of descent' when egg or sperm donation or surrogacy creates 'third party reproducers' (Thompson 2006a: 271).

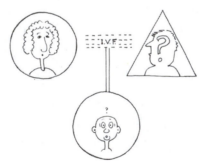

Cultural differences are also the focus of Brigitte Jordan's studies of women and birthing practices. Her work with four different groups showed how these practices depend on a range of cultural ideas about life and death, gender, power and authority, and religion:

> Jordan's work opened up a whole area of research in applied medical anthropology and, equally importantly, provided women, their families, and their

medical assistants with knowledge of alternative ways to situate the birth...
For many women, this research transformed the birth experience into a positive
and emotionally significant moment in their lives. (Jordan, in Whiteford and
Bennett 2005: 126)

As noted in Chapter 2, cultural variations are equally evident in approaches to
child rearing, and this is also an area in which 'the long view' is informative. Some
researchers look not only at the prehistoric, but also at the pre-human. For example,
Sarah Hardy (2003) works with primates in considering some of the fundamentals
of human behaviour in child rearing. She suggests that the stereotypical 'Flintstones'
view of early humans, in which men are presented as 'the hunters' and women as 'the
nurturers', is wrong, and that the evolutionary record actually points to biological
and cultural mechanisms that engender cooperation in child rearing. She also looks
at contemporary human cultures where this model pertains, and extended family
members – both female and male – have a major role in raising children. Her
research emphasizes the importance of social cooperation in child rearing, both for
individuals and for society as a whole.

BUILDING BODIES OF KNOWLEDGE

Patricia Hammer

Center for Social Well Being, Peru

I first encountered anthropology by chance. I had enrolled in a body-building class at the local community
college, with the idea of getting into shape to apply for a job as a firefighter. While waiting to sign up for
the course, I began to peruse the teaching schedule, and was attracted by an offering entitled 'Chinese culture'.
Although I had very little idea what anthropology was, I decided to take the class. The professor was Chinese
born and, faced with rural conflict, had fled to Hong Kong as a refugee. Eventually the family immigrated to
California where she studied anthropology.

In this initial exposure, I was amazed at the breadth of the discipline. With an interest in music I focused
my class paper on the history and styles of traditional Chinese music. My classmates selected themes that
included Chinese cultural systems of healing, early education, calligraphy, fishing and dinghy construction. Our
professor insisted that gaining a sensory understanding of a culture required that 'you eat it', therefore, after
our final exam, we all went out for a Chinese meal, with the professor guiding us through the dishes as well as
explaining Chinese dining symbolism and etiquette. The course was a fulfilling introduction to anthropology.

Extinguishing my firefighter ambitions and applying myself to undergraduate study, I resumed an earlier
interest in Spanish. I became aware of opportunities for 'study-abroad' programmes that would combine my
ambitions to acquire language skills and to experience a different culture and society. In my third year in

college I left the North American continent for the first time to attend university in Lima, Peru. Here, I expressed to my professor my enthusiasm to 'get my feet wet'. Within a month I was in contact with linguists in the Andes, and lost no time in travelling to the region. I was warmly received by the researchers, who invited me to accompany them to the rural agricultural villages where they worked.

Although my anthropology and Spanish classes were held at the university in Lima, I took advantage of long weekends and school breaks to spend time in a particular Quechua-speaking rural village. I observed and participated in daily activities, while taking extensive notes. I was thrilled to be able to explore the social interactions and cultural practices of a small Andean farming village, so different from my own US-urban orientations.

The inductive nature of experiential learning came to the fore in this initial exposure to fieldwork. Because I had been introduced to the community by established linguists, people associated me with language learning. When asked why I had come to their village, I commonly replied that I wanted to learn the language, thinking of my tedious word lists, reference dictionary and grammar texts. However, often I was met with the unexpected response: 'Ah, that's easy! All you have to do is drink the water, breathe the air, eat the food — and soon you'll be speaking Quechua just like us!' This revealed a kind of participatory acquisitive notion of 'learning culture'. Beyond ingesting communal substances, locals also convinced me that by wearing traditional dress and joining in with daily and ritual activities that I would (in a way) become 'one of them'.

As a female undergraduate, with little guidance about fieldwork, I took my cues from the community members who instructed me on what to do, what to wear, what to say, with whom to speak (or not), etc., and all the other details vital for young unmarried women in rural villages. It's not surprising that, although I went into the field with no specific research topic, I returned with a keen interest in Andean gender relations.

Having completed a BA, I was convinced that I wanted to pursue a career in anthropology, but was left pondering what that would entail. I was still intrigued by the Andes region: if I asked the people in the community what I should study, what would they say? Something that would be of practical use to them, I thought.

My studies in Peru had improved my Spanish, so while trying to figure out what to study in graduate school, I took a job as a medical interpreter in a prenatal clinic. This awakened an interest in cross-cultural perspectives on women's reproductive experiences. I wasn't only called upon for literal interpretation, but found myself having to explain Latin American customs, beliefs and practices to the clinic personnel. For example, women patients felt it a priority to tell nurses about significant emotional upsets they had suffered (such as bad news from their home country), in the belief that sudden strong feelings have ill effects on the developing baby. During that time I also worked as a translator for a lay midwife who attended home births. I began to search for studies on cross-cultural midwifery, and discovered medical anthropology.

Finally, I sensed the potential for a career with practical applications for understanding, and perhaps improving, maternal health. I could have trained as a nurse-midwife to pursue a similar goal. However, I chose anthropology because of its appreciation for different kinds of knowledge. I did my graduate research in Peru and Bolivia exploring Quechua-speaking women's concepts and practices to manage menstruation, pregnancy, birth and post-partum health. Fundamental to this was a focus on cultural conceptions of the workings of the body, known as 'ethnophysiology'. This would later underpin participatory research in international health projects, to improve communication between health workers and community members.

During my graduate study I also looked at the work of other social science professionals, with an eye to developing a career outside academia. I was pleasantly surprised to find that when I inquired about projects with international non-profit organizations, as well as with state institutions, they were enthusiastic about my research, often inviting me to speak at workshops. I began sending my CV to international health organizations. Early one morning I received a call from a women's reproductive health project coordinator in Lima. We spoke at length about effective participatory research, and soon I was flying off to Peru to start my first job as an international health consultant.

Since 1996, I have worked as an applied medical anthropologist with ministries of health and education, and NGO projects, primarily in Peru and Bolivia. I am also the director of a rural institute dedicated to the promotion of indigenous healing knowledge and practices in the north-central Peruvian Andes.

Learning from other cultural groups allows us to question the practices that our own culture regards as 'normal'. Elizabeth Whitaker observes that, 'culture determines the way we have children and how we raise children... Rarely do we question our cultural traditions, especially when there are experts and expert opinions' (Whitaker 2003: 38). Using evolutionary, biological and cultural perspectives, her work examines breastfeeding practices across cultures, and suggests that American approaches fail to acknowledge that mothers and infants form a biological pair not just during pregnancy, but also in the child's infancy:

> Mothers and infants are physiologically interconnected from conception to the termination of breastfeeding. While this mutual biological relationship is obvious during pregnancy, to many people it is less clear in the period following birth. In Western society, individuals are expected to be autonomous and independent, and this idea extends to mothers and their babies. Individual autonomy is a core value in our economy, society, and family life: even to our understanding of health and disease. However, it is not a widely shared notion, as more sociocentric conceptions of personhood are very common in other cultures. (Whitaker 2003)

Many transitions in life have cultural importance, and there is a wealth of ethnographic research considering the diverse ideas and rituals that surround shifts into puberty, adulthood, marriage, birth, 'mature' status, professional advancement, retirement, and of course death. Each society handles these life stages differently, but all mark important transitional points, often with elaborate ceremonies that reveal core cultural ideas and values. These influence how groups manage not only childbirth and parenting, but also later stages, for example the care of the elderly. With the 'baby boomers' born in the 1940s reaching retirement age, greater attention is being given to the issues surrounding geriatric care. Anthropologists have been closely involved in work examining how old age is imagined and experienced in different groups; how people think about ageing; what kinds of activities they undertake in old age; and how different generations interact.

There is also considerable ethnographic research on institutions for the short- and long-term care of the elderly, such as nursing homes and hospitals. Robert Harman (2005: 312) comments that 'nursing home treatment is frequently unsatisfactory and sometimes inhumane', and he notes that a number of anthropologists have acted as advocates for the inhabitants of such institutions, or worked to influence policy. They have also contributed to the education of carers in institutions and at home, producing guidance videos and manuals, and organising seminars and workshops for them.

LONG-TERM CARE

Sherylyn Briller

Assistant Professor of Anthropology, Institute of Gerontology, Wayne State University

I come from a family of urban teachers. My father taught for thirty years in the New York City public school system. While he truly made a difference in his students' lives, this job was very demanding. He often came home bone-weary and said, 'You can pick any profession you like, just don't be a teacher. It's too exhausting.' Today, despite my father's warning, I teach anthropology at Wayne State, a large urban university in Detroit. However, I really love the job, especially teaching applied anthropology and preparing students for their future professional roles. On the first day of each course, I always tell students 'my story'.

As a twenty-one-year-old undergraduate anthropology major, I did not know what I wanted to do after I finished college, but I thought that I might work in a field related to aging. In my family there were many elders, including grandparents and great aunts and uncles. Some were childless and my nuclear family served as the 'children' and 'grandchildren' in their lives. I relished spending time with them and hearing their stories.

This strong interest in working with elders and oral history pushed me in the direction of gerontology, and my first job after college was working in a nursing home as an Activities Assistant. This was very anthropological, as you were charged with learning about people and their interests, and trying to incorporate what you found into making their institutional lives more palatable. I would like to say that I was hired because of my kind personality and rapport with elders, but the reality was that my boss thought that a college graduate might keep up with the enormous amount of paperwork that the job required. This job also introduced me to working on special care units and the 'culture of dementia care'.

After nearly two years, I went to work as the program coordinator for a large community senior centre in an economically depressed neighbourhood in Minneapolis. This involved running an activity programme that encouraged elders to come to the centre, where they ate hot lunch, socialized, and were linked to supportive services. Technically, I was supposed to have a Masters of Social Work (MSW) for this job. When I began working in the senior centre, I planned to go back to graduate school and get this degree. However, I shared an office with the programme's social worker and got to see her job first-hand. In my opinion, there were strong pros and cons to it. On the positive side, she got to work with elders 1:1 every day. On the negative side, she spent much time telling seniors about their eligibility for services. Frequently, the regulations were problematic, and the process was frustrating for all. Watching these experiences kindled my interest in research and policy. I was advised that to work in a policy-related area, I needed to go to graduate school and get an advanced degree. No one said that this had to be in a specific field, so I chose to stick with anthropology.

I entered the graduate program at Case Western Reserve University in Cleveland, where several faculties specialized in medical anthropology and the anthropology of ageing. My dissertation research focused on familial and governmental old-age support mechanisms in Mongolia. I consider myself very lucky to have had this traditional long-term ethnographic fieldwork experience in Asia as part of my graduate education. While in graduate school, I also worked on an interdisciplinary research team focused on improving United States' long-term care environments. We did research, staff education and consulting for numerous facilities, and published a book series about creating successful dementia care settings (Briller et al. 2002).

While finishing my dissertation, I was offered a one-year replacement position as an anthropology lecturer at Wayne State University, then the next year I was offered a tenure-track job as an assistant professor. My current research focuses mainly on ageing and end-of-life issues in the United States, and I am interested in using anthropology to address ageing and health-related issues in a range of groups. My job also involves training other anthropologists to work effectively in a broad range of community settings.

I tell this story to my classes partly to reassure them that it is OK to study anthropology because you are interested in the subject, even if you do not know precisely how you will use the knowledge in the future. It also illustrates how the path into a field like medical anthropology is very often not linear. With a degree in anthropology and the set of usable skills that this provides, it is possible to remain consistently employed with a degree in anthropology in academic and non-academic settings. I also use the story to highlight a number of important characteristics involved in working as an anthropologist in diverse settings namely, broad research interests, flexibility, creativity and being willing to work under a series of different job titles. I then encourage students to go on and create their own stories, in which they put their anthropological education to use.

It is also useful to understand social beliefs and values in relation to the diseases that often accompany (and sometimes precede) ageing. Ideas about cancer, disability, and dementia are critical in defining how these are treated or managed at a social level, and an awareness of 'under-the-surface' beliefs can often help in developing new ways to cope with health problems in these areas. Thus Jeannine Coreil's (2004) work looks at different cultural models of illness, and how these affect recovery in breast cancer support groups.

Because of the discipline's cross-cultural utility, anthropologists are often employed to assist in the health care of elderly refugees and immigrants. Robert Harman notes research in several related areas: Elzbieta Gozdziak working on problems specific to older refugees and programmes designed to support them; Neil Henderson's development of ethnically specific Alzheimer's support groups for Hispanic and African Americans; and Kay Branch's work as an Elder Rural Services Planner for a Native Tribal Health Consortium in Alaska (Harman 2005).

As noted in earlier chapters, anthropologists also work with aid agencies, many of which focus on bringing medical aid to parts of the world (and diverse cultural contexts) where health care systems are failing. More often than not, a lack of resources for health care is coupled with difficulties in the provision of sufficient food and clean water.

FOOD AND LIFESTYLE

The anthropology of food has long been a major area of research. Ethnographers have focused on the social and cultural diversities with which human societies approach this central aspect of life, looking at the history of food; how food is produced, cooked and shared; what foods mean in different societies; how food is used in rituals; how food contributes to the construction of social identity and status; the use of food for medicinal purposes; and of course the various health issues relating to food security, nutrition and diet.

AN ANTHROPOLOGICAL JOURNEY

Nancy Pollock

Victoria University, Wellington, New Zealand

My anthropological journey began in the Caribbean, but led me to establish my research in the Pacific, where I have been fortunate to benefit from the hospitality and tolerance of many host families who put up with my seemingly inane questions, fed me a range of foods, and shared times of shortage and times of relative plenty. Many flights and boat trips have taken me through the skies and waters of the Pacific to islands that are each beautiful in their own way. The environment of each atoll and island provides a setting that challenges an outsider's understanding and necessitates local explanation. My fieldwork has followed two overlapping research interests, food habits as they affect health, and development. These two areas of research have led me to exchange information with many non-social scientists, particularly nutritionists, epidemiologists, lawyers and health physicists.

Food consumption was not a popular or accepted area of anthropological research when I wrote my Ph.D. dissertation in 1969, but it has come to the fore in the last 20 years. For me, collecting dietary data in an atoll community in the Marshall Islands provided a platform for subsequent field research and yielded a rich source of ethnographic data about social life on an atoll still under US jurisdiction. The data also presented interesting contrasts with later research on food habits in other Pacific island communities.

In the 1990s, a Wallisian colleague and I conducted research on Wallis and Futuna for the South Pacific Commission (as it was then) and the New Zealand Medical Council. One project focussed on understanding obesity from a local perspective, where body size (BMI) is considered large by Western medical standards. One informant told us she would feel weak if she lost any of her 96 kg, and this 'comfort size' was an important consideration for her health. Contributors also asserted the strong focus on food as a social pathway to integrate communities. The islands of Wallis and Futuna are still heavily reliant on local root crops and fish they provide for their families, and so represent an economy that is 'pre-commercial'.

A second project undertaken at the suggestion of French Medical officials looked at the drinking habits of young Wallisian men, some of whom had injured themselves and others when driving cars. The close restrictions on social life and lack of alternative 'entertainment' were revealed as major reasons for binge parties in the bush, together with ready access to alcohol at any corner store.

These two projects, and a subsequent one in Fiji, became training exercises in anthropological fieldwork with local researchers. In Fiji we collected data on food consumption and then, working with Samoan and Maori students from Victoria University, we demonstrated ethnic differences in food selection, timing of eating and feasts. This led to a project in Wellington sponsored by the Ministry of Social Development, focussed on the criteria participants used to select foods at the supermarket when they had $100 a week (or less) to spend on food. From this I went on to investigate the social issues around use of food banks in New Zealand, and this work became part of a series of studies assessing poverty in New Zealand society.

Working on food consumption in Pacific communities also drew me into two major projects focussed on the aftermath of nuclear testing in the Marshall Islands, where the US exploded Bravo and other nuclear devices in the 1950s. The Nuclear Claims Tribunal was established in 1987 to assess claims for damage to Marshallese people and to the environment resulting from fallout from these tests. The tribunal held compensation hearings between 2001 and 2003, to hear evidence from each of the four atoll communities affected. Food contamination is the major source of health problems being treated today, particularly the large number of goitre cancers experienced by Marshallese islanders. Research by nuclear physicists, agriculturalists, epidemiologists and others assessed the amount of ingested radiation some fifty years after the people were exposed, in order to calculate compensation levels in dollar amounts. My earlier food research in the area provided ethnographic background to food use and lifestyle, and thus provided an indication of the circumstances in which people were likely to have been exposed to radiation. I presented material at each of the four Tribunal hearings, using historical, environmental and sociological evidence particular to each atoll's case. Compensation claims have now been awarded to each of the atoll communities, although at the time of writing the US has yet to complete the payments.

On another Pacific island, Nauru, people also sought compensation, but in this case it was for the effects of the phosphate mining carried out since 1906. In 1919 the British Phosphate Commission (consisting of government nominees by Australia, New Zealand and Great Britain) took over management of the mine from Germany, selling the phosphate mainly to Australian and New Zealand farmers to enhance sheep and cattle production. As mining has rendered the interior (four-fifths) of the island unusable, after independence in 1968 Nauruan landowners sought compensation from the former Commissioners for the very low payouts they had received since mining began. Their case was heard before the International Court of Justice who awarded Nauru financial compensation to be paid by Australia, New Zealand and Britain, together with advice on rehabilitation. A Commission of Enquiry was charged with documenting means of rehabilitating the island, and this commission asked me to provide background documentation to the land claims. I was the only social scientist (and only woman) on an eighteen-member team, and I performed the role of liaison person between this team and the Nauruan people. My Nauruan counterpart and I convened meetings around the island, interviewing people about their ideas of Nauru in the future, and making a video of the issues.

More recently my interest in food habits and health has resulted in a series of research projects addressing food security and poverty issues, often in multi-disciplinary projects. Collaborating with colleagues across a wide spectrum of disciplines encourages us all to think laterally. Nutritional colleagues now include social issues such as meal structures and local food values in their bio-medical approach to nutrition education, and understand the importance of social data, for example in calculating food intake, or in approaches to obesity.

Anthropologists can and do bridge many disciplinary boundaries. In doing so they try to use language that overcomes the jargon of specialist communication. I see a very important future for students of anthropology to draw on their training to bridge the statistical/qualitative gulf; to interweave the subjective with the objective, and to offer new lines of thought.

Cultural beliefs and practices around food are critical in defining what people eat. David Himmelgreen and Deborah Crooks point out that many anthropological studies of food have practical applications in dealing with nutrition-related problems: for example, a study examining the high consumption of Coca-Cola in the

Yucatan revealed a belief that it is healthy, and the importance of local perceptions of it as a Western (and therefore high-status) item. As they say: 'anthropological studies on the marketing of fast-food chains like McDonald's are especially relevant today' (Himmelgreen and Crooks 2005: 155). In more general terms:

> Applied nutritional anthropology has the potential to make significant con-tributions in addressing the nutritional problems of the twenty-first century. These problems include the global obesity epidemic, the intersection of diet and physical activity in the development of obesity related diseases (e.g. type 2 diabetes), the continuing problems with undernutrition and micronutrient deficiencies, the ongoing problem of food insecurity in a food-rich world… [And] the contribution of globalization on food consumption patterns. (Himmelgreen and Crooks 2005: 178–9)

Anthropologists often find themselves working in regions where food security is major issue: for example, David Pelletier's (2000, 2005) research in Latin America, Vietnam and Bangladesh is concerned with how malnutrition affects levels of child mortality, with a view to improving policies in this area. Ann Fleuret (1988) researched food aid and its implications for development in Kenya and became involved in the American Anthropology Association's Task Force on Famine. In research on health there are often intersections with other issues: for example, Mike Mtika's (2001) work illustrates how, in poor countries, the AIDS epidemic has had major implications for household food security.

Researchers also work in areas where the over-consumption of poor quality food along with sedentary lifestyles creates obesity. Nurgül Fitzgerald, David Himmelgreen and their colleagues (Fitzgerald *et al.* 2006) became involved in developing educational programmes to promote better dietary habits through nu-trition in impoverished American communities; Barry Popkin (2001) has been tracing dietary changes and a shift towards higher levels of obesity in the developing world; and Hannah Bradby's (1997) ethnographic study on the dietary choices of Punjabi women in Glasgow highlighted the social issues that contribute to a relationship between health, eating and heart disease.

There is also a growing anthropological literature on health foods, their mean-ings and what they reveal about the concepts that people use in thinking about their health. Thus Rosalind Coward's work on health foods also points to growing concerns about the inclusion of undesirable substances in modern food production:

> The pursuit of a healthy diet is the principal site where we can exercise conscious control over our health. Diet is the privileged arena where the sense of personal responsibility for our health can be worked out. No wonder there has been such panic as the facts about adulteration of food at source have become widely

known... In the mythology of alternative health, food and health have become inextricably linked as if it would be impossible to be healthy without serious attention to our diet... Food and its relation to health has totally replaced sex as the major source of public anxiety about the body. (Coward 2001: 50–1)

This work resonates with my own research on drinking water, examining why many people are willing to pay vastly more for bottled spring water rather than drink tap water that they fear may have been chemically polluted in the course of its treatment, and during its journey through an industrial farming landscape (Strang 2004).

Anthropologists can therefore provide insights into many aspects of food use and into wider behavioural issues, such as the way that people think about physical exercise, and the extent to which this is encouraged (or not) in their economic and social practices. And as mentioned in Chapter 5, in relation to social marketing, anthropologists are well situated to work in areas such as health education, where the major aim is to understand cultural beliefs and values with a view to encouraging behavioural change. Some culturally embedded ideas encourage people to adopt habits that are harmful, and the only way to combat such problems is to understand the underlying factors. Thus Florence Kellner's research (2005) seeks an in-depth understanding of how the processes of self-construction and self-presentation that are part of 'coming of age' in most Western societies actually encourage many young women to take up smoking.

PIECING STORIES TOGETHER

Rachael Gooberman-Hill

Department of Social Medicine, University of Bristol

I work as an anthropologist researching health, illness and healthcare. I look at what 'good' and 'bad' health is, and I describe how doctors and other health care providers look after people. My work aims to improve the health care that people in developed countries receive, because although there are plenty of excellent treatments out there, people who need them don't always get them. I run projects that involve talking to people about their health and their experience of health care. My colleagues and I do this through one-to-one interviews, group interviews (focus groups) and observations. The topics have ranged from long-term illness and joint surgery to how people living with cancer feel about taking morphine for pain.

It's a real privilege to be entrusted with people's own stories about things that are often very private and personal. But my work is about more than just listening; it's about piecing many people's stories together to make bigger stories that policy makers, doctors and other researchers might listen to. To present those 'bigger stories' I write articles for medical journals, in which I usually describe what it is like to live and cope with particular health problems. For instance I've published an article explaining why people do or do not like to use walking sticks, and another one about what it's like to live with the pain of arthritis. It's often very moving to spend time listening to people, but it's also exciting to be able to present their stories, and I enjoy the time I spend writing up my research.

An equally important part of my job involves working alongside people from different professions: for example doctors, psychologists and statisticians. Even though we're sometimes in different countries, we work together to think about areas that need research, and we design new projects accordingly. Our aim is to shed light on issues that have both local and international importance. For me, every day is different, and having the research skills of an anthropologist opens doors all the time.

UNDERSTANDING DISEASE

Behavioural change is also, quite literally, a matter of life and death in responses to infectious diseases, and in this area, as in others, local understandings are critical. The comparative nature of anthropological research underlines the reality that there are many specifically cultural ways of handling epidemics, some of which may be better suited to a particular context than imposed western models. Curtis Abraham (2007) describes how Barry Hewlett's work illustrates this point. Hewlett examined some of the problems that arose following an outbreak of the Ebola virus in central West Africa in 1995 and 1996. Medical aid was sent, but there was little communication or coordination with the local community, and people became so suspicious of outsiders that when they returned with the second outbreak, there was armed resistance to their activities. The research showed how the problem lay in the aid agencies' lack of understanding of local history, how diseases were perceived and also how they were managed. They were also misled by stereotypes about African medicine. 'Western public health officials ignored the fact that indigenous people have their own strategies for disease control and prevention' (Abraham 2007: 35). Partly as a result of this work, the World Health Organisation (WHO) revised its guidelines for responding to Ebola outbreaks.

Curtis Abraham also points to Ted Green's work, which further affirms the need for treating local understandings with respect. Green has spent several decades working in sub-Saharan Africa, and is familiar with indigenous contagion theories. He notes that people are well aware of the causes of disease, and how contagion spreads, and have specific protocols for quarantine. Programmes that cohere with local methods and actively support and make use of them are far more likely to work. WHO has also taken this advice on board, and is now directing its efforts towards working with and incorporating indigenous medical practices into aid programmes (in Abraham 2007).

Understanding local perspectives is particularly critical in dealing with issues such as the AIDS epidemic, which has been so devastating in Africa. Adam Ashforth's work looks at how the spread of this disease is entangled with ideas about witchcraft, which has been seen, traditionally, as a central factor in illness. 'Cases of premature death or untimely illness in Africa are almost always attributed to the action of invisible forces, frequently those described as "witchcraft". Thus the HIV/AIDS epidemic is also 'an epidemic of witchcraft' (Ashforth 2004: 147). Because of the distrust this engenders, the disease therefore poses a threat not only to human health, but also to the stability of democratic governance in the region:

> The implications of a witchcraft epidemic are quite different from those of a 'public health' crisis ... when suspicions of witchcraft are at play in a community, problems of illness and death transform matters of public health from questions of appropriate policies into questions concerning the fundamental character and legitimacy of public power in general – questions relating to the security, safety and integrity of the community. (Ashforth 2004: 142)

DRUG CULTURES AND CRIME

Understanding local cultural perspectives is vital in considering how best to combat AIDS, wherever this disease occurs. Merrill Singer, Ray Irizarry and Jean Schensul (2002) conducted research into AIDS prevention in America, looking at needle sharing among drug users. Their central question was whether this group would use free needles if these were made available, and whether this would be an effective way of slowing the spread of HIV/AIDS. However, they also had to consider anxieties in local communities that handing out needles might increase intravenal drug use, and the political realities that surround policy making: 'Needle exchange is one of a number of controversial strategies that have appeared in recent years (widespread street distribution of condoms and bleach for needle cleaning are others) in an effort to halt the spread of AIDS to the drug-using sector of the population' (Singer, Irizarry and Schensul 2002: 208).

Their research showed that concerns about needle exchanges increasing drug use were unfounded, and that the scheme had some potential as an effective measure against the spread of infection.

As these examples imply, anthropologists tend to ask *why* people do what they do, rather than merely condemning what many people regard as antisocial behaviour. Like other social scientists, they think that getting under the surface to see the cause of problems is more likely to lead to effective solutions. Researchers bring this approach to investigating a range of difficult social issues, such as the use of drugs and alcohol, prostitution, violence and crime, which have major effects not only on social life in general, but more specifically on people's health and wellbeing. Linda Bennett's (1995) work, for example, looks at different cultural perspectives on alcohol, and the impacts of alcoholism on families. Linda Whiteford and Judy Vetucci (1997) have examined the effects of substance abuse in pregnancy, and how this might be prevented and Philippe Bourgois's (1995) investigations in New York's Harlem reveal the subaltern economy surrounding crack dealing.

THE QUALITY OF PUBLIC HEALTH

Richard Chenhall
Menzies School of Health Research, Charles Darwin University, Northern Territory, Australia

I become involved in the evaluation of residential treatment centres, through my Ph.D. studies. After completing an undergraduate and postgraduate degree in anthropology, my first 'proper' job entailed teaching and doing research in a public health research institute. As the only social scientist working in this centre, I was bewildered by the language spoken by public health researchers, who were mostly epidemiologists. I did not know anything about the bacterium *Burkholderia pseudomallei*, I was not too sure what a chronic disease actually was and I knew that public health was something that dealt with the health of populations and mainly used statistics. Everyone talked about some doctor who, in the 1840s, halted a cholera epidemic by sealing a particular water pump in London. So I stumbled my way through various lectures and discussions with medical doctors, and often felt pretty silly as I rarely understood what they were talking about.

I found that public health researchers were quite interested in the kind of information they thought an anthropologist would be able to provide, but in a research context dominated by epidemiology (which relies mainly on statistical data), qualitative methods such as participant observation were unfamiliar. Complex social analysis does not fit easily into public health models designed to provide very specific interventions. Anthropological research seeks to expand understandings of health issues by going beyond clinical knowledge and statistical comparisons, to examine a range of social and cultural influences in people's lives: those aspects of illness and treatment which cannot be reduced to variables and measured. However, in understanding population health we need to tackle the more complex aspects of human behaviour and the social systems within which we are enmeshed.

Things have moved on since I first began working in this area, and qualitative research and anthropological methodologies have become increasingly popular in the health sciences. I now teach in a public health postgraduate degree programme, and the majority of students go on to work as project managers or research assistants in health-related projects, or find employment in government departments. Many make use of the methodological tools of anthropology, finding their training in qualitative research methods to be one of the key skills they use in their workplaces.

In the last few years I have worked in three main settings. First, in extending my Ph.D. research, I assisted in the development of culturally appropriate evaluations of indigenous residential alcohol and drug treatment centres. Acute and chronic social and health problems associated with substance misuse among indigenous people is regarded as a national issue, and while residential treatment programs are seen as essential, health professionals, researchers and indigenous people running these programs say that they lack the tools to assess their effectiveness. My research was designed to explore and measure appropriate outcomes both during and post treatment. It drew upon participatory action research, and was initiated and controlled by the organizations themselves (Chenhall 2007, 2008). The research, which was part of a National Health and Medical Research training fellowship in Aboriginal and Torres Strait Islander health, now informs national and international debate. It has demonstrated that the process of designing health evaluations can lead to organizational change related to both the focus and delivery of treatment.

Australia has low rates of tuberculosis but there are still high rates in immigrant and indigenous communities. A few years ago, a colleague and I conducted a study of tuberculosis in a North Arnhem Land community (Grace and Chenhall 2006). We found that the limited level of awareness and knowledge about the cause and symptoms of tuberculosis, and the reluctance of Aboriginal people to visit health clinics, contributed to late presentation of active TB, and lack of compliance with treatment. A number of issues were related to this, including cultural understandings of healing, lack of funding to support dedicated treatment, and the difficulties that local Aboriginal community leaders face in trying to influence the way in which funding is allocated and policies determined.

My other major research interest is in changing trends in substance misuse in remote indigenous communities, with a specific focus on youths. In recent research in the Northern Territory, another anthropologist and I have explored a number of issues related to the growing use of cannabis, petrol sniffing, and teenage pregnancy (Chenhall and Senior 2006, 2007; Senior and Chenhall 2008).

Given the recent 'interventionist' policies of the Australian government around restricting access to alcohol within indigenous communities, our research showed that other types of drug use, specifically cannabis use, has grown. The research therefore elicited significant media and political attention, and an unintended result was the introduction of harsher penalties and fines associated with the possession and trafficking of cannabis. This did not align with our recommendations, which focused on the provision of health and education services to address the underlying social determinants of substance misuse (Carson et al. 2007). So the translation of research to effective policy change is not as simple as it seems.

Drug and alcohol abuse and prostitution often occur in the same socio-economic arena. Pamela Downe's work involves both advocacy and research with prostitutes in Costa Rica (1999) and Edward Laumann's (2004) research in Chicago considers the complexity of 'sex markets' and how these intersect with social networks and sexually transmitted diseases. He also considers sexual violence and its social and cultural context.

Many social problems are related to mental health issues and, while these are often regarded as an individual matter, how they are dealt with at a social level is critical. There are wide cultural variations in how mental health problems are understood and encompassed, and anthropological insights into these variations are useful in informing both the management and treatment of problems. They also reveal changing attitudes: for example, Emily Martin's work examines attitudes to mental conditions like manic depression and ADHD (attention deficit hyperactivity disorder). She observes that, because ideas about 'what makes an individual' are becoming more open to constant change and fluidity, these conditions 'have been undergoing a dramatic revision in American middle-class culture, from being simply dreaded liabilities, to be especially valuable assets that can potentially enhance one's life' (Martin 2006: 84). Cultural attitudes to mental health also have to be considered in relation to physical issues: not just genetic, diet and lifestyle factors, but also wider social, cultural and ecological influences requiring what Roger Sullivan and his research collaborators have called a 'bio-cultural analysis'. Their research in Palau was directed towards trying to discover why there was, most particularly among the men in the population, one of the highest incidences of schizophrenia in the world (Sullivan *et al.* 2007).

More extreme mental health issues often intersect with crime, and there has been considerable media interest in analyses of the social causes of crime, and, more particularly, in the solving of crimes. Forensic anthropology features regularly in novels, television programmes and films, and has been made famous by programmes such as *Silent Witness*. The role of the forensic anthropologist is usually to identify bones and determine the cause of death: she or he will begin by determining whether the bones are human, and will then look for indications of age, gender, and ancestral origin. Dental records are useful, as are old fractures and signs of diseases, hair samples, blood type, and of course DNA. In general, this work is not as dramatic as that depicted on television, but there are some famous cases: for example Alfred Harper (1999) describes the role of forensic anthropology in identifying tiny bone and tooth fragments and thus solving a case in Connecticut, after a murderer had disposed of his wife's body in an industrial woodchipper. In recent years, forensic anthropologists have also been involved in identifying the victims of genocide in countries such as Rwanda and, unfortunately, the need for this kind of work is increasing.

It will be plain from the above account that there is enormous diversity in the range of work done by anthropologists in relation to health, and a range of sub-disciplinary areas of expertise have emerged – for example, medical anthropology, biological anthropology, nutritional anthropology and forensic anthropology. Because anthropology invariably considers the context of social behaviour, there is also a considerable body of work concerned with the institutions that deal with health issues.

NURSING A HOLISTIC UNDERSTANDING

Marion Droz Mendelzweig

Chargée de Recherche, Haute Ecole de la Santé La Source, Lausanne

I have always want to know about what people do and why they do it. Sometimes I want to ask 'how do they manage to behave like this?' I guess being an anthropologist implies a capacity to preserve a childish curiosity.

My research is oriented towards the past rather than towards an ethnological 'other'. I did my first degree in history but moved to studying anthropology when, while working for the International Red Cross in 1994, I was faced with the abomination of the genocide in Rwanda. As a member of a family that, like so many others, was subjected to the genocide perpetuated by the Nazis, I found that the Rwandan experience resonated with my own history and shed new light on the relationship between individuals and the societies that determine their identity. After seeing the results of genocide in Rwanda, I turned to anthropology hoping for an explanation to keep me from despairing about humanity. I can't say that it has given me more optimism, but I am convinced that gaining anthropological tools in order to look at humankind helps us to be more intelligent in considering what is going on in the world, and in imagining the future.

To study anthropology, I joined the Ethnology Institute at the Neuchâtel University in Switzerland. It was a very attractive place for young scholars eager to learn about the infinite richness of human cultures. My studies there were a continual voyage of discovery, not so much from the topics we studied, but rather from the way I learned to look at them. Each new research perspective was a trigger to more exploration: would I continue in the anthropology of religion; in the anthropology of food; or in the anthropology of material culture? Among so many possible avenues, the word 'health' acquired new meaning and complexity.

The subject of my MA thesis — on medically assisted procreation — opened a door for working in the medical realm as a research fellow in a school for nursing. Broadly, the difference between nursing and a medical approach is that the first is centred on the person and the second on the disease. From the nursing point of view, the interest lies not so much in the biological causes for a disease, but on the ill person's understanding of it and on the social and environmental conditions that affect its progress and treatment. It is therefore not surprising that nursing schools include in their teaching programmes anthropological approaches to health, culture, kinship and social groups, or that nursing as a discipline is keen to draw professional knowledge from anthropology. There is a common objective: gaining the capacity to understand 'the other'.

My tasks at the school are twofold: I teach anthropological approaches to students and conduct research projects, for example looking at health networks for migrants. I see anthropology's major contribution to nursing as providing a holistic understanding of the social phenomenon around health and medical care.

MANAGING HEALTH

I noted earlier the utility of anthropology in considering health institutions such as nursing homes, where anthropologists consider the issues surrounding the long-term care of elderly or disabled people. Some researchers have also turned an analytic eye on the health professions themselves, examining their political, social and economic dynamics. Elizabeth Hart, for example, is particularly interested in the anthropology of organizations, and has turned her attention to the way that the institutional cultures of health care facilities enable some people to have more 'voice' than others. She looks at 'people's experiences of speaking in organizational contexts where they feel themselves to be in some way suppressed, or marginalized, or even describe themselves as 'invisible' – as nurses often do when speaking of their caring skills' (Hart 2006: 146). Hart works mostly with women in the British National Health Service, but also with senior male managers, who she found face similar dilemmas in speaking up, being required sometimes to profess confidence in the policies they were implementing, despite serious misgivings regarding their efficacy.

Gender issues also surfaced in Joan Cassell's (2003) research, which considered the realities for women surgeons in a male-dominated area of health care, where metaphors about practice are highly aggressive, employing images of war and invasion, and valorising courage and rapid decision-making. Her research raises questions about whether women actually display the assumed 'traditional' female characteristics, such as sensitivity, warmth, compassion, and whether (and how) this affects the operating theatre.

The research also made it plain that women are often not welcome as equals in this arena, which – as comparative ethnographies have shown – is a far from unusual

dynamic in male dominated arena: 'Similar distrust and exclusion of women is found in all the 'adrenalized vocations ... such masculine thinking is familiar to anthropologists: the sacred flutes, trumpets, bull-roarers, will lose their potency if women learn their mysteries' (Cassell 2003: 275).

Many social and moral values permeate health care. For example, Deborah Lupton's work is closely concerned with 'medicine as culture' and she is particularly interested in how medical professionals classify patients unofficially, as 'good' or 'bad' depending on whether their illness is 'self-inflicted' (for example via smoking, or promiscuity); whether they are compliant to treatment; and whether they question the doctor's authority, or are hostile and complaining.

> While medicine is predicated on scientific principles of objectivity and the ethical tenet of altruism, moral values are suffused throughout the medical encounter. In doctors and other medical professionals' interaction with patients, it is not only the biomedical model and the imperatives of time which shape medical judgements, but value judgements about the patient based on gender, social class, ethnicity, age, physical attractiveness and the type of illness (for example, whether it is 'deserved' or not). (Lupton 2003: 134)

Lupton also considers how alternative therapies challenge medical authority, often by rejecting simple 'mind-body' dualisms and recognising the importance of a wider human-environmental interaction. This returns us to the original point in this chapter, that there are many different cultural models of health and well-being. In contemporary multicultural societies, such diversity requires careful governance, and a number of anthropologists are involved in needs assessment and the development of health policy.

Eric Bailey, for example, worked with an organization called United Health Care, which co-sponsors annual health fairs throughout Detroit (Bailey 1998). The organization found that it had had little success with the African American communities – in fact their participation in health services was declining. Bailey's cultural-historical research revealed that many institutions providing health care for this sector of the population were in decline, and often depended on large teaching hospitals, with high staff turnover. This engendered little trust or use of their services. Additionally, many people did not participate in the provision of free health screenings because charity care was seen as demeaning to individuals. The medical staff conducting them (often in unsuitable settings) were generally from non-African ethnic backgrounds. Neither they, nor the promotional materials they used, were culturally sensitive to local perspectives. With these problems made visible, it became feasible to organize the delivery of health services in a more effective way (in Ferraro 1998).

Similarly, Merry Wood was employed in British Colombia, by the Greater Vancouver Health Service Society, an organization with 400 staff members in nine mental health teams. Wood's work focused on long-term planning, assessing needs and evaluating programmes, and she produced a short manual for people to use in reviewing their policies and programs, with a view to improving services and responding to the needs of diverse cultural groups (Wood, in Ervin 2005: 106).

While also critical in other areas, ethics are of particular importance in medical and health-related research. There are major emotive issues, such as abortion, which remain a focus for intense conflict (see Ginsburg 1989). As touched on earlier in this volume, there are complex ethical issues in human organ replacement too, where a severe shortage of organs for transplantation has opened the door to marketing approaches and the idea of organs as commodities has raised some major 'social and moral issues' (Marshall, Thomasma and Daar 1996: 1). New techniques in gene analysis and potential gene therapies have also opened up a large set of ethical concerns. For example anthropologists such as Rayna Rapp (1989) and Aviad Raz (2004) have considered the discourses around genetic counselling and how this reframes medical ideas; and Kathryn Taylor's (1988) work considers the issues around the disclosure of medical information.

As this chapter illustrates, although many people think of 'health' as a specialized category, it is an intensely social and cultural area of life and, as such, all of its aspects benefit from ethnographic analysis which reveals the underlying ideas and beliefs that direct human action, and the social, economic and political realities that form the context in which health is upheld or compromised. There are many fascinating and worthwhile research opportunities in this area.

8 ANTHROPOLOGY, ART AND IDENTITY

DEFINING IDENTITY

Human beings spend a lot of time and energy 'creating' themselves and others, and formulating ideas about social identity: who 'we' are, and who 'they' are. They do this in a host of ways: through language, performance, art, material culture, ritual and other media. Every human society, small or large, has a vision of its own characteristics, and defines these in comparison to others. There are many sub-divisions of identity according to things like gender and sexuality, age, class, education, political ideology, religious beliefs and so on. Larger societies contain sub-cultural groups: indigenous communities; ethnic groups; immigrant populations; rural and urban inhabitants. And there are more specialized groupings, defined by profession, or by their interest in particular sporting activities. Some years ago, Benedict Anderson (1991) coined the now well-known phrase 'imagined communities' to describe how people identify themselves, and there are many such communities: social, professional and ideological. They can be quite specific: for example the scientific communities that span the globe are not large, but they share a common professional identity. And people are linked by other common interests, for example in music or art.

While there is a tendency to assume that the arts (in whatever form) are a kind of non-essential 'add-on' to culture, anthropologists take the arts seriously. They see identity and how it is represented as a vital part of human life, and recognize that it plays a key role in conflicts between groups at a local, national and international

level; in arguments over land and resources; and in the maintenance of cultural diversity. Understanding how people deal with issues of identity and representation is therefore practical as well as absorbing, and many anthropologists are thus closely engaged in understanding the processes through which identity is constructed and expressed. This chapter considers some of the work that researchers do in this area.

GENDER AND SEXUALITY

One of the most fundamental aspects of human identity is that of gender, but cross-cultural comparison reveals that there are wide variations in ideas about how many genders exist, and how these are composed, whether by genital anatomy (as in most Western societies), by density of flesh and bone (as in Nepal) or by inclination and behaviour (as in societies where gender categories are more fluid). Harriet Whitehead's (1981) early research with Native American cultures, for example, observed that is common for three gender categories to be accepted: male, female, and a third, more mixed, category. And Sharyn Graham Davies' (2004) research with the Bugis in Indonesia describes a system in which five gender categories are defined.

Human societies have equally diverse ideas about sexuality and how this is constituted. Jennifer Robertson's (2005) comparative research with lesbian and gay cultures in different societies reveals many cultural differences in how sexuality is perceived, represented and experienced, and she notes wide variations in the extent to which same-sex unions are considered to be acceptable.

The anthropology of gender often focuses on how ideas about masculinity or femininity are upheld in different cultural contexts. Henrik Ronsbo (2003: 157), for example, working with young male footballers in Central America, concluded that sport plays a key role in creating their local identities, providing a process similar to that previously offered by religious brotherhoods. 'Young men, when playing football, and other villagers, when watching it, embody personal and social identities' (Ronsbo 2003: 157). I became interested in similar issues when working with young stockmen in northern Australia, observing the intensive socialization through which they learned 'how to be men' in a very tough arena (Strang 2001b). In fact, as illustrated by Barry Smart's (2005) work on sporting celebrities, there is now an entire 'anthropology of sport' that considers the many social meanings that are expressed through sporting activity.

Rita Astuti's (1998) work in Madagascar, examining the different attitudes to the birth of boys and girls, underlines the importance of gender identity in defining social status and power. This is further illustrated in Lila Abu-Lughod's work, which describes the intense social pressure through which, in Egypt, successful female movie stars have been criticized for neglecting their husbands and families and forced to 'repent', giving up their careers and conforming to Islamic ideas about femininity. There is

> ... a sentiment being widely disseminated in the press and other media, especially in the last two decades of increasing unemployment, that women's proper place is in the home with their families. Actresses and other show business personalities epitomize the challenge to that domestic model and are targeted in part because they are the most extreme and visible cases of a widespread phenomenon: working women. (Abu-Lughod 1997: 505)

Issues of equality for women in the workplace can be found everywhere. Gillian Ranson, for example, conducts research with female engineers in Calgary 'looking at the ramifications of increasing female participation in one of the last bastions of male domination' (Ranson 2005: 104). One of her major questions was whether they would remain in this field 'for the long haul' (Ranson 2005), and what their experiences revealed about gender relations and professional opportunities for women in contemporary Canada.

There are many ways to consider the effects of gender relations in different societies. As we saw in earlier chapters, gender is also an important factor in defining ownership of and access to resources, and it commonly affects access to education too, as is illustrated by Anna Robinson-Pant's research on women and literacy in India and Africa, which draws a relationship between literacy and the degree of equality that women are able to achieve (Robinson-Pant 2004).

RACE, NATIONALISM AND SOCIAL MOVEMENTS

The other key marker of identity that exerts a major influence on people's lives is that of race. Although most anthropologists would say that the idea of race is an invention – a cultural device for describing 'the other', which has little or no genetic foundation – the concept nevertheless retains a lot of popular currency. Citing Levi-Strauss, one of anthropology's founding fathers, Clifford Geertz (1986) pointed out that every culture hopes to define itself by resisting those that surround it. This idea is very evident in discourses about race, which speak directly to fundamental ideas about what human beings are composed of: in a literal sense, blood and genes, but also in a wider sense, knowledge, beliefs and ideologies – all of which can be seen as containing an identity vulnerable to 'pollution' by otherness (see Douglas 2002[1966], Strang 2004).

Part of what anthropologists do in relation to race is to consider how ideas about it are created and upheld. For example, Carolyn Fluehr-Lobban's (2005) work examines 'how racism happens' in America, looking at the biological and cultural ideas, and the social and spatial arrangements that allow racist assumptions to persist in many communities. Gillian Cowlishaw's (1998) research charts how ideas about race are expressed in relationships between Aboriginal people and the wider Australian population; and Peter Wade (2002) considers the implications of concepts of race in the United Kingdom's increasingly multicultural society.

Popular ideas about racial identity have rarely produced positive visions of 'the other', and many anthropologists, whose profession necessarily includes an appreciation of diversity, have worked hard to combat racist stereotypes and their effects: for example – as we have seen in previous chapters – acting as advocates for beleaguered minority communities, openly criticizing racist policies and practices, and mediating in conflicts. As in other areas of research, an essential part of this task is cultural translation: the communication of different realities and experiences of life, creating a more fully informed 'representation' of identity that serves as a positive alternative to the stereotypes that sometimes appear in the media. In Australia, for example, Bain Attwood and Andrew Markus (1999) have been part of a lively intellectual movement to make visible the hidden history of Aboriginal people since colonization. In the UK, Brian Street (1975) wrote critically about the way that 'savages' have been portrayed in English literature over time, and Jeremy MacClancy (2002) has be at pains to show that 'the other' is 'exotic no more'.

However, ideas about racial identity are not invariably negative: for example Carol Trosset's (1993) classic ethnography of Welsh communities shows that where stereotypes originate within – where people identify themselves as a racial group with certain characteristics – then this can be a positive and binding mechanism. Thus the Welsh people have revived their own language and brought it back into everyday use, and, in doing so, have achieved a stronger sense of identity. On the other side of the planet, Aboriginal Australians have been astute in subverting negative media stereotypes of themselves as 'primitive', 'pre-modern' people, reconstructing them in more positive terms that valorize 'traditional' ecological knowledge, long-term, sustainable environmental management and 'harmony with nature' (Hendry 2006), and which stress the artistic creativity that their culture enables (Kleinert and Neale 2000).

Like race, nationalism is also a potentially double-edged sword. It can serve as a way of thinking about identity that encourages solidarity and a sense of community; or as a way of defining 'the other' in negative terms and dealing with them aggressively. Robert Foster's (2002) work traces how, through engagement with Western material culture, disparate (and often warring) communities in Papua New Guinea have begun to develop the idea of a 'nation' which can engage more collectively – and perhaps more effectively – with a wider global context. Alternatively, anthropologists such as Jane Cowan (2000), working in Macedonia, and Joel Halpern and David Kideckel (2000), working in the former Yugoslavia, have focused on how ideas of nationhood have led neighbouring communities into bitter internal conflicts. This is a complex issue in post-colonial settler societies too. In New Zealand and Australia, for example, indigenous groups have long fought for an egalitarian bicultural approach, but as Erich Kolig's (2004) research has shown, contemporary pressures to encompass multiculturalism can often override these negotiations.

In addition to races and nations, there are other cultural and sub-cultural groups that share a common identity. As noted in Chapter 4., large social movements such as environmentalism also form distinct communities, linked by a shared ideology. Such movements can be based on class: for example, Sharryn Kasmir (2005) conducted research in a large automobile factory in Tennessee, examining how class identities were mobilized to resist a labor-management partnership and assert worker identification. Religions have often formed the basis of large social movements, and many ethnographers have turned their attention to the study of religious groups, thus Joel Robbins' (2007) work considers the anthropology of Christianity, and Simon Coleman's (2007) research on religious language and ritual has led him to consider new forms of worship via technologies such as the Internet. Tanya Luhrmann works with neo-Pagan communities in London, and notes the long history of 'alternative' social and religious movements:

> I took myself off to London to conduct fieldwork among a subculture of people
> – several thousand at least – who thought of themselves as, or as inspired by,
> the witches, wizards, druids, kabbalists and shamans of mostly European lore.

They met in different kinds of group: 'covens', 'lodges', 'brotherhoods' – which all ultimately descended from a nineteenth century group – the Golden Dawn – created by three dissident Freemasons in the heyday of spiritualism and psychical research. (Luhrmann 2002: 121)

There are other 'virtual' communities enabled by Internet connections too. For example, Steven Klienknecht conducts research on the transnational subculture of computer 'hackers' whose common interest lies in breaching the boundaries of institutions and their systems. Given the potential mayhem that such hacking can create, understanding the motivations of this group is important.

REPRESENTING IDENTITY

How do people 'show and tell' who they are? As implied in the previous section on education, language itself is a key 'plank' of identity, containing specifically cultural categories, concepts and values, and this is why retaining traditional languages is often seen as central to the ability of minority groups to 'hold their own' in larger multicultural societies. Just as reviving the Welsh language has been an important development in defining Welshness, indigenous communities all around the world struggle to keep their own languages alive. Linguistic anthropologists have long played a vital role in this endeavour, often recording entire language 'orthographies' so that they are available to younger generations even if local language usage lapses for a while (as often happens when small-scale societies are disrupted by colonialism).[1]

In Australia, prior to the colonial era, there were several hundred different language groups, many of which also had special 'religious' languages for ritual occasions, so there is a lot of work to be done to preserve what remains of this extraordinary diversity. In the Aboriginal community where I work in North Queensland, for example, there are three different language groups: Yir Yoront, Kokobera and Kunjen. Since the 1930s, a number of linguistic specialists have worked there: Barry Alpher (1991) wrote a vast lexicon of the Yir Yoront language; Phillip Hamilton (1994) compiled an orthography for the Kokobera people, and Bruce Sommer (1972) did long-term research on the Kunjen language.

Similar kinds of work have been done for a long time in many parts of the world: in New Zealand, for instance, Joan Metge's (1976) work has underlined why an insistence on the teaching and use of Maori is central to the indigenous community's identity and, in North America, Keith Basso's (1996) research with the Western Apache also draws attention to the importance of seeing how language relates to 'place', which he maintains is essential to understanding people's belief systems and their relationships with their environment.

Because minority groups often find that their traditions are subsumed by those of the larger societies they inhabit, language retention and political resistance to absorption or assimilation are often closely intertwined. At times, language use itself becomes a point of contention, and this is amply illustrated by Jacqueline Urla's (2006) research on the Basque language revival movement in northern Europe. She has been chronicling the Basque people's efforts to preserve Euskara, reputedly the oldest living language in Europe. Her research reports the government's closure of the Euskara language newspaper and the arrest of its editorial board (who were accused of collaborating with the terrorist group, ETA). The local populace was outraged, and tens of thousands of people took to the streets to demonstrate against the government's decision:

> To the many protesters, the closing of the Basque newspaper signifies an entirely new level of intervention, namely an extension of the anti-ETA clampdown into the domain of media and culture, and effectively the criminalisation of Euskara itself... Now that terrorism is perceived to be everywhere, we can expect to see an increase in this kind of repressive action ... [but] the determined citizens of the Basque Country have not been easily silenced. They have raised money and organised to set up a new Basque-language newspaper. (Urla 2006: 2–3)

Closely aligned with language is the importance of oral histories as a form of identity construction and self-representation. There is a classic phrase that 'history is written by the winners'. Thus the histories of colonized communities or those defeated in war have often been omitted from official records. The phrase also underlines the reality that official 'history' is often 'his-story', rendering women's contributions to events invisible. And it assumes that history is *written*, leaving little room for the stories of people who do not write. In non-writing cultures particularly (but also in others) oral history is a vital part of everyday life, transmitting knowledge from one generation to the next, and enabling people to describe themselves to themselves and to others. Paul Connerton, whose classic monograph focused on 'how societies remember', described even village gossip as a means by which 'a village informally constructs a continuous communal history of itself' (Connerton 1989: 17).

Over the last few decades ethnographers have increasingly recorded oral histories in order to move beyond the limitations of officially sanctioned accounts. In Australia, anthropologists such as Jeremy Beckett (1988) and Dawn May (1994) have made use of oral accounts to critique the way that Aboriginal history has been excluded from the 'official' colonial record, and to describe Aboriginal perspectives on the colonial experience. 'Instead of an authorised version of Aboriginality in Australia, there has been a medley of voices, black and white, official and unofficial, national and local, scientific and journalistic, religious and secular, interested and disinterested, all offering or contesting particular constructions of Aboriginality' (Beckett 1988: 7).

Similar issues arise in other post-colonial societies, as illustrated, for example, by the work of Marie Mauzé, Michael Harkin and Sergei Kan with north-west coast communities in North America (2004), and Ranginui Walker's (2004) depictions of Maori history in New Zealand.

Whether oral or written, history is essentially a narrative about personal and collective experience. Thus Paul Antze and Michael Lambek's work focuses on memory as 'the ground for cultural reproduction' (1996: xxi):

> Memory serves as both a phenomenological ground of identity (as when we know implicitly who we are and the circumstances that have made us) and the means for explicit identity construction (as when we search our memories in order to understand ourselves or when we offer particular stories about ourselves in order to make a certain kind of impression). (Antze and Lambek 1996: xvi)

ART AND PERFORMANCE

Cultures create narratives about who they are not only through language, oral history and written media, but also through a range of visual media. The anthropology of art thus offers us a rich source of ideas about how people uphold and communicate their identities, beliefs and values. There is some overlap with the discipline of art history, which tends to focus on the art of larger societies, tracing particular artistic 'movements' over time, and with Cultural Studies, which focuses on a range of media, usually in industrialized societies (see Power and Scott 2004). Anthropologists who specialize in the analysis of art are also interested in these shifts, but because of their professional focus on local or specific communities, they are more often involved in work relating to the art production of smaller groups and more concerned to locate their analyses in an explanatory ethnographic context.

Australia again provides a lively research area in this regard. As anthropologists such as Howard Morphy (1998), Fred Myers (2002, 2006) and Peter Sutton (1989) have shown, Aboriginal art provides an excellent avenue through which to understand the complexities of indigenous culture. As this art has become internationally renowned and marketed transnationally, it has become an important source of income for indigenous communities. Thus contemporary studies also consider not only how art functions 'at home', but also how it mediates relationships between local communities and the larger societies with which they interact (see Klienart and Neale 2000, Morphy and Perkins 2006).

> The production, circulation, and consumption of Aboriginal acrylic paintings constitutes an important dimension of self-production of Aboriginal people and of the processes of 'representing culture'... This is a hybrid process of

cultural production, bringing together the Aboriginal painters, art critics, and ethnographers, in addition to curators, collectors and dealers: in short, an 'artworld'. (Myers 2006: 495)

There are many other approaches to the study of art in anthropology. Ruth Phillips (2006), for example, looks at the 'souvenir art' produced for tourists by indigenous communities, and Robert Thompson explores traditions of artistic criticism in sub-Saharan Africa: 'Yoruba art critics are experts of strong mind and articulate voices who measure in words the quality of works of art . . . Yoruba artistic criticism may occur at a dance feast where the excellence of sculpture and motion becomes a matter of intense concern' (Thompson 2006b: 242).

As Thompson's work implies, not all 'art' is concerned with paintings or sculpture. Many groups wear clothes and objects that are major identity signifiers, and there is also the ultimate form of social identification, in which people paint, tattoo or scarify culturally meaningful designs onto their own bodies. All of these things serve to manifest people's identities – to concretize them in physical terms.

Less tangible expressions of identity are equally important, and performances of songs, dances, stories, plays and so on are often a central part of community self-expression. For instance, Pernille Gooch's (1998) work with the Van Gujjar people of Uttar Pradesh showed how public performances offered positive opportunities for them to present beneficial representations of their culture as 'the voice of nature'.

Similar functions are apparent in anthropological research on dance, as illustrated by John Norman's (1970) classic text on the 'Ghost Dance' of the Sioux, and Joy Hendry's (2006) survey of a number of indigenous communities, which underlined the importance of dance and performance in their efforts to communicate a particular cultural identity. As Simone Abram, Jacqueline Waldren and Don MacLeod point out, identity often comes to the fore when local communities 'perform' for tourists:

'People continue to represent their 'identity' in terms of folkloric costumes ... and practices such as music, dance, cuisine, etc. and assert the authority of their local knowledge by claiming their status in terms of identity' (Abram, Waldren and MacLeod 1997: 5).

A NATURAL TURN TO THE ANTHROPOLOGY OF DANCE

Jonathan Skinner

Lecturer in Social Anthropology, Queen's University Belfast

I want to tell you about how I came to anthropology and what it means to me being an anthropologist. I was very lucky when I was growing up: the only son of parents who loved travelling. I travelled with them a lot, and with a number of youth groups. I didn't really know what I was doing, but I kept diaries of my travels, did exchanges with people in Finland, Israel and Canada, and retraced Marco Polo's trade caravan route (yes, some people do win those cornflake packet competitions). I even spent a year on exchange in a school in Canada after finishing school in England before taking up my place at the University of St Andrews in Scotland (I fell in love with the castle when visiting). At university I chose anthropology, psychology and philosophy for my first year subjects because I wanted to see what they were like. I didn't know anything about any of them. They were all challenging in different ways: anthropology was weird and made me think a lot about my travels and exchanges; philosophy taught me the consequences of my thoughts and actions; and psychology was interesting but all statistics and multiple-choice tests. Sometimes anthropology and psychology came together as we looked at aggression in societies and in human nature; I would then get frustrated by the psychologists talking generally when I was reading about the Yanomamo and the Ik, and how it was so different in different parts of the world.

In my summers at the University of St Andrews I continued to travel and did some English Language teaching in Romania. That experience turned into an undergraduate anthropology dissertation looking at ethnic tensions between Romanians and Hungarians living in Transylvania (a part of Romania near Vlad Dracul's castle). I liked the anthropology department at St Andrews more and more as an undergraduate. I enjoyed myself and wrote for student newspapers, acted, did lots of sport and worked in the students' union. The dissertation got me out of the university and mixing with all sorts of people, asking questions, talking, drinking and dancing — and all in the name of research.

When I graduated I thought about continuing with all this. I liked the mix between people and books. I liked the emphasis anthropology has upon real people living real lives in a particular context. I was addicted to sampling different worlds. Edmund Leach calls this 'butterfly collecting' and was critical of anthropologists doing too much of it. But I didn't want to go back to Romania — I'd liked it, but had also been very ill after having to drink homemade vodka at the start of all the meals, even breakfast (to kill off all the bugs, of course).

In my first year as a post-graduate at St Andrews, supporting myself financially by giving tutorials and teaching English to Japanese students, I read a lot about British colonialism and I changed my research direction.

There are only a few British colonies left, so I found an island in the Caribbean called Montserrat. Hey, I was paying my way with loans and teaching, so I felt entitled to such a fieldwork destination.

Montserrat was amazing! A small, tear-shaped island in the Caribbean with very friendly people, little tourism, lots of Carnival and calypso, and an unusual connection with Ireland — some Montserratians are known controversially as 'the Black Irish' of the Caribbean. I was there looking at colonial relations when suddenly a volcano erupted. I was evacuated and left most of my clothes and possessions behind except for my notebooks. I came back to St Andrews and experienced all sorts of culture shock in reverse. I'd left the island so quickly that part of me was still there. Every time I did the laundry, the vibrations from the spin cycle would give me palpitations, and I would sweat as my body took me back to the island, the eruption and the earth tremors.

After writing my Ph.D. thesis I got a job in a Sociology department as the token anthropologist. My work shifted to looking at reactions to the volcano, and living with risk. I then took over the editorship of the journal *Anthropology in Action* and began working with groups of anthropologists around the world, going to conferences and bringing conference panels to press by encouraging them to publish their latest applied anthropology in the journal. Check it out online!

To cut a longer story short, in 2003 I moved to Belfast where I currently teach anthropology. Having taken up dancing as a hobby while writing my Ph.D. thesis, I found lots of interesting connections with my work in the Caribbean, examining people's ideas about risk and community: who to dance with, who to avoid, and why, and how people narrate and order their everyday lives. I still write about what is going on on Montserrat, but am also more broadly interested in people who dance. At the moment I'm writing about dance as an informal therapy for getting over clinical depression, comparing dancers in Belfast with dancers in Sacramento, CA (I know — that choice of fieldsite again, but someone has to do it). In Belfast the salsa dancers come together and it is a way for Protestants and Catholics to integrate and get over the past Troubles; in Sacramento the salsa dancers come together and it is a way for latino migrants to recreate their 'everynight life' and to feel at home in a different country, even if it is just for a few hours. Same dance, different meanings. This fascinates me.

I'd do it all the same again if I could. Anthropology gives me that space/excuse to explore. I've never regretted the anthropology route, although I have worried about what would have happened if I had missed the subject entirely.

Tourism has, in many ways, replaced the colonial frontier as the place where different cultures meet and perform their identities to each other. With globalization it has become a major industry (see Reid 2003), and one in which major political and economic inequalities become highly visible (Coleman and Crang 2002). Less powerful groups face difficult choices about engaging in tourist industries in order to make a living, or resisting pressure to 'perform themselves' for the gratification of wealthier groups. Thus Xianghong Feng asks 'who benefits?' when areas are opened up to tourism:

The Chinese government is making tourism an important rural development strategy. Local governments and outside developers jointly manage and develop natural and cultural resources to increase tourism revenues. The government sells development and management rights to large for-profit corporations... Pleasant climate, stunning views, 'colorful' ethnic minority cultures, and the newly discovered and partially restored Ming Dynasty 'Southern China Great Wall' are the primary tourist attractions in Fenghuang County. This project impacts 374,000 people, made up of 29 national minorities and representing 74 percent of the local population. Some researchers argue that this public-private partnership successfully produces profits for developers and creates economic growth. The present research uses a power and scale perspective to identify the preliminary socioeconomic impacts of this capital-intensive development model on local communities [and] to identify the decision-makers, document the distribution of social power, and identify the flow of costs and benefits through the tourism system. (Feng 2008: 207)

However, unless subject to a repressive regime, host communities are not passive recipients of the effects of tourism: they often find multiple ways to negotiate relationships in ways that also fulfil their own needs. This is nicely illustrated by Assa Doron's research in the city of Varanasi:

Contemporary studies of tourism in the 'Third World' often focus on the far-reaching economic, cultural and environmental consequences of tourism on local populations. Scholars have argued that guest/host interactions reflect a relation of domination in which ... wealthy Western tourists travel in search of the exotic Orient. The tourists are then served and catered to by local communities who are dependent on their business. Such polarities tend to privilege the 'guests' as the purveyors of change, while the creative and innovative practices of the host group are rendered invisible ... I examine the boatmen of Varanasi and their role as culture brokers, negotiating the sacred city for visitors ... I look at the multiple strategies and tactics that boatmen have developed to satisfy their needs and desires to their own advantage ... the boatmen are quick to 'tune in' to those with whom they are dealing. Moreover, the close encounters that boatmen have with tourists enable them to view Western culture as well as their own local culture critically. (Doron 2005: 32)

Tourism is therefore a fruitful site for research into the representational issues that these 'cultural meetings' engender and into the complex social, economic and political relationships that ensue

Along with dance and performance, music is an important part of representational expression, and there is a large anthropological subfield of 'ethnomusicology' devoted to studying music in communities all around the world. This field is very diverse, containing, for example, Fiona Magowan's (2007) research, which examines

the songs and rituals used for mourning in Northern Australia, and Greg Booth's (2000) work on the music of Bollywood.

The study of art and performance builds on a longstanding anthropological interest in formal rituals and ceremonies. All human societies have rituals: these are often religious or semi-religious in nature, and intensely laden with cultural meanings. As the influential theorist Victor Turner said, the performance of a ritual celebrates the 'values, common interests and moral order' of a group, and so transcends its divisions, binding it together (Turner 1982: 10). Rituals are therefore very revealing of cultural ideas, offering an abiding source of insights into particular worldviews. Thus Pnina Werbner has used her research on Christmas rituals in Western societies to consider how these create a 'moral economy' of honour and debt and reproduce social relations. They also, it would appear, establish hierarchical relations between parents and children and between rich and poor, as well as excluding non-Christian ethnic groups from the performance of 'the nation' at Christmas time (Werbner 1996).

Rituals are wonderfully expressive of cosmological ideas, and any ethnographic account examining a society's beliefs must surely consider how these are manifested in formal ceremonies. The ethnographic canon abounds with examples that provide insights into the intangible: for example, Silvia Rodgers' research on the rituals that are carried out to launch Navy ships considers how these animate and personify a belief in the ship as a female being:

> If the ceremony of launching looks at first sight like the transition rite that accompanies the ship as she passes from land to water, it soon becomes clear that the critical transition is from the status of an inanimate being to that of an animate and social being. From being a numbered thing at her launch, the ship receives her name and all that comes with the name. This includes everything that gives her an individual and social identity, her luck, her life essence and her femininity... This ceremony is unique in our society ... in that it symbolically brings to life an artefact. Members of the Royal Navy, and indeed the merchant

navies, talk about a ship as having a life, a soul, a spirit, a personality and a character of her own. (Rodgers 2006: 231)

As this example illustrates, material culture is inevitably encoded with cultural values, and there are many anthropologists involved in research that explores 'the meaning of things'. This links with the work on human-environmental relationships that we considered in Chapter 4, which suggests that people find meaning in all of the material objects that surround them, including 'natural' things such as water (Strang 2004), or trees (Rival 1998), as well as the artefacts they have made themselves, which serve to maintain their social and economic relationships and express particular cultural identities.

MUSEUMS AND CULTURAL HERITAGE

Ethnographic research has often involved collecting images and material culture as well as social data. As well as providing a useful focus for analysis these are an important part of how cultural identities are represented. As noted at the beginning of this chapter, identity is a comparative business, which invariably involves self-representations and representations of 'the other'. Who controls the representation of a group is intensely revealing of power relations. This is readily evident in areas such as photography, film and museum studies, which intersect with 'what anthropologists do' in a variety of ways. Since the early days of the discipline there has been a steady shift away from a somewhat distanced anthropological view of 'other' societies to more collaborative co-produced representations (see Mills, Babiker and Ntarangwi 2006). This reflects changes in the relationships between anthropologists and their host communities, which, since the fierce critiques of the 1960s and 1970s offered by feminist anthropologists and indigenous groups, have become keenly aware of the need to establish mutually beneficial working relationships that are characterized by equality and shared control over the representational process. It has now become standard for representational projects to be carried out in collaboration with local experts and indigenous scholars.

This shift is particularly obvious in the museum sphere. Museums have always sought to represent cultural realities, and they are a primary site at which many people first come into contact with ideas about 'other' cultural groups. Ethnographic museums bring material ideas into a space in which these can be examined and, ideally, explained and understood. The role of cultural translator is obviously critical in this process: 'Ethnographic museums and applied anthropologists have played a fundamental role in the representation and interpretation of indigenous peoples, both in the colonial and post-colonial periods' (Stanton 1999: 282).

For anthropologists, working in museums is not just about designing and explaining exhibitions; it is also about mediating relationships and exchanges of information between different cultural groups. John Stanton works at the Berndt Museum at the University of Western Australia, and notes two major developments: first, the ethical need, coupled with demands from the cultural groups being represented, for greater participation of these communities in the direction and management of museums. Second, the development of research, exhibition and education programmes that link museums more closely with the communities that are (or were) the source of the artefacts on display, and involve them directly in exhibition design and research (Stanton 1999). Thus, as Mary Bouquet and Nuno Porto observe (2005), museums are now involved in a collaborative and dynamic process of cultural production (see also Bouquet 2001).

Anthropologists work for or advise all kinds of museums, ranging from the large established national museums, to the small museums that communities initiate in order to represent themselves. There is a rapidly increasing number of the latter in many local and indigenous communities, sparked by political desires for self-representations, and by the enlarging tourist trade around the world.

A natural extension of museum research is the wider arena of 'cultural heritage', in which many anthropologists and archaeologists are now employed (see Shackel and Chambers 2004). This is concerned with the ways in which heritage is manifested: through landscapes, architecture, customary practices, the use of resources, the designation of sacred sites, archaeological remains or indeed any object or activity that can be said to encapsulate culture over time.

Cultural heritage is a fast expanding area, and there are several reasons for this. Many indigenous or ethnic communities have become keen to define and articulate their identity for social, political and economic reasons, and a lot of cultural heritage work is done to support claims for land or resources. The aforementioned tourist trade has also been influential in encouraging communities to depict their identities more actively, and sometimes to commodify and market their 'culture' in order to gain an income from tourists.

But cultural heritage is not just something that small ethnic minorities or indigenous communities are interested in: it is also something that larger societies use to affirm their own claims to land (most particularly in post-colonial environments) and to generate income from tourism. In addition, it provides a way in which, in an increasingly mobile and fragmented world, people can construct a locally rooted and meaningful sense of identity and feel that they are part of a community. It is an old adage in anthropology that active self-representations are most often made by minorities who feel that their identity may be under threat in some way, but now, in an increasingly cosmopolitan social environment, this pressure is felt by many groups of people.

A useful example is provided by Mary La Lone's (2001) work, which led her to become involved in an effort to preserve mining heritage from the coal-mining era in the Appalachian mountains. Knowledge about that era was fading away, until a group of former miners and families formed a local heritage association:

> As an anthropologist at Radford University in the New River Valley, I witnessed the group's activities and recognized the need to lend anthropological assistance in the form of an oral history project designed to document and preserve knowledge of the mining heritage. Few written records have survived... The bulk of knowledge about mining life existed in the minds of aging members of the mining families who, ranging in age from their late 50s up, were beginning to pass away without their memories being recorded. (La Lone 2001: 403)

La Lone set up a university-community partnership, which, once established as a foundation for the project, began working to create a Coal Mining Heritage Park, to commemorate mining heritage as a community focal point in the landscape.

A lot of cultural heritage work is generated by development and the legislative requirement, in many countries, to ascertain whether important cultural artefacts or landscapes will be disturbed or destroyed by the physical rearrangement that development entails. Philip Moore's work as a heritage consultant is typical in this regard: 'I worked intensively as a consultant between 1987 and 1991 and sporadically since then. My work was done primarily, though not exclusively, for mining companies seeking to meet their obligations regarding Aboriginal heritage so that resource development projects could proceed' (Moore 1999: 230).

Cultural heritage is not just about the past: anthropologists also consider how people create places and objects that memorialize and try to make sense of the present. Thus Sylvia Grider's research examines the difficult process in which people created public memorials while trying to make sense of the shootings at Columbine High School in 1999 (Grider 2007), and Peter Margry and Cristina Sanchez-Carretero have observed how spontaneous shrines have become increasingly important as a way of dealing with tragic events:

The tragic death of Diana, Princess of Wales in 1997 firmly placed improvised memorial sites or spontaneous shrines as a phenomenon on the world map. In the collective emotional outpouring that followed, memorial sites were erected all over the world with flowers, candles, letters, drawings, messages, stuffed animals and toys... Similar behaviour was displayed in reaction to the untimely death of other beloved public personalities – for example Elvis Presley in 1977 and Olof Palme in 1986 ... however it was not until after Princess Diana's death that public memorialisation of death found an elaborate format with an enduring ritual form and symbolic repertoire... Such memorials therefore make ideal subjects for case studies of how national (and international) memory is constructed. (Margry and Sanchez-Carretero 2007: 1)

FILM AND PHOTOGRAPHY

Many kinds of representational activity involve the use of film and photography and, as with museums and other mechanisms through which identity is communicated, much depends on who controls the process, and whether it involves a freely chosen self-representation, or one decided by someone else. The colonial era produced a number of visions of indigenous or tribal communities that supported evolutionary ideas about 'primitive', 'savage' and 'exotic' others, and upheld highly disparate power relations. This is still an issue: Elizabeth Edwards' (1996) research on postcards from around the world shows that many of these ideas persist in current portrayals of indigenous or ethnic minorities. And David Turton's (2004) work throws up similar issues in examining tourist photographs of the Mursi people, who wear large lip-plates which tourists find fascinating and of course highly photogenic.

The kinds of issues that surround photography are equally relevant in relation to film. Ethnographic film is a major tool for communicating knowledge about cultures, and debates about the ethics of portraying host communities have paralleled those that have been taking place in museums, with increasing involvement and control by the people being represented. Some communities, such as the Kayapo in South America, have been highly active in taking charge of and making use of video and film to create their own self-representations (Turner 1992), or collaborating with anthropologists in this endeavour. Aboriginal scholars such as Marcia Langton (1993: 10) have argued that 'one of the important interventions is the act of self-representation itself and the power of aesthetic and intellectual statements'.

The portrayal of different cultural groups in popular film and media is also an important area of study for anthropologists, providing useful data on ideas about race, identity and 'the other'. Pat Caplan recently turned an analytic eye on the ways that 'others' are represented in TV series such as 'Tribe' and its imitators, in which television presenters go to 'live' with tribal peoples (albeit for just a few weeks) and present this as 'anthropology' (Caplan 2005).

Who is in charge of the representational process remains important: consider, for example, some of the images of indigenous people in films such as *Walkabout* (1971), *Crocodile Dundee* (1986), or *The Gods Must be Crazy* (1980), and more recent portrayals, such as *The Rabbit Proof Fence* (2002) or *Ten Canoes* (2006), which either involved or (in the latter case) were wholly produced by Aboriginal people themselves.

Whatever its potential to provide stereotypical visions of cultural identity, as Jun Xing and Lane Hirabayashi (2003) point out, film remains a powerful educational tool that can foster cross-cultural communications, as can all of the representational forms described here. In broader terms, Thomas Hylland Eriksen (2006) is convinced that anthropologists need to engage proactively with all media. Certainly there is a lot of good (and interesting) work to be done in this arena.

GOING TO THE MOVIES

Richard Chalfen

Center on Media and Child Health, Children's Hospital/Harvard Medical School, Boston

What do we know about the beginnings of human life? What did people do with their time on an everyday basis? These were the questions that led me to become an undergraduate major in anthropology at the University of Pennsylvania. A college friend pointed me in the direction of those *National Geographic* pictures depicting daily Paleolithic life — a little like what one can now see in feature films such as *Quest for Fire* and *Clan of the Cave Bear, 10,000 B.C.* and even cartoons such as *The Flintstones*. Where do these images come from? How do we know anything about these conditions, or is it all pure fiction?

Before long, curiosity about variations in contemporary life took over. I realized that social and cultural anthropology had become more central to my interests than biological questions. I recall several documentary films about the lives of people living in distant and exotic parts of the world. As fascinating as these portraits were, I became sceptical: why should I believe what I was seeing in these films about these other ways of life? Was I just 'going to the movies' or was this different? Issues about pictures and pictorial representation in general remained with me: I needed to know more about who made these films and how they were made. Then I discovered the existence of something called 'visual anthropology', and the possibility of combining anthropology and filmmaking skills. In short, more school was necessary.

Graduating as both an anthropology major and a pre-med student initially offered a frustrating choice. I came from a medical family with both my father and brother graduating from the same medical school. I thought maybe I should do the same thing. Instead I signed up for a graduate degree in anthropology at Tulane University and, later, for studies in film and visual communication, again at the University of Pennsylvania.

At Penn's Annenberg School, one of my professors needed a cultural anthropologist because he had a research grant from the National Science Foundation for fieldwork that gave cameras to Navajo people. He intended to ask them to make 16 mm films about their own lives. So, during the summer of 1966, I became a research assistant for a project, *Through Navajo Eyes* (Worth and Adair 1997). This yielded a kind of excitement that has lasted for over 40 years.

As a recent graduate, following my experience with the Navajo, I approached the Pennsylvania Hospital and the Philadelphia Child Guidance Clinic with a proposal to make 16 mm films with local teenagers. Seeking an integration of urban anthropology and visual anthropology, and with methods, results and new questions from the Navajo Project, I wanted to demonstrate that one did not need to travel 2,000 miles and work with an indigenous group to record cultural differences in films. My colleagues and I theorized that, as a multicultural society, Philadelphia contained many different ways of seeing the 'same' surroundings. My intention was to demonstrate that if filmmaking was introduced in a 'neutral' manner (at least in theory), the technology could be sensitive enough to record this diversity. I asked how different groups of teenagers saw themselves and understood their own lives, living within an urban environment. For instance, how might ethnicity, social class and gender influence their filmmaking? In this way I began to research the relationships among socio-cultural variables and patterns of visual communication.

As a consultant at the clinic, I was able to develop the concept of 'socio-documentary filmmaking' with culturally diverse groups of adolescents. The first project was with a group of African-American girls, former gang members (the 'Dedicated Soul Sisters') who had been identified as potential teenage mothers. When the film they created was presented to clinic personnel, the psychologists, psychiatrists and social workers were delighted that they could get to know their client populations in new and significant ways. The films offered them what they felt was a transparent 'window on life' view of their ethnically diverse patrons. In this way, clinic staff appropriated my academically driven efforts to their own needs relating to the practical matters of a child guidance clinic, and I was thrown into doing applied visual anthropology.

In 1995 I went to work with Michael Rich, a medical practitioner in Boston who had introduced VIA (Video Intervention/Prevention Assessment), a research method in which children and adolescents with chronic medical conditions are given the opportunity to create video diaries, and asked to 'teach your clinicians what it means to live with your condition'. The narratives address their experience of illness, health and health care, and are used to improve both in-take clinical procedures (especially questionnaires) and several phases of medical education, both of which are aimed at improving patient care.

My research has remained focused on the relationships between medical, visual and applied anthropology, and this has satisfied several long-term interests. Early questions about anthropology and film communication find a comfortable home next to medical concerns and a need to contribute new knowledge to the problems of 'being human'. In a world that seems to be increasingly visual, new understandings and applications of how people look at something, how they see and understand the world and, in turn, how they communicate that information to others through visual technology take on a parallel significance. Combining forms of photography and videography with anthropology for use in applied contexts has proven to be fascinating and challenging work in a field that is still in its infancy.

CONCLUSION

APPLYING ANTHROPOLOGY

In this text, I have simply tried to give a brief overview of the kinds of things that anthropologists do in some of the main areas of human social and cultural activity. However, with a theoretical and methodological 'toolkit' that enables researchers to understand and articulate social behaviour, there is really no area of human life in which anthropology cannot be applied, and it is potentially useful in any and all of them.

THE POTENTIAL SEEMS VIRTUALLY LIMITLESS

Robert Trotter

Northern Arizona University

From my perspective, there are people applying good anthropological theory and methods in almost all areas. I am doing both medical anthropology and corporate anthropology, but have engaged in other major areas in the past (such as education, migration, traditional healing). The potential seems virtually limitless. Lots of fun things are being done; more are available every day. My ex-students are running their own businesses, working for both federal and state government, working for or heading up non-profit organizations ranging from small groups and small focuses to international groups and international causes, and also working for corporations as anthropologists.

> I have been doing applied anthropology for 30 years. I have had a wonderful time and plan on continuing to do so, since I get to work with outstanding people in many different fields, and get to work cross-culturally on many different projects.

In the examples that I have given about 'what anthropologists do', I have deliberately not drawn a distinction (which I think is a false one) between anthropologists located in universities, those who are employed by other institutions, or those who freelance as consultants or advisors. In reality, all of us apply anthropology in a variety of ways: those of us in university posts – because we generally conduct research directly with communities – often do research that can readily be described as 'applied', and even the most abstract theorizations filter into policy and practice. Anthropologists working as consultants or employed by other kinds of institutions also have a contribution to make to theoretical developments in the discipline, and to the ethnographic canon.

INTERDISCIPLINARY ANTHROPOLOGY

A discussion about interdisciplinarity is really beyond the scope of this book, but it is worth saying a few things about it. Anthropologists often find themselves working in collaboration with people from other scientific disciplines: not just within the social sciences, but increasingly with the natural sciences too: in the environmental arena with botanists, biologists, ecologists, hydrologists and climatologists; in areas of governance with political scientists and economists; in education and health with sociologists and psychologists; in the health field with medical specialists; in urban planning and housing with architects and engineers; in museums and other representational spaces with art historians and archaeologists; in the legal arena with lawyers. The list could go on, with a fairly infinite diversity of possible disciplinary combinations.

Collaborative research is a challenging undertaking, especially in conjunction with natural science disciplines, whose conceptual approaches are much more specialized than the broader frame offered by anthropological theory. Like any relationship between very different parties, it takes some effort to achieve a good balance (see Strang 2007). However, interdisciplinary projects can also be immensely creative and rewarding, leading to new and imaginative solutions to complex problems. Some people feel that interdisciplinarity is the shape of things to come. With larger, more complex issues they say, such as environmental degradation and globalization, we need to bring a range of analytic approaches to bear in order to get anywhere. In response to this trend, funding agencies are encouraging collaborative approaches, and pushing the natural and social sciences to work together.

Anthropologists have an advantage when it comes to engaging with other disciplines: their training in cultural translation means that they are well prepared to learn the 'inside' perspective of other disciplinary languages and ways of thinking. This not only makes them good collaborators, it can also make them good mediators between disparate groups in an interdisciplinary project. Intellectually, anthropology offers several major contributions to interdisciplinary research. A holistic 'let's see the whole picture' theoretical approach can provide a helpful frame for more specialized disciplinary models. Anthropology also provides useful ethnographically grounded insights into the complexities of the local context in which the work is taking place, illuminating 'the people side of the equation' and revealing the social and cultural issues that drive human behaviour. For example, in my own work with UNESCO I work mainly with ecologists and hydrologists who chart the physical effects of human activities on river systems. Part of the task of the social scientists in the programme is to consider what drives these activities in social and cultural terms. In reality, it has been equally important for us to develop conceptual frameworks that everyone can engage with, and to do a lot of 'cross-cultural translation' (and sometimes conflict resolution) between the various disciplines.

TRANSFERRING ANTHROPOLOGY

Not everyone who trains in anthropology goes on to employment as 'an anthropologist'. Some use it as a strong foundation for further training; others simply carry their anthropological skills into different areas of work. One of the beauties of the discipline is that it provides forms of expertise that are eminently transferable to other career paths. The most obvious directions are the 'people oriented' careers, such as social work, human resources, counselling, conflict resolution, mediation, education, charity/NGO work, diplomacy, government, conservation, tourism, legal work... Anthropological skills even come in useful for politicians, for example Mo Mowlam studied anthropology at Durham University before rising to a senior position as New Labour's Northern Ireland Secretary. She was

> ...a refreshingly different politician who gave New Labour a lot of its original zing. She helped to modernize her party and to beat a new path towards peace in Northern Ireland. Much of this stemmed from her personality, but the breadth of her political understanding and her effectiveness in handling people and communities demonstrate the continued value of training in anthropology for policy makers and politicians. (Bilsborough 2005: 28)

There are many less obvious avenues opened up by training in anthropology too, such as employment in social science publishing, science writing, and journalism. Marcus Helbling, for instance, found it easy to make use of his anthropological training in becoming a sports journalist:

> I've never worked as an anthropologist: I started working as a sports journalist during my studies. But I've always tried to find anthropological issues in sports. I just got the chance to start working as a print journalist for a newspaper. Today I work as a TV-journalist for Swiss television. Most anthropologists are open minded, with sensitivity and interest for 'the other'. They have the advantage of being scientists with a broad approach – and research methods in anthropology can often be used in journalism as well. (personal communication, 2006)

Robert Morais put his anthropological career to one side for quarter of a century before finding it irresistible to start analysing and writing about the meetings in which he participated (see Chapter 6):

> In 1981, I left academic anthropology and became an advertising executive... In mid-2006, I joined a marketing research and consulting firm. After a quarter of a century of work in the field, this is my first report... Based upon participation in thousands of creative meetings between 1981 and 2006 while employed at large and mid-sized American advertising agencies [it] aligns closely to what Sherry ... terms 'observant participation' and to Kemper's assertion that 'advertising executives are ethnographers in the strict sense of the word'. (Morais 2007: 150)

In reality, an ability to analyse situations critically, and understand how groups and organizations work is a major advantage in any career, even those that don't focus directly on 'people' issues.

RITES OF PASSAGE

Miranda Irving

School of Oriental and African Studies (SOAS), University of London

After successfully completing a first degree in anthropology I was lucky enough to go on to do some postgraduate research in Palembang, Sumatra. Fieldwork was fun, challenging, emotionally intense, stimulating, gruelling and inspiring all at once. It was a true 'rite of passage'. The plan was to go on to work in social research, preferably abroad. At the time, however, I found that I couldn't continue on to complete a Ph.D.

Nevertheless, the experience of learning and 'doing' anthropology gave me a particular perspective, which I carried into other areas of work. For example, soon after my postgraduate research, I found work as a temporary secretary for several months. My longest assignment was in a government typing pool in Bedford. The typing pool was a great example of 'culture' in the workplace. As I sat at my desk, in a room with rows of other typists, tapping away at the typewriter keys, I observed the group of which I had become a temporary part. The 'pool' was just like a society in microcosm: it had its own rituals, behavioural codes, hierarchies, divisions and conflicts. Though my observations added little to my work, being part-participant and part-observer of this mini society livened up what was otherwise an extremely boring job.

At other times, my anthropological background has been more directly useful. Several years on, I was employed as a research assistant on a community care project, commissioned by a local community council in Sussex. The job involved straightforward fieldwork: participant observation and face-to-face interviewing of elderly people and members of their support network to ascertain their perceptions of the provision of care. I travelled to three idyllic villages, attended day care centres, sat in on community functions and went into people's homes. The elderly people I interviewed were so unique, each one with their own particular strategies for staying healthy, connected, useful and safe. Lots of cups of tea were consumed, and interviews — which should have taken only an hour — went on for much longer as we fell into deep conversation.

On a personal level I found it intriguing how each person had built up networks of support to ensure they were cared for, and it was a lesson for my own future old age.

But there was also a more practical side to the research. I spent another month writing up a report for the community council, and along with my supervisor, made some policy recommendations on the basis of our findings and analysis. The report was published by the community council and distributed nationally and internationally. As a 'voice of the people on the ground', anthropology can have a valid and important role in the implementation of policy, and I like to think that my report played some part in this.

Fate then took me to Oman. I was there as an expatriate wife, but soon made contacts and landed a job as a consultant sociologist with a major engineering consultancy. They were undertaking an irrigation project in the rural areas of the country, and needed input from a social scientist. At first I was asked to help design a farm survey. They wanted to develop a broad questionnaire, which would be taken to all the farmers in the area. The aim was to get a general idea of the social and familial structures within the region, and how these relate to both farming practices and the very complex existing irrigation systems known as *falaj*. On the strength of this work, I was put forward for a couple of other projects: one, looking at traditional fishing practices along the coast, and another assessing the viability of placing dams in a remote and mountainous part of the country.

Since that time I have moved countless times. As a 'trailing spouse', always on the move, I have not been able to pursue a coherent career let alone find jobs in social research. This does not mean that my anthropological skills and experience have gone to waste though. For me, anthropology is a way of viewing life and you bring this with you, whatever you do. Anthropology helps us to understand ourselves and our interactions with others from within a broader framework. It leads us to comprehend another point of view, see the many sides of an argument and never assume that ideas, or ways of being, are fixed. It reveals the richness of life and enables an acceptance of diversity.

When I returned to the UK I decided to take a more journalistic path. My background in anthropology was extremely useful in this too, not only in terms of researching and interviewing techniques, but in having note taking, observation and general analytical abilities too. And finally, twenty-three years on, I have managed to return to university get on with finishing that Ph.D.

WHAT KIND OF PEOPLE BECOME ANTHROPOLOGISTS?

As suggested by the range of examples in this book, anthropology is a rather multi-cultural and diverse profession, and rapidly becoming more so. The discipline originally grew out of exchanges between European scholars and a vast range of host communities, but there are now professional anthropologists in all nations and in many sub-cultural groups, and a number of indigenous anthropologists. The diversity of 'what anthropologists do' means that the discipline attracts people with equally diverse cultural backgrounds, interests, beliefs, ideologies and aims.

However, it is possible to say a few things about what anthropologists have in common. More than anything, I think they share a burning curiosity to understand how the world works and why people act in the ways that they do. They want to see 'the whole picture' so that they can make sense of what is going on. Along with this lively intellectual curiosity, they have to be able to gather, manage and analyse a lot of data systematically and rigorously, which suggests a need for considerable organizational ability and discipline. Even if they work 'at home', anthropologists have to be comfortable with change: being in strange places, dealing with strangers, embarking on unfamiliar activities, eating different foods, and above all, engaging in a non-judgemental way with ideas and beliefs that may be very different from their own. Obviously, it helps if they are generally inclined to like people and are good at getting along with them!

Although the aim of this text has been to describe 'what anthropologists do', and to demonstrate the practical applications of anthropology and the potential career directions that it offers, I'd like to conclude with a comment about '*why* anthropologists do'. Why do people choose to spend their lives doing something that is plainly pretty demanding? Some motivations have peeped through in the autobiographies included in the text. There are plainly some pragmatic reasons: anthropological training gives practitioners a lot of choice in the range of careers open to them, as well as making them very employable. It is also flexible – something that can be put to use in just about any context. But there are deeper motivations too: for some, anthropology is about understanding and potentially leading social change. As Kay Milton said: 'I would advise anyone who wants to change the world to go for anthropology. The better we understand ourselves, the better our chances of making changes that lead to a better future' (see her autobiography in Chapter 4). So for many of us, doing anthropology is about doing something that makes a difference: something that helps things along in a positive way.

Being able to feel that one's time is usefully spent, and not wasted on something pointless is certainly a major bonus. Another major reward is the pleasure of unravelling the puzzle of human behaviour. To understand what is going on beyond the superficial is immensely satisfying. And perhaps above all, anthropology is exciting: humans are sufficiently complicated and diverse that there is always more to learn and intriguing things to consider. Fieldwork brings a host of new experiences. So a career in anthropology is often intellectually and sometimes literally an adventure: a journey to interesting ideas, people and places.

APPENDIX 1
STUDYING ANTHROPOLOGY

In most educational systems there are three major levels of study in anthropology: undergraduate degrees, master's degrees, and doctorate degrees. At an undergraduate level anthropology can be readily combined with 'sister' subjects like archaeology, history, political science, sociology, human geography, and potentially with other areas, such as development studies, environmental studies, education, psychology, business management, architecture and urban planning. Many undergraduate courses also have an honours year, which leads students towards research and further study.

It is sometimes possible to shift across to anthropology from other disciplines at a master's level, by doing an intensive taught course, possibly followed by a second year focused on research.

An honours undergraduate degree, or a master's in anthropology are both useful qualifications for carrying anthropological skills into a variety of careers. With either one of these it is also feasible to consider doing the doctoral research that is the major qualification for practising as a professional anthropologist. When students reach this stage, they usually look for a university department that can provide experienced supervision in the area that they want to study. Sometimes they make a direct approach to the person whose research they feel their interests relate to most closely. As anthropology is one of the 'original' scholarly disciplines, it is offered in most good universities. In thinking about where to study, prospective students should consider whether a university has a well-established anthropology department, and whether this is staffed by professional anthropologists who, as well as being teachers, are also active researchers.

All of this information is readily available on university web sites, and a quick search will find lists of universities in each country, and their contact details. Most are also happy to send prospective students further information, and many hold open days and career days at which it is possible to meet and talk to staff. University web sites also list the people who are specifically responsible for student applications at each level of study.

Prospective students might also want to visit the web sites of anthropology associations and the journals that publish anthropological research to get a wider view of what is going on in the field (see Appendix 3 for a list of these).

APPENDIX 2
SOME SUGGESTIONS FOR FURTHER READING

GENERAL TEXTS ABOUT ANTHROPOLOGY

Auge, M. and Colleyn, J. (2006), *The World of the Anthropologist*, transl. J. Howe, Oxford: Berg.

Coleman, S. and Simpson, B. (eds) (1998), *Discovering Anthropology: A Resource Guide for Teachers and Students*, London: Royal Anthropological Institute.

Ember, C., Ember M. and Peregrine, P. (2005), *Anthropology*, Upper Saddle River, NJ: Pearson, Prentice-Hall.

Eriksen, T. (2001), *Small Places, Large Issues: An Introduction to Social and Cultural Anthropology*, Sterling, VA: Pluto Press.

Eriksen, T. (2004), *What is Anthropology?*, Oxford: Berg.

Haviland, W. (2000), *Anthropology*, Fort Worth, TX: Harcourt College Publishers.

Haviland, W., Gordon, R. and Vivanco, L. (eds) (2006), *Talking about People: Readings in Contemporary Cultural Anthropology*, Boston: McGraw-Hill.

Hendry, J. (1999), *An Introduction to Social Anthropology: Other People's Worlds.* Basingstoke: Palgrave-Macmillan.

MacClancy, J. (ed.) (2002), *Exotic No More: Anthropology on the Front Lines*, Chicago: Chicago University Press.

Metcalf, P. (2005), *Anthropology: the Basics*, New York: Routledge.

Peacock, J. (1986) *The Anthropological Lens: Harsh Light, Soft Focus*, Cambridge: Cambridge University Press.

Toussaint, S. and Taylor, J. (eds) (1999), *Applied Anthropology in Australasia*, Nedlands: University of Western Australia Press.

GENERAL TEXTS ABOUT CAREERS IN ANTHROPOLOGY

Camenson, B. (2000), *Great Jobs for Anthropology Majors*, Lincolnwood, IL: VGM Career Horizons.

Ervin, A. (2005), *Applied Anthropology: Tools and Perspectives for Contemporary Practice*, Boston: Allyn & Bacon.

Ferraro, G. (1998), *Applying Cultural Anthropology: Readings*, Belmont, CA: Wadsworth.

Gwynne, M. (2003a), *Applied Anthropology: A Career-oriented Approach*, Boston: Pearson Education Inc.

Gwynne, M. (2003b), *Anthropology: Career Resources Handbook*, New York, London: Pearson Education.

Kedia, S. and Van Willigen, J. (2005), *Applied Anthropology: Domains of Application*, Westport, CT: Praeger.

McDonald, J. (2002), *The Applied Anthropology Reader*, Boston: Allyn & Bacon.

Morris, B. and Bastin, R. (2004), *Expert Knowledge: First World Peoples, Consultancy, and Anthropology*, New York: Berghahn Books.

National Association for the Practice of Anthropology (2001), 'Careers in Anthropology: Profiles of Practitioners', *National Association for the Practice of Anthropology Bulletin*, 20, www.anthrosource.net.

Nolan, R. (2003), *Anthropology in Practice: Building a Career Outside the Academy*, Boulder, CO: Lynne Rienner Publishers.

Omohundro, J. (2000), *Careers in Anthropology*, London: McGraw-Hill Humanities.

Pink, S. (2006), *Applications of Anthropology: Professional Anthropology in the Twenty-first Century*, London: Berghahn Books.

Podolefsky, A. and Brown, P. (eds) (2003), *Applying Anthropology: An Introductory Reader*, 7th edn, Boston: McGraw-Hill.

Sabloff, P. (2000), *Careers in Anthropology: Profiles of Practitioner Anthropologists*, NAPA Bulletin 20, Washington, DC: American Anthropological Association.

Society for Applied Anthropology (1949–) *Human Organization: Journal of the Society for Applied Anthropology*, Washington, DC: Society for Applied Anthropology.

Society for Applied Anthropology (1978–), *Practising Anthropology*, Oklahoma City: Society for Applied Anthropology.

Stephens, R. (2002), *Careers in Anthropology: What an Anthropology Degree can Do for You*, Boston: Allyn & Bacon.

Sunderland, P. and Denny, R. (2008), *Doing Anthropology in Consumer Research*, Oxford: Berg.

ETHNOGRAPHIC METHODS

Agar, M. (1996), *The Professional Stranger: An Informal Introduction to Ethnography*, 2nd edn, New York: Academic Press.

Pawluch, D., Shaffir, W. and Miall, C. (eds) (2005), *Doing Ethnography: Studying Everyday Life*, Toronto: Canadian Scholars' Press.

ANTHROPOLOGY AND ADVOCACY

Attwood, B. and Markus, A. (1999), *The Struggle for Aboriginal Rights: A Documentary History*, St Leonards, NSW: Allen & Unwin.

Cowan, J., Dembour, M.-B., Wilson, R. (2001), *Culture and Rights: Anthropological Perspectives*, New York: Cambridge University Press.

Howard, B. (2003), *Indigenous Peoples and the State: The Struggle for Native Rights*, DeKalb, IL: Northern Illinois University Press.

Nagengast, C. and Vélez-Ibáñez, C. (2004), *Human Rights: The Scholar as Activist*, Oklahoma City: Society for Applied Anthropology.

Nash, J. (ed.) (2005), *Social Movements: An Anthropological Reader*, Malden, MA: Blackwell.

Paine, R. (ed.) (1985), *Advocacy and Anthropology*, St John's Newfoundland: Institute of Social and Economic Research.

Rodríguez-Piñero, L. (2005), *Indigenous Peoples, Postcolonialism, and International Law: The ILO Regime, 1919–1989*, Oxford: Oxford University Press.

Rumsey, A. and Weiner, J. (eds) (2001), *Mining and Indigenous Lifeworlds in Australia and Papua New Guinea*, Hindmarsh, South Australia: Crawford House Publishing.

Sillitoe, P., Bicker, A. and Pottier, J. (eds) (2002), *Participating in Development: Approaches to Indigenous Knowledge*, London: Routledge.

Toussaint, S. (ed.) (2004), *Crossing Boundaries: Cultural, Legal, Historical and Practice Issues in Native Title*, Carlton, Victoria: Melbourne University Press.

Walker, R. (2004), *Ka whawhai tonu matou: Struggle without End*, London: Penguin.

Wolfe, A. and Yang, H. (eds) (1996), *Anthropological Contributions to Conflict Resolution*, Athens, GA: University of Georgia Press.

ANTHROPOLOGY AND AID

Atlani-Dualt, L. (2007), *Humanitarian Aid in Post-Soviet Countries: An Anthropological Perspective*, London: Routledge.

Corsin-Jimenez, A. (ed.) (2007), *The Anthropology of Organisations*, London: Ashgate.

De Mars, W. (2005), *NGOs and Transnational Networks: Wild Cards in World Politics*, Ann Arbor, MI: Pluto Press.

Mosse, D. (2005), *Cultivating Development: An Ethnography of Aid Policy and Practice*, London: Pluto Press.

Mosse, D. and Lewis, D. (eds) (2005), *The Aid Effect: Giving and Governing in International Development*, London: Pluto.

Munger, F. (2002), *Laboring Below the Line: The New Ethnography of Poverty, Low-wage Work, and Survival in the Global Economy*, New York: Russell Sage Foundation.

ANTHROPOLOGY AND DEVELOPMENT

Arce, A. and Long, N. (eds) (1999), *Anthropology, Development, and Modernities: Exploring Discourses, Counter-tendencies, and Violence*, London: Routledge.

Bicker, A., Sillitoe, P. and Pottier, J. (eds) (2004), *Development and Local Knowledge: New Approaches to Issues in Natural Resources Management, Conservation and Agriculture*, London: Routledge.

Carrier, J. (2004), *Confronting Environments: Local Understanding in a Globalizing World*, Walnut Creek, CA: Altamira Press.

Cohen, J. (ed.) (2002), *Economic Development: An Anthropological Approach*, Walnut Creek, CA: Altamira Press.

Edelman, M. and Haugerud, A. (eds) (2005), *The Anthropology of Development and Globalization: From Classical Political Economy to Contemporary Neoliberalism*, Malden, MA, Oxford: Blackwell.

Eriksen, T. (2003), *Globalisation: Studies in Anthropology*, London: Pluto Press.

Escobar, A. (1995), *Encountering Development: the Making and Unmaking of the Third World*, Princeton, NJ: Princeton University Press.

Hobart, M. (ed.) (1993), *An Anthropological Critique of Development: The Growth of Ignorance*, London: Routledge.

Khagram, S. (2004), *Dams and Development: Transnational Struggles for Water and Power*, Ithaca, NY: Cornell University Press.

Nolan, R. (2002), *Development Anthropology: Encounters in the Real World*, Boulder, CO: Westview Press.

Olivier de Sardan, J.-P. (2005), *Anthropology and Development: Understanding Contemporary Social Change*, New York: Zed Books.

Reid, D. (2003), *Tourism, Globalization and Development*, London: Pluto Press.

Robinson-Pant, A. 2004. *Women, Literacy, and Development: Alternative Perspectives*, New York: Routledge.

Sillitoe, P., Bicker, A. and Pottier, J. (eds) (2002), *Participating in Development: Approaches to Indigenous Knowledge*, London: Routledge.

ANTHROPOLOGY AND THE ENVIRONMENT

Anderson, D. and Berglund, E. (eds) (2003), *Ethnographies of Conservation: Environmentalism and the Distribution of Privilege*, New York: Berghahn Books.

Berglund, E. (1998), *Knowing Nature, Knowing Science: An Ethnography of Environmental Activism*, Knapwell: The White Horse Press.

Descola, P. and Palsson, G. (eds) (1996), *Nature and Society: Anthropological Perspectives*, London: Routledge.

Diamond, J. (2005), *Collapse: How Societies Choose to Fail or Succeed*, New York: Penguin.

Dominy, M. (2001), *Calling the Station Home: Place and Identity in New Zealand's High Country*, Lanham, MD: Rowman & Littlefield.

Feld, S. and K. Basso (eds) (1996), *Senses of Place*, Santa Fe, NM: School of American Research Press.

Haenn, N. and Wilk, R. (2006), *The Environment in Anthropology: A Reader in Ecology, Culture and Sustainable Living*, New York: New York University Press.

Harrison, G. and Morphy, H. (1998), *Human Adaptation*, Oxford: Berg.

Howes, D. (2005), *Empire of the Senses: A Sensual Culture Reader*, Oxford: Berg.

Milton, K. (ed.) (1993), *Environmentalism: The View from Anthropology*, London: Routledge.

Milton, K. (2002), *Loving Nature: Towards an Ecology of Emotion*, London: Routledge.

Milton, K and Svasek M. (eds) (2005), *Mixed Emotions: Anthropological Studies of Feeling*, Oxford: Berg.

Serpell, J. (1996), *In the Company of Animals: A Study of Human-animal Relationships*, Cambridge: Cambridge University Press.

Strang, V. (1997), *Uncommon Ground: Cultural Landscapes and Environmental Values*, Oxford: Berg.

Yearley, S. (2005), *Cultures of Environmentalism: Empirical Studies in Environmental Sociology*, New York: Palgrave Macmillan.

ANTHROPOLOGY AND GOVERNANCE

Gledhill, J. (2000), *Power and its Disguises: Anthropological Perspectives on Politics*, London, Sterling, VA: Pluto Press.

Gupta, A. and Sharma, A. (2006), *The Anthropology of the State: A Reader*, Malden, MA: Blackwell.

Haller, D. and Shore, C. (2005), *Corruption: Anthropological Perspectives*, London, Ann Arbor, MI: Pluto Press.

Richard, M. and Emener, W. (2003), *I'm a People Person: A Guide to Human Service Professions*, Springfield, IL: C. C. Thomas.

Shore, C. (2000), *Building Europe: The Cultural Politics of European Integration*, London: Routledge.

Shore, C. and Nugent, S. (2002), *Elite Cultures: Anthropological Perspectives*, London, New York: Routledge.

Shore, C. and Wright, S. (eds) (1997), *Anthropology of Policy: Critical Perspectives on Governance and Power*, London: Routledge.

Wright, S. (ed.) (1994), *Anthropology of Organisations*, London, New York: Routledge.

ANTHROPOLOGY, BUSINESS AND INDUSTRY

Ferraro, G. (2006), *The Cultural Dimension of International Business*, Upper Saddle River, NJ: Prentice Hall.

Fisher, M. S. and Downey, G. (eds) (2006), *Frontiers of Capital: Ethnographic Reflections on the New Economy*, Durham, NC: Duke University Press.

Malefyt, T. and Moeran, B. (eds) (2003), *Advertising Cultures*, Oxford: Berg.

Mariampolski, H. (2006), *Ethnography for Marketers: A Guide to Consumer Immersion*, Thousand Oaks, CA: Sage Publications.

Nixon, S. (2003), *Advertising Cultures: Gender, Commerce, Creativity*, London: Sage.

Squires, S and Byrne, B. (eds) (2002), *Creating Breakthrough Ideas: The Collaboration of Anthropologists and Designers in the Product Development Industry*, Westport, CT: Bergin & Garvey.

Stewart, P. and Strathern, A. (eds) (2005), *Anthropology and Consultancy: Issues and Debates*, New York: Berghahn Books.

ANTHROPOLOGY AND HEALTH

Caplan, P. (ed.) (1997), *Food, Health and Identity*, London: Routledge.

Joralemon, D. (1999), *Exploring Medical Anthropology*, Boston: Allyn & Bacon.

Goodman, A. Dufour, D. and Pelto, G. (eds) *Nutritional Anthropology: Biocultural Perspectives on Food and Nutrition*, Mountain View, CA: Mayfield Publishing.

Lupton, D. (ed.), (2003), *Medicine as Culture: Illness, Disease and the Body in Western Societies*, London: Sage Publications.

Raz, A. (2004), *The Gene and the Genie: Tradition, Medicalization, and Genetic Counselling in a Bedouin Community in Israel*, Durham, NC: North Carolina Academic Press.

ANTHROPOLOGY, ART AND IDENTITY

Abram, S., Waldren, J. and Macleod, D. (eds) (1997), *Tourists and Tourism: Identifying with People and Places*, Oxford: Berg.

Beckett, J. (ed.) (1988), *Past and Present; The Construction of Aboriginality*, Canberra: Aboriginal Studies Press.

Bender, B. (ed.) (1993), *Landscape, Politics and Perspectives*, Oxford: Berg.

Bender, B. (1998), *Stonehenge: Making Space*, Oxford: Berg.

Bouquet, M. (2001), *Academic Anthropology and the Museum: Back to the Future*, New York: Berghahn Books.

Bouquet, M. and Porto, N. (2005), *Science, Magic, and Religion: The Ritual Process of Museum Magic*, New York: Berghahn Books.

Chambers, E. (ed.) (1997), *Tourism and Culture: An Applied Perspective*, Albany, NY: State University of New York Press.

Coleman, S. and Crang, M. (2002), *Tourism: Between Place and Performance*, Oxford: Berghahn Books.

Coote, J. and Shelton, A. (eds) (1992), *Anthropology, Art and Aesthetics*, Oxford: Clarendon Press.

Cowan, J. (2000), *Macedonia: The Politics of Identity and Difference*, London: Pluto Press.

Donnan, H. (ed.) (2002), *Interpreting Islam: A Theory, Culture and Society Series*, New York: Sage.

Dyck, N. and Archetti, E. (eds) (2003), *Sport, Dance and Embodied Identities*, Oxford: Berg.

Fluehr-Lobban, C. (2005), *Race and Racism: An Introduction*, Lanham, MD: Rowman & Littlefield.

Gell, A. (1998), *Art and Agency: An Anthropological Theory*, Oxford: Clarendon Press.

Hendry, J. (2006), *Reclaiming Culture: Indigenous People and Self-representation*, New York: Palgrave Macmillan.

Kleinert, S. and Neale, M. (eds) (2000), *The Oxford Companion to Aboriginal Art and Culture*, Oxford: Oxford University Press.

Morphy, H. (1998), *Aboriginal Art*, London: Phaidon.

Morphy, H. and Perkins, M. (eds) (2006), *The Anthropology of Art: A Reader*, Oxford: Blackwell.

Power, D. and Scott, A. (2004), *Cultural Industries and the Production of Culture*, London, New York: Routledge.

Robertson, J. (2005), *Same-Sex Cultures and Sexualities: An Anthropological Reader*, Malden, MA: Blackwell Publishing.

Selwyn, T. (ed.) (1996), *The Tourist Image*, Chichester: Wiley.

Shackel, P. and Chambers, E. (eds) (2004), *Places in Mind: Public Archaeology as Applied Anthropology*, London: Routledge.

Smart, B. (2005), *The Sport Star: Modern Sport and the Cultural Economy of Sporting Celebrity*, London: Sage.

Trosset, C. (1993), *Welshness Performed: Welsh Concepts of Person and Society*, Tucson: University of Arizona Press.

Wade, P. (2002), *Race, Nature and Culture*, London: Pluto Press.

APPENDIX 3
OTHER RESOURCES

ANTHROPOLOGY ASSOCIATIONS AND NETWORKS

American Anthropological Association (AAA)
http://www.aaanet.org/

Anthropology Matters Postgraduate Network
http://www.anthropologymatters.com/

Association of Social Anthropologists of Aotearoa/New Zealand (ASAANZ)
http://asaanz.rsnz.org/

Association of Social Anthropologists of the UK and the Commonwealth (ASA)
http://www.theasa.org/

Australian Anthropological Society
http://www.aas.asn.au/

Bureau of Applied Research in Anthropology (BARA)
http://barabeta.bara.arizona.edu/instruction/

Canadian Anthropological Society (CASCA)
http://www.cas-sca.ca/

C-SAP (Birmingham)
http://www.c-sap.bham.ac.uk

(The Higher Education Academy Subject Network for Sociology, Anthropology, Politics)
http://www.c-sap.bham.ac.uk/

European Association of Social Anthropologists
http://www.easaonline.org/

Network of Applied Anthropologists UK
http://www.theasa.org/networks/apply.htm

Political Ecology Society (PESO)
http://jpe.library.arizona.edu/eco~1.htm

Royal Anthropological Institute
http://www.therai.org.uk/

Society for Applied Anthropology, USA
http://www.sfaa.net/

Wenner-Gren Foundation
http://www.wennergren.org/

World Council of Anthropological Associations
http://www.wcaanet.org/

ANTHROPOLOGY JOURNALS

American Anthropologist
http://www.aaanet.org/publications/ameranthro.cfm

Anthropology in Action
http://Berghahn Booksbooksonline.com/journals/aia/

Anthropology Matters Journal
http://www.anthropologymatters.com/journal/

Anthropology Today
http://www.therai.org.uk/pubs/at/anthrotoday.html

Cultural Anthropology (Journal of the Society for Cultural Anthropology)
http://www.culanth.org

Current Anthropology
http://www.journals.uchicago.edu/toc/ca/current

Human Organization (Journal of the Society for Applied Anthropology)
http://www.sfaa.net/ho/

Irish Journal of Anthropology
http://www.anthropologyireland.org/ijajournal1.htm

Journal of Anthropological Research
http://www.unm.edu/~jar/

Journal of Political Ecology
http://jpe.library.arizona.edu/

Oceania
http://www.arts.usyd.edu.au/publications/oceania/oceania1.htm

Practicing Anthropology
http://www.sfaa.net/pa/pa.html

Sites: A Journal of Social Anthropology and Cultural Studies
http://asaanz.rsnz.org/

The Asia Pacific Journal of Anthropology
http://rspas.anu.edu.au/anthropology/tapja/

The Australian Journal of Anthropology
http://www.aas.asn.au/aas_taja.php

'VIRTUAL' LIBRARIES IN ANTHROPOLOGY
http://www.intute.ac.uk/socialsciences/anthropology/

http://www.aaanet.org/publications/anthrosource/

http://vlib.anthrotech.com/

GLOSSARY

Alternative Dispute Resolution (ADR), mediated conflict resolution framework, presented as an alternative to adversarial legal methods.

cosmology, cosmological beliefs, a particular group's or society's vision of 'how the world works', which may be religious and/or secular.

counter-mapping, the creation of culturally specific maps that present an alternative to dominant representations of landscape.

cultural landscape, a physical and ideational landscape formed by specific cultural beliefs, values and practices.

cultural mapping, a process of collecting data on a specific cultural landscape, sometimes linked with 'counter-mapping'.

cultural translation, a role often carried out by anthropologists, which entails interpreting the realities of a particular cultural group to others (and possibly vice versa).

diaspora, a cultural, religious or ethnic community dispersed internationally.

discourse, a specific, culturally and historically produced way of describing the world.

discourse analysis, the process of analysing and revealing the ideas and values embedded in particular discourses.

empirical, based on evidence: experience or experiment.

epidemiology, the scientific study of epidemics.

epistemology, the science of knowledge.

ethnobotany, ethnobiology, ethnoscience, local (often indigenous) forms of knowledge relating to flora and fauna, and to the material environment. Can be subsumed under the broader term, 'traditional ecological knowledge'.

ethnography, an in-depth, holistic account of a particular group or community.

globalization, the transformation of local or regional phenomena to a global scale; an idea of a unified global society and economy.

governance, the control and direction of a society or group.

hypothesis, a theory to be proved or disproved by reference to evidence, a provisional explanation.

lexicon, dictionary.

life course analysis, an ethnographic method that involves examining people's life histories within a particular context.

NGO-graphy, the study of non-governmental organisations and their activities.

orthography, a word list recording an oral language, and applying linguistic expertise in ensuring consistent spelling and pronunciation.

participant observation, a research method that entails participating in the daily life of the study community, and observing and recording events.

participatory action research (PAR), collaborative research that assists communities in the achievement of their aims.

pedagogy, the science of education, methods of teaching and learning.

political ecology, the study of how social, political and economic factors affect environmental issues.

positive correlation, a statistical term defining factors that occur simultaneously, suggesting a causal relationship between them.

social movements, the spread of ideologies across groups nationally or internationally, creating agitation for change.

social organization, the particular system of social relations pertaining in a society or cultural group; its forms of descent and inheritance.

spatial relations, the spatial distribution of people in relation to a material environment and/or landscape in accord with specific cultural norms.

traditional ecological knowledge (TEK), specifically cultural (often indigenous) knowledge about local ecosystems (see also ethnobotany, ethnobiology and ethnoscience).

NOTES

Acknowledgements

1. In order of appearance in the text these are: Markus Weilenmann, Marzia Balzani, Mary-Ellen Chatwin, Yongjun Zhao, Ruth Dearnley, Scarlett Epstein, Ted Green, Paul Sillitoe, Kay Milton, Danny Dybowski, Saffron James, Cris Shore, Stuart Kirsch, Ralph Bishop, Patricia Sachs, Patricia Hammer, Sherylyn Briller, Nancy Pollock, Rachael Gooberman-Hill, Richard Chenhall, Marion Droz-Mendelzweig, Jonathan Skinner, Richard Chalfen, Robert Trotter, Miranda Irving.

Introduction

1. Shore (1996) and MacClancy (2005) have written about how anthropology has often been portrayed in the media.
2. There are some excellent introductory texts providing more detail on 'what anthropology is' – for example Eriksen's *What is Anthropology?* (2004) and Coleman and Simpson's *Discovering Anthropology* (1998) (see also Hendry 1999, Metcalf 2005, Haviland *et al.* 2006).
3. In America, for example, archaeologists regard their profession as coming under the larger umbrella of anthropology, while in the UK and Europe these are seen as separate (albeit closely related) disciplinary areas.
4. Anthropology is sometimes regarded as having two major strands: social anthropology and cultural anthropology. The differences between these vary from country to country, reflecting the different trajectories that the discipline has taken over time.
5. Professional anthropology associations have detailed ethical guidelines, and these are regularly updated to keep pace with changes in the kind of work that practitioners do. Most universities also have strict research-ethics codes and meeting these is a formal prerequisite for any research activity. Professional and institutional codes generally require social researchers to try to ensure that their work with communities is mutually beneficial. They provide guidance on issues such as asking permission to do research, consulting host communities about the design of research projects, maintaining the confidentiality of data when necessary, and ensuring that the people who provided the data have access to the research findings. They also cover more complex issues, for example relating to intellectual property rights. The ethical guidelines of associations are generally available on their web sites, some of which are listed in the appendices to this volume.
6. There have been long-running discussions amongst educators about the potential for introducing students to anthropology at a secondary school level. It has begun to make an appearance in various forms, as 'social studies' and so forth, and at the time of writing there are moves, for example in the UK, to bring it into the curriculum more formally.

Chapter 1 Anthropology and Advocacy

1. 'Ethnobotany', 'ethnobiology' and 'ethnoscience' are all terms describing the localized expertise accumulated through a group's engagement with a particular environment over many centuries. These are can be subsumed under the broader heading of 'traditional ecological knowledge'.
2. See his autobiography in Chapter 6.
3. Globalization is the transformation of local or regional phenomena to a global scale; an idea of a unified global society and economy.
4. 'Social movements' occur when ideologies spread across groups, nationally or internationally, encouraging pressure for change. Other (loosely related) examples include the feminist movement; the civil rights movement; the peace movement; and the New Age movement. More recently, anthropologists have considered the 'counter-movements' opposing globalization, initiated by indigenous networks and other groups critical of this process.
5. The process of creating culturally specific maps, which often challenge dominant representational forms, has also been called 'counter-mapping'.

Chapter 2 Anthropology and Aid

1. Obviously government funding comes with some 'strings attached' too, and most funding agencies give a clear remit as to the kind of research they will support. However in applying for these kinds of resources researchers can at least design their own projects and – in general – they have considerable independence in conducting the research.
2. This was renamed as the Department for International Development. It also has formal links with the United Kingdom's Commonwealth Development Corporation, which has been heavily criticized recently for its shift away from support for Third World agriculture into other areas of investment, such as shopping malls and mobile phones, which are more profitable (for the Corporation).
3. Work on such transient communities was pioneered by Judith Okely's work on European gypsies in the early 1980s (Okely 1983).
4. There are some complex ethical considerations in relation to this issue, as professional codes of practice preclude spying on communities, or using ethnographic data collected from them to their detriment. At the same time there are – potentially conflicting – moral issues raised by the need to prevent terrorism and harm to other groups. These issues – and the propriety of working for national agencies involved in intelligence gathering – have generated considerable debate with the discipline.

Chapter 3 Anthropology and Development

1. *Zenzele* translates as 'do-it-yourself'.
2. Darrell Posey died in 2001. He is remembered by many of us as a committed activist, who spent his life assisting indigenous peoples in their efforts to preserve and protect their traditional knowledges.

Chapter 4 Anthropology and the Environment

1. Quite apart from being one of the best job titles I have ever had, this is a really useful Fellowship which the RAI awards every year, to enable anthropologists to do 'urgently needed' research, for example, recording cultural data that is held only orally, by older generations, or researching in areas of pressing social need.
2. The term 'cosmology' is simply a society's understanding of 'how the world works'. This might be based on religious beliefs, forms of science, or indeed both.

3. 'Traditional' is a somewhat disputed term academically but I use it here as indigenous groups often do, to indicate the customs, beliefs and knowledges that prevailed prior to colonization.

4. See also Posey and Plenderlieth (2004), Hornborg and Kurkiala (1998).

5. A film was made about Lansing's work in 1989 for the United Kingdom's Channel 4 *Fragile Earth* series. Directed by Andrew Singer, it is called 'The Water Goddess and the Computer'.

6. 'Political ecology' is the study of how social, political and economic factors affect environmental issues.

7. Fortun (1999: 240) charted the long-term outcomes for the various groups involved in the Bhopal disaster of 1984, in which an explosion at a Union Carbide plant in India released pesticides over the city, killing an estimated 10,000 people and creating long-term physical and economic harm to a further 600,000.

8. 'Discourse analysis' is the process of analysing and revealing the ideas and values embedded in particular discourses.

9. See also Strang (1997).

Chapter 6   Anthropology, Business and Industry

1. To some extent this issue runs parallel to the discussion in Chapter 2 about the way that unelected NGOs have replaced services and activities that were previously the responsibility of government bodies.

2. See also Malefyt and Moeran (2003).

Chapter 8   Anthropology, Art and Identity

1. As far back as 1873, E. B. Tylor wrote about indigenous languages and, working with oral cultures, many early anthropologists painstakingly set down written records of their languages. Bejamin Whorf's work, 'Some Verbal Categories of Hopi', published in 1938, typifies these efforts.

BIBLIOGRAPHY

Abraham, C. (2007), 'Western Medicine Doesn't Have All the Answers', *New Scientist*, 31 July, pp. 35–7.

Abram, S., Waldren, J. and Macleod, D. (eds) (1997), *Tourists and Tourism: Identifying with People and Places*, Oxford: Berg.

Abu-Lughod, L. (1997), 'Movie Stars and Islamic Moralism in Egypt', in R. Lancaster and M. Di Leonardo (eds), *The Gender/Sexuality Reader: Culture, History, Political Economy*, New York: Routledge, pp. 502–12.

Acheson, J. (1987), 'The Lobster Fiefs Revisited: Economic and Ecological Effects of Territoriality in the Maine Lobster Industry', in B. McCay and J. Acheson (eds), *The Question of the Commons: The Culture and Ecology of Communal Resources*, Tucson: University of Arizona Press.

Acosta, R. (2004), *The Halfhearted Politics of NGOs*, paper presented to NGO Study Group Seminar, 'Ethnography of NGOs: Understanding Organisational Processes', Oxford, 28 April 2004.

Agar, M. (1996), *The Professional Stranger: An Informal Introduction to Ethnography*, 2nd edition, New York: Academic Press.

Albro, R. (2005), '"The Water is Ours, Carajo!" Deep Citizenship in Bolivia's Water War', in J. Nash (ed.) (2005), *Social Movements: An Anthropological Reader*, Malden, MA: Blackwell Publishing, pp. 249–68.

Alikhan, F., Kyei, P. Mawdsley, E., Porter, G., Raju, S., Townsend, J. and Varma, R. (2007), *NGOs and the State in the Twenty-First Century: Ghana and India*, Oxford: INTRAC.

Alpher, B. (1991), *Yir-Yoront Lexicon: Sketch and Dictionary of an Australian Language*, Trends in Linguistics Documentation 6, Berlin: Mouton de Gruyter.

Anderson, B. (1991), *Imagined Communities: Reflections on the Origins and Spread of Nationalism*, London: Verso.

Anderson, D. and Berglund, E. (eds) (2003), *Ethnographies of Conservation: Environmentalism and the Distribution of Privilege*, New York: Berghahn Books.

Anthropology Today (2004), 'IBM Hires Anthropologist', *Anthropology Today*, 20(3): 29.

Antze, P. and Lambek, M. (eds) (1996), *Tense Past: Cultural Essays in Trauma and Memory*, New York, London: Routledge.

Arce, A. and Long, N. (eds) (1999), *Anthropology, Development, and Modernities: Exploring Discourses, Counter-tendencies, and Violence*, London: Routledge.

Ashforth, A. (2004), 'AIDS as Witchcraft in Post-Apartheid South Africa', in V. Das and D. Poole (eds), *Anthropology in the Margins of the State*, Santa Fe, NM: School of American Research Press, pp. 141–63.

Astuti, R. (1998), '"It's a boy!", "It's a girl!" Reflections on Sex and Gender in Madagascar and Beyond', in A. Strathern and M. Lambek, *Bodies and Persons: Comparative Perspectives from Africa and Melanesia*, Cambridge: Cambridge University Press, pp. 29–52.

Atlani-Dualt, L. (2007), *Humanitarian Aid in Post-Soviet Countries: An Anthropological Perspective*, London: Routledge.

Attwood, B. and Markus, A. (1999), *The Struggle for Aboriginal Rights: A Documentary History.* St Leonards, NSW: Allen & Unwin.

Auge, M. and Colleyn, J. (2006), *The World of the Anthropologist*, translated by J. Howe, Oxford: Berg.

Avruch, K. and Black, P. (1996), 'ADR, Palau, and the Contribution of Anthropology', in A. Wolfe and H. Yang (eds), *Anthropological Contributions to Conflict Resolution*, Athens, GA: University of Georgia Press, pp. 47–61.

Baba, M. (2005), 'Anthropological Practice in Business and Industry', in S. Kedia and J. Van Willigen (eds), *Applied Anthropology: Domains of Application*, Westport, CT: Praeger, pp. 221–61.

Bailey, E. (1998), 'The Medical Anthropologist as Health Department Consultant', in G. Ferraro, *Applying Cultural Anthropology: Readings*, Belmont CA: Wadsworth, pp. 7–10.

Basso, K. (1996), *Wisdom Sits in Places: Landscape and Language among the Western Apache*, Albuquerque, NM: University of New Mexico Press.

Beckett, J. (ed.) (1988), *Past and Present; The Construction of Aboriginality*, Canberra: Aboriginal Studies Press.

Bender, B. (1998), *Stonehenge: Making Space*, Oxford: Berg.

Bender, B. (ed.) (1993), *Landscape, Politics and Perspectives*, Oxford: Berg.

Bennett, L. (1995), 'Accountability for Alcoholism in American Families', *Social Science and Medicine*, 40(1): 15–25, in S. Kedia and J. van Willigen (eds) *Applied Anthropology: Domains of Application*, Westport, CT: Praeger, p. 134.

Bennett, V. (1995), *The Politics of Water: Urban Protest, Gender and Power in Monterrey, Mexico.* Pittsburgh: University of Pittsburgh Press.

Benthall, J. (2002), 'Organised Charity in the Arab-Islamic World', in H. Donnan (ed.) *Interpreting Islam: A Theory, Culture and Society Series*, New York: Sage, pp. 150–65.

Berglund, E. (1998), *Knowing Nature, Knowing Science: An Ethnography of Environmental Activism*, Knapwell: The White Horse Press.

Bestor, T. (2003), 'How Sushi Went Global' in A. Podolefsky and P. Brown (eds), *Applying Anthropology: An Introductory Reader*, 7th edn, London: McGraw-Hill, pp. 367–73.

Bhattacharjee, A. (2006), 'The Public/Private Mirage: Mapping Homes and Undomesticating Violence in the South Asian Immigrant Community', in A. Sharma and A. Gupta (eds), *The Anthropology of the State: A Reader*, Malden, MA: Blackwell, pp. 337–56.

Bicker, A., Sillitoe, P. and Pottier, J. (eds) (2004), *Development and Local Knowledge: New Approaches to Issues in Natural Resources Management, Conservation and Agriculture*, London: Routledge.

Bilsborough, A. (2005), Obituary, in *Anthropology Today*, 21 (5): 28.

Booth, G. (2000), 'Religion, Gossip, Narrative Conventions and the Construction of Meaning in Hindi Film Songs', in *Popular Music*, 19: 125–45.

Bouquet, M. (2001), *Academic Anthropology and the Museum: Back to the Future*, New York: Berghahn Books.

Bouquet, M. and Porto, N. (2005), *Science, Magic, and Religion: The Ritual Process of Museum Magic*, New York: Berghahn Books.

Bourgois, P. (1995), 'Workaday World, Crack Economy', in J. McDonald (ed.) (2002), *The Applied Anthropology Reader*, Boston: Allyn & Bacon, pp. 149–56.

Bradby, H. (1997), 'Health, Eating and Heart Attacks: Glaswegian Punjabi Women's Thinking about Everyday Food', in P. Caplan (ed.), *Food, Health and Identity*, London: Routledge, pp. 213–33.

Bräuchler, B. (2004), 'Islamic Radicalism Online: the Moluccan Mission of the Laskar Jihad in Cyberspace', in *The Australian Journal of Anthropology*, 15(3): 267–85.

Briller, S., Marsden, J., Perez, K. and Profitt, M. (2002), *Creating Successful Dementia Care Settings*, Baltimore, MD: Health Professions Press.

Brown, C. (2002), 'Anthropology and Social Marketing: A Powerful Combination', in J. McDonald (ed.) *The Applied Anthropology Reader*, Boston: Allyn & Bacon, pp. 414–18.

Buchli, V., Lucas, G. and Cox, M. (eds) (2001), *Archaeologies of the Contemporary Past*, London: Routledge,

Camenson, B. (2000), *Great Jobs for Anthropology Majors*, Lincolnwood, IL: VGM Career Horizons.

Caplan, P. (ed.) (1997), *Food, Health and Identity*, London, New York: Routledge.

Caplan, P. (ed.) (2003), *The Ethics of Anthropology: Debates and Dilemmas*, New York: Routledge.

Caplan, P. (ed.) (2005), 'In Search of the Exotic: A Discussion of the BBC2 series Tribe', *Anthropology Today*, 21(2): 3–7.

Caplan, P. (2006), *Discussion: Madonna and the Malawian 'Orphan'*, The Ferguson Centre for African and Asian Studies at the Open University, http://www.open.ac.uk/Arts/ferguson-centre/discussion-docs/disc-pcaplan-madonna-02nov06.htm.

Carrier, J. (2004), *Confronting Environments: Local Understanding in a Globalizing World*, Walnut Creek, CA: Altamira Press.

Carson, B., Dunbar, T., Chenhall, R. and Bailie, R. (2007), *Social Determinants of Indigenous Health*, Allen & Unwin: Sydney.

Carsten, J. and Hugh-Jones, S. (eds) (1995), *About the House: Levi-Strauss and Beyond*, Cambridge: Cambridge University Press.

Cartmill, M. (1993), *A View to a Death in the Morning: Hunting and Nature through History*, Cambridge, MA: Harvard University Press.

Casagrande, D., Hope, D. Farley-Metzger, E. Cook, W., Yabiku, S. and Redman, C. (2007), 'Problem and Opportunity: Integrating Anthropology, Ecology, and Policy through Adaptive Experimentation in the Urban US Southwest', *Human Organization*, 66(2): 125–40.

Cassell, J. (2003), 'Doing Gender, Doing Surgery: Women Surgeons in a Man's Profession', in A. Podolefsy and P. Brown (eds), *Applying Anthropology: An Introductory Reader*, Mountain View, CA: Mayfield, pp. 274–82.

Cernea, M. (2000), 'Risks, Safeguards, and Reconstruction: A Model for Population Displacement and Resettlement', in M. Cernea and C. McDowell (eds), *Risk and Reconstruction: Experiences of Settlers and Refugees*, Washington, DC: World Bank, in S. Kedia and J. van Willigen (eds), *Applied Anthropology: Domains of Application*, Westport, CT: Praeger.

Chambers, E. (1985), *Applied Anthropology: A Practical Guide*, Englewood Cliffs, NJ; London: Prentice-Hall.

Chambers, E. (ed.) (1997), *Tourism and Culture: An Applied Perspective*, Albany: State University of New York Press.

Cheater, A. (1995), 'Globalisation and the New Technologies of Knowing: Anthropological Calculus or Chaos?', in M. Strathern (ed.), *Shifting Contexts: Transformations in Anthropological Knowledge*, London: Routledge, pp. 117–30.

Chenhall, R. (2007), *Benelong's Haven: Recovery from Alcohol and Drug Misuse in a Residential Treatment Centre*, Melbourne: Melbourne University Press.

Chenhall, R. (2008), 'What's in a Rehab? Ethnographic Evaluation Research in Indigenous Residential Alcohol and Drug Rehabilitation Centres', *Anthropology and Medicine*, 15(2): 91–104.

Chenhall, R. and Senior, K. (2006), '"Stuck Nose": Experiences and Understanding of Petrol Sniffing in a Remote Aboriginal Community', *Journal of Contemporary Drug Problems*, 33: 451–72.

Chenhall, R. and Senior, K. (2007), '"Stopping sniffing is our responsibility": Community Ownership of a Petrol Sniffing Program in Arnhem Land', *Health Sociology Review*, 16(3–4): 315–27.

Chiapetta-Swanson, C. (2005), 'The Process of Caring: Nurses and Genetic Termination', in D. Pawluch, W. Shaffir and C. Miall (eds), *Doing Ethnography: Studying Everyday Life*, Toronto: Canadian Scholars' Press, pp. 166–76.

Chicago Field Museum, (2008), http://www.fieldmuseum.org/ccuc/default.htm.

Cohen, J. (ed.) (2002), *Economic Development: An Anthropological Approach*, Walnut Creek, CA: Altamira Press.

Colchester, M. (2004), 'Conservation Policy and Indigenous Peoples', *Cultural Survival Quarterly*, 28 (1): 17–22.

Coleman, S. (2007), *The Globalisation of Charismatic Christianity: Spreading the Gospel of Prosperity*, Cambridge: Cambridge University Press.

Coleman, S. and Crang, M. (2002), *Tourism: between Place and Performance*, Oxford: Berghahn Books.

Coleman, S. and Simpson, B. (eds) (1998), *Discovering Anthropology: A Resource Guide for Teachers and Students*, London: Royal Anthropological Institute.

Colson, E. and Kottak, C. (1996), 'Linkages Methodology for the Study of Sociocultural Transformations', in E. Moran (ed.) *Transforming Societies, Transforming Anthropology*, Ann Arbor: University of Michigan Press, pp. 103–34.

Combs, H. (2006), 'In Search of How Real Consumers Live', *Furniture Today*, 30(42): 1–2.

Connerton, P. (1989), *How Societies Remember*, Cambridge: Cambridge University Press.

Cooper, P. (2004), 'The Gift of Education: An Anthropological Perspective on the Commoditization of Learning', *Anthropology Today*, 20(6): 5–8.

Coote, J. and Shelton, A. (eds) (1992), *Anthropology, Art and Aesthetics*, Oxford: Clarendon Press.

Coreil, J. (2004), 'Cultural Models of Illness and Recovery in Breast Cancer Support Groups', in *Qualitative Health Research.* 14(7): 905–23. Cited in S. Kedia and J. van Willigen (eds) (2005), *Applied Anthropology: Domains of Application*, Westport, CT: Praeger, p. 131.

Corsin-Jiménez, A. (ed.) (2007), *The Anthropology of Organisations*, London: Ashgate.

Cowan, J. (1990), *Dance and the Body Politic in Northern Greece*, Princeton, NJ: Princeton University Press.

Cowan, J. (2000), *Macedonia: The Politics of Identity and Difference*, London: Pluto Press.

Cowan, J., Dembour, M.-B., Wilson, R. (2001), *Culture and Rights: Anthropological Perspectives*, New York: Cambridge University Press.

Coward, R. (2001), 'The Meaning of Health Foods', in D. Miller (ed.) *Consumption: Critical Concepts in the Social Sciences*, London: Routledge, pp. 50–72.

Cowlishaw, G. (1998), 'Erasing Culture and Race: Practising "Self-determination"', *Oceania*, 68(3): 145–69.

Croll, E. and Parkin, D. (eds) (1992), *Bush Base, Forest Farm: Culture, Environment and Development*, London: Routledge.

Crosby, A. (1994), *Germs, Seeds and Animals: Studies in Ecological History*, Armonk, NY: M.E. Sharpe.

Crosby, A. (2004), *Ecological Imperialism: the Biological Expansion of Europe, 900–1900*. Cambridge: Cambridge University Press.

De Gaetano, Y. (2007), 'The Role of Culture in Engaging Latino Parents' Involvement in School', *Urban Education*, 42(2): 145–62.

De Mars, W. (2005), *NGOs and Transnational Networks: Wild Cards in World Politics*, Ann Arbor, MI: Pluto Press.

Descola, P. and Palsson, G. (eds) (1996), *Nature and Society: Anthropological Perspectives*, London: Routledge.

Diamond, J. (2005), *Collapse: How Societies Choose to Fail or Succeed*, New York: Penguin.

Dominy, M. (2001), *Calling the Station Home: Place and Identity in New Zealand's High Country*, Lanham, MD: Rowman & Littlefield.

Donahue, J. and Johnston, B. (eds) (1998), *Water, Culture and Power: Local Struggles in a Global Context*, Washington, DC: Island Press.

Donnan, H. and McFarlane, G. (1989), *Social Anthropology and Public Policy in Northern Ireland*, Aldershot: Avebury.

Donnan, H. (ed.) (2002), *Interpreting Islam: A Theory, Culture and Society Series*, New York: Sage.

Doron, A. (2005), 'Encountering the "Other": Pilgrims, Tourists and Boatmen in the City of Varanasi', *Australian Journal of Anthropology*, 17 (1): 32–46.

Douglas, M. (1987), *How Institutions Think*, London: Routledge & Kegan Paul.

Douglas, M. (2002 [1966]), *Purity and Danger: An Analysis of Concepts of Pollution and Taboo*, London: Routledge.

Douglas, M. and Mars, G. (2007), 'Terrorism: A Positive Feedback Game', in A. Corsin-Jimenez (ed.), *The Anthropology of Organisations*, London: Ashgate, pp. 763–86.

Downe, P. (1999), 'Participant Advocacy and Research with Prostitutes in Costa Rica', in *Practicing Anthropology*, 21(3): 21–4.

Drazin, A. (2006), 'The Need to Engage with Non-Ethnographic Research Methods', in S. Pink (ed.), *Applications of Anthropology: Professional Anthropology in the Twenty-first Century*, London: Berghahn Books, pp. 90–108.

Dwivedi, R. (1999), 'Displacement, Risks and Resistance: Local Perceptions and Actions in the Sardar Sarovar', *Development and Change*, 30(1): 43–78.

Eaton, S. B. and Konner, M. (2003), 'Ancient Genes and Modern Health' in A. Podolefsy and P. Brown (eds), *Applying Anthropology: An Introductory Reader*, 7th edn, Boston: McGraw-Hill, pp. 52–5.

Ebrahim, A. (2003), *NGOs and Organizational Change: Discourse, Reporting, and Learning*, Cambridge: Cambridge University Press.

Edelman, M. and Haugerud, A. (eds) (2005), *The Anthropology of Development and Globalization: from Classical Political Economy to Contemporary Neoliberalism*, Malden, MA, Oxford: Blackwell.

Edwards, E. (1996), 'Postcards: Greetings from Another World', in T. Selwyn (ed.), *The Tourist Image*, Chichester: Wiley, pp. 197–221.

Ember, C., Ember M. and Peregrine, P. (2005), *Anthropology*, Upper Saddle River, NJ: Pearson, Prentice-Hall.

Eriksen, T. (2001), *Small Places, Large Issues: An Introduction to Social and Cultural Anthropology*, Sterling, VA: Pluto Press.

Eriksen, T. (2003), *Globalisation: Studies in Anthropology*, London: Pluto Press.

Eriksen, T. (2004), *What is Anthropology?*, Oxford: Berg.

Eriksen, T. (2006), *Engaging Anthropology: The Case for a Public Presence*, Oxford: Berg.

Ervin, A. (2005), *Applied Anthropology: Tools and Perspectives for Contemporary Practice*, Boston: Allyn & Bacon.

Escobar, A. (1991), 'Anthropology and the Development Encounter: the Making and Marketing of Development Anthropology', *American Ethnologist*, 18(4): 658–82.

Escobar, A. (1995), *Encountering Development: the Making and Unmaking of the Third World*. Princeton, NJ: Princeton University Press.

Fairhead, J. (1990), *Fields of Struggle: Towards a Social History of Farming Knowledge and Practice in a Bwisha Community, Kivu, Zaire*, London: University of London.

Fairhead, J. (1993), 'Representing Knowledge: the "New Farmer" in Research Fashions', in J. Pottier (ed.) *Practising Development: Social Science Perspectives*, London: Routledge, pp. 187–204.

Fairhead, J. and Leach, M. (1996), *Misreading the African Landscape: Society and Ecology in a Forest-savanna Mosaic*, Cambridge: Cambridge University Press.

Feld, S. and K. Basso (eds) (1996), *Senses of Place*, Santa Fe, New Mexico: School of American Research Press.

Feng, X. (2008), 'Who Benefits? Tourism Development in Fenghuang County, China', *Human Organization*, 67(2): 207–21.

Ferraro, G. (1998), *Applying Cultural Anthropology: Readings*, Belmont, CA: Wadsworth.

Ferraro, G. (2006), *The Cultural Dimension of International Business*, Upper Saddle River, NJ: Prentice Hall.

Fisher, M.S. and G. Downey (ed.). (2006), *Frontiers of Capital: Ethnographic Reflections on the New Economy*, Durham, NC: Duke University Press.

Fitzgerald, N., Himmelgreen, D., Damio, G., Segura-Pérez, S., Peng, Y. and Pérez-Escamilla, R. (2006), 'Acculturation, Socioeconomic Status, Obesity and Lifestyle Factors among Low-income Puerto Rican Women in Connecticut US, 1998, 1999', *Pan American Journal of Public Health*, 19(5): 306–13.

Fleuret, A. (1988), 'Food Aid and Development in Rural Kenya', in D. Brokensha and P. Little (eds), *The Anthropology of Development and Change in East Africa*, Boulder, CO: Westview Press, pp. 77–97.

Fluehr-Lobban, C. (2003), *Ethics and the Profession of Anthropology: Dialogue for Ethically Conscious Practice*, Walnut Creek, CA: AltaMira Press.

Fluehr-Lobban, C. (2005), *Race and Racism: An Introduction*, Lanham, MD: Rowman & Littlefield.

Forbes, K. (2007), 'Bureaucratic Strategies of Exclusion: Land Use Ideology and Images of Mexican Farmworkers in Housing Policy', *Human Organization*, 66(2): 196–210.

Forth, G. (2003), *Nage Birds: Classification and Symbolism among an Eastern Indonesian People*, New York: Routledge.

Fortun, K. (1999), 'Locating Corporate Environmentalism: Synthetics, Implosions and the Bhopal Disaster', in G. Marcus (ed.) *Critical Anthropology Now: Unexpected Contexts, Shifting Constituencies, Changing Agendas*, Santa Fe, NM: School of American Research Press, pp. 203–43.

Foster, R. (2002), *Materializing the Nation: Commodities, Consumption, and Media in Papua New Guinea*, Bloomington, IN: Indiana University Press.

Fratkin, E. and Roth, E. (2005), *As Pastoralists Settle: Social, Health, and Economic Consequences of the Pastoral Sedentarization in Marsabit District, Kenya*, New York: Kluwer Academic/Plenum Publishers.

Gardner, K. (2002), *Age, Narrative and Migration: The Life Histories of Bengali Elders in London*, Oxford: Berg.

Geertz, C. (1986), 'The Uses of Diversity', *Michigan Quarterly Review*, 25: 105–23.

Gell, A. (1998), *Art and Agency: An Anthropological Theory*, Oxford: Clarendon Press.

Giblett, R. (1996), *Postmodern Wetlands: Culture, History, Ecology*, Edinburgh: Edinburgh University Press.

Gibson, M. (1988), *Accommodation Without Assimilation: Sikh Immigrants in an American High School*, Ithaca, NY: Cornell University Press.

Ginsburg, F. (1989), *Contested Lives: The Abortion Debate in an American Community*, Berkeley: University of California Press.

Glantz, M. (2001), *Currents of Change: Impacts of El Nino and La Nina on Climate and Society*, 2nd edn, Cambridge: Cambridge University Press.

Glantz, M. (2003), *Climate Affairs: A Primer*, Wasington, DC: Island Press.

Gledhill, J. (2000), *Power and its Disguises: Anthropological Perspectives on Politics*, London, Sterling, VA: Pluto Press.

Goldman, L. (ed.) (2000), *Social Impact Analysis: An Applied Anthropology Manual*, Oxford: Berg.

Goldman, M. (ed.) (1998), *Privatizing Nature: Political Struggles for Global Commons*, London: Pluto Press.

Gooch, P. (1998), 'The Van Gujjars of Uttar Pradesh: A Voice that Made a Difference', in A. Hornborg and M. Kurkiala (eds) (1998), *Voices of the Land: Identity and Ecology in the Margins*, Lund: Lund University Press. pp. 247–88.

Grace, J. (1999), 'Damned if You Do, Damned if You Don't: The Dilemma of Applied Anthropology', in S. Toussaint and J. Taylor (eds), *Applied Anthropology in Australasia*, Nedlands. University of Western Australia Press, pp. 124–40.

Grace J. and Chenhall, R. (2006), 'A Rapid Anthropological Assessment of Tuberculosis in Remort Aboriginal Community in Northern Australia', *Human Organization*, 65(4): 387–99.

Graham Davies, S. (2004), It's Like One of Those Puzzles: Conceptualising Gender among Bugis', *Journal of Gender Studies*, 13(2): 107–16.

Green, E. (ed.) (1986), *Practising Development Anthropology*, Boulder, CO: Westview Press.

Green, E. (ed.) (1998), 'Women's Groups and Income Generation in Swaziland', in G. Ferraro (ed.), *Applying Cultural Anthropology: Readings*, Belmont, CA: Wadsworth, pp. 216–21.

Green, E. (2003), *Rethinking AIDS Prevention: Learning from Successes in Developing Countries*, Westport, CT: Praeger.

Green, E. and Iseley, R. (2002), 'The Significance of Settlement Pattern for Community Participation in Health: Lessons from Africa', in J. McDonald (ed.) *The Applied Anthropology Reader*, Boston: Allyn & Bacon, pp. 215–30.

Green, J. (1998), 'Who's Watching the Children? Anthropology in Child Care', in G. Ferraro (ed.) *Applying Cultural Anthropology: Readings*, Belmont, CA: Wadsworth, pp. 161–5.

Grider, S. (2007), 'Public Grief and the Politics of Memorial: Contesting the Memory of the "Shooters" at Columbine High School', *Anthropology Today*, 23(3): 3–7.

Griffin, C. (2008), *Nomads Under the Westway: Irish Travellers, Gypsies and Other Traders in West London*, Hatfield: University of Hertfordshire Press.

Grillo, R. and Stirrat, R. (1997), *Discourses of Development: Anthropological Perspectives*, Oxford: Berg.

Grobsmith, E. (2002), 'Applying Anthropology to American Indian Correctional Concerns', in J. McDonald (ed.) *The Applied Anthropology Reader*, Boston: Allyn & Bacon, pp. 165–71.

Guest, G. (2003), 'Anthropology in the Technology Industry', in A. Podolefsky and P. Brown (eds), *Applying Anthropology: An Introductory Reader*, 7th edn, London: McGraw-Hill, pp. 259–60.

Gupta, A. and Sharma, A. (2006), *The Anthropology of the State: A Reader*, Malden, MA: Blackwell.

Gutmann, M. (2006), 'For Whom the Taco Bells Toll: Popular Responses to NAFTA South of the Border', in W. Haviland, R. Gordon and L. Vivanco (eds), *Talking about People: Readings in Contemporary Cultural Anthropology*, Boston: McGraw-Hill, pp. 170–80.

Gwynne, M. (2003a), *Applied Anthropology: A Career-oriented Approach*, Boston: Pearson Education Inc.

Gwynne, M. (2003b), *Anthropology: Career Resources Handbook*, New York: Pearson Education Inc.

Haenn, N. and Wilk, R. (2006), *The Environment in Anthropology: A Reader in Ecology, Culture and Sustainable Living*, New York: New York University Press.

Haller, D. and Shore, C. (2005), *Corruption: Anthropological Perspectives*, London: Pluto Press.

Halpern, J. and Kideckel, D. (2000), *Neighbours at War: Anthropological Perspectives on Yugoslav Ethnicity, Culture, and History*, University Park, PA: Pennsylvania State University Press.

Hamilton, P. (1994), *Uw Oykangand and Olgol: An Early Dictionary*, Kowanyama: Kowanyama Aboriginal Land and Natural Resources Management Office.

Hammer, P. (2008), *Action Research in the Andes*, Lima: Centre for Social Well Being. http://www.socialwellbeing.org.

Hammond, R. (1998), 'Environmental Health and Anthropology in a County Health Department', in G. Ferraro (ed.) *Applying Cultural Anthropology: Readings*, Belmont, CA: Wadsworth, pp. 196–9.

Hansen, A. (2002), 'The Illusion of Local Sustainability and Self-Sufficiency: Famine in a Border Area of Northwestern Zambia', in J. McDonald (ed.) *The Applied Anthropology Reader*, Boston: Allyn & Bacon, pp. 260–76.

Hardy, Sarah. (2003), 'Mothers and Others', in A. Podolefsky and P. Brown (eds), *Applying Anthropology: An Introductory Reader*, 7th edn, London: McGraw-Hill, pp. 25–31.

Hargreaves, A., Lieberman, A., Fullan, M. and Hopkins, D. (1998), *International Handbook of Educational Change*, New York: Springer.

Harman, R. (2005), 'Anthropology and the Aged', in S. Kedia and J. Van Willigen (eds), *Applied Anthropology: Domains of Application*, Westport, CT: Praeger, pp. 307–40.

Harper, A. (1999), 'Forensic Archaeology and the Woodchipper Murder' in K. Feder (ed.). *Lessons from the Past: An Introductory Reader in Archaeology*, Mountain View, CA: Mayfield, pp. 189–93.

Harrison, G. and Morphy, H. (1998), *Human Adaptation*, Oxford: Berg.

Hart, E. (2006), '"Speaking of Silence" Reflections on the Application of Anthropology in the UK Health Services', in S. Pink (ed.) *Applications of Anthropology: Professional Anthropology in the Twenty-first Century*, London: Berghahn Books, pp. 145–68.

Haviland, W. (2000), *Anthropology*, Fort Worth, TX: Harcourt College Publishers.

Haviland, W., Gordon, R. and Vivanco, L. (eds) (2006), *Talking about People: Readings in Contemporary Cultural Anthropology*, Boston: McGraw-Hill.

Hayden, C. (2007), 'A Generic Solution? Pharmaceuticals and the Politics of the Similar in Mexico', *Current Anthropology*, 48(4): 475–95.

Heatherington, T. (2005), 'As if Someone Dear to Me Had Died': Intimate Landscapes, Political Subjectivity and the Problem of a Park in Sardinia', in K. Milton and M. Svasek (eds), *Mixed Emotions: Anthropological Studies of Feeling*, Oxford: Berg, pp. 145–59.

Hedican, E. (1995), *Applied Anthropology in Canada: Understanding Aboriginal Issues*, Toronto: University of Toronto Press.

Hegmon, M., and Eiselt, B. (eds) (2005), *Engaged Anthropology: Research Essays on North American Archaeology, Ethnobotany, and Museology*, Ann Arbor, MI: University of Michigan Museum of Anthropology

Hendry, J. (1999), *An Introduction to Social Anthropology: Other People's Worlds*, Basingstoke: Palgrave-Macmillan.

Hendry, J. (2006), *Reclaiming Culture: Indigenous People and Self-representation*, New York: Palgrave Macmillan.

Henning, A. (2005), 'Climate Change and Energy Use: The Role for Anthropological Research', *Anthropology Today*, 21(3): 8–12.

Henze, R. and Davis, K. (1999), 'Authenticity and Identity: Lessons from Indigenous Language Education', *Anthropology and Education Quarterly*, 30(1): 3–21.

Herman, P. and Kuper, R. (2003), *Food for Thought: Towards a Future for Farming*, For the Confederation Paysanne, London: Pluto Press.

Herrmann, G. (2006), 'Garage Sales Make Good Neighbours: Building Community through Neighborhood Sales', *Human Organization*, 65(2): 181–200.

Herzfeld, M. (1992), *The Social Production of Indifference: Exploring the Symbolic Roots of Western Bureaucracy*, Oxford: Berg.

Heyman, J. (2004), 'The Anthropology of Power-Wielding Bureaucracies', *Human Organization*, 63: 487–500.

Hill, D. (2003), *Body of Truth: Leveraging What Consumers Can't or Won't Say*, Hoboken, NJ: Wiley.

Hills, M. (2006), 'Anthropology at the Centre: Reflections on Research, Policy Guidance and Decision Support', in S. Pink (ed.) *Applications of Anthropology: Professional Anthropology in the Twenty-first Century*, London: Berghahn Books, pp. 130–44.

Himmelgreen, D. and Crooks, D. (2005), 'Nutritional Anthropolgy and its Application to Nutritional Issues and Problems', in S. Kedia and J. Van Willigen (eds), *Applied Anthropology: Domains of Application*, Westport, CT: Praeger, pp. 149–88.

Hobart, M. (ed.) (1993), *An Anthropological Critique of Development: The Growth of Ignorance*, London: Routledge.

Hopper, K. (1991), 'More Than Passing Strange: Homelessness and Mental Illness in New York City', *American Ethnologist*, 15(1): 155–67.

Hornborg, A. and Kurkiala, M. (eds) (1998), *Voices of the Land: Identity and Ecology in the Margins*, Lund: Lund University Press.

Howard, B. (2003), *Indigenous Peoples and the State: The Struggle for Native Rights*, DeKalb, IL: Northern Illinois University Press.

Howes, D. (2005), *Empire of the Senses: A Sensual Culture Reader*, Oxford: Berg.

International NGO Training and Research Centre (INTRAC) (2007), *Resources Database*, http://www.intrac/org.resources_database.php?last=15.

Jackall, R. (1983), 'Moral Mazes: Bureaucracy and Managerial Work', *Harvard Business Review*, 61: 118–30.

Jing, J. (1999), 'Villages Dammed, Villages Repossessed: A Memorial Movement in Northwest China', *American Ethnologist*, 26(2): 324–43.

Johnston, B. (1994), *Who Pays the Price? The Sociocultural Context of Environmental Crisis*, Washington, DC: Island Press.

Joralemon, D. (1999), *Exploring Medical Anthropology*, Boston: Allyn & Bacon.

Kane, K. (1996), 'Anthropologists Go Native in the Corporate Village', *Fast Company*, 5: 60.

Kaplan, C. (1995), 'A World Without Boundaries: the Body Shop's Trans/national Geographics', *Social Text*, (43): 55–66.

Kasmir, S. (2005), 'Activism and Class Identity: the Saturn Auto Factory Case', J. Nash (ed.) *Social Movements: An Anthropological Reader*, Malden, MA: Blackwell, pp. 78–96.

Kedia, S. and Van Willigen, J. (2005), *Applied Anthropology: Domains of Application*, Westport, CT: Praeger.

Kellner, F. (2005), 'Smoking and Self: Tobacco Use Effects on Young Women's Constructions of Self and Other', in D. Pawluch, W. Shaffir and C. Miall (eds), *Doing Ethnography: Studying Everyday Life*, Toronto: Canadian Scholars' Press, pp. 226–37.

Kenney, S. 'Conducting Qualitative Research On Emotionally Upsetting Topics: Homicide and Those Left Behind', in D. Pawluch, W. Shaffir and C. Miall (eds), *Doing Ethnography: Studying Everyday Life*, Toronto: Canadian Scholars' Press, pp. 118–26.

Khagram, S. (2004), *Dams and Development: Transnational Struggles for Water and Power*, Ithaca, NY: Cornell University Press.

Kielich, Andrea, and Miller, Leslie. (1998), 'Cultural Aspects of Women's Health Care', in G. Ferraro (ed.) *Applying Cultural Anthropology: Readings*, Belmont, CA: Wadsworth, pp. 32–40.

Kirsch, S. (2001), 'Changing Views of Place and Time along the Ok Tedi', in Alan Rumsey and James Weiner (eds), *Mining and Indigenous Lifeworlds in Australia and Papua New Guinea*, Adelaide: Crawford House Publishing, pp. 145–56.

Kirsch, S. (2003), 'Mining and Evironmental Human Rights in Papua New Guinea', in F. Jedrzej and S. Pegg (eds), *Transnational Corporations and Human Rights*, Basingstoke: Palgrave Macmillan, pp. 115–36.

Kirsch, S. (2006), *Reverse Anthropology: Indigenous Analysis of Social and Environmental Relations*, Stanford, CA: Stanford University Press.

Kleinert, S. and Neale, M. (eds) (2000), *The Oxford Companion to Aboriginal Art and Culture*, Oxford: Oxford University Press.

Klienknecht, S. 'Ethnographic Insights Into the Hacker Subculture', in D. Pawluch, W. Shaffir and C. Miall (eds), *Doing Ethnography: Studying Everyday Life*, Toronto: Canadian Scholars' Press, pp. 212–24.

Kolig, E. (2004), 'Deconstructing the Waitangi Treaty Narrative: Democracy, Cultural Pluralism and Political Mythmaking in New Zealand/Aotearoa', *Sites*, 1(2): 84–118.

Kottak, C. (1996), The Media, Development and Social Change', in E. Moran (ed.) *Transforming Societies, Transforming Anthropology*, Ann Arbor, MI: University of Michigan Press, pp. 135–63.

Kressel, G. (2003), *Let Shepherding Endure: Applied Anthropology and the Preservation of a Cultural Tradition in Israel and the Middle East*, Albany, NY: State University of New York Press.

Kwiatkowski, L. (2005), 'NGOs, Power and Contradiction in Ifugao, the Philippines', in *Urban Anthropology and Studies of Cultural Systems and World Development*, 34

Laabs, J. (1998), 'Corporate Anthropologists', in G. Ferraro (ed.) *Applying Cultural Anthropology: Readings*, Belmont, CA: Wadsworth, pp. 61–5.

La Lone, M. (2001), 'Putting Anthropology to Work to Preserve Appalachian Heritage', *Practicing Anthropology*, 23(2): 5–9.

Langton, M. (1993), *'Well I Heard it on the Radio and I Saw it on the Television': An Essay for the Australian Film Commission on the Politics and Aesthetics of Filmmaking by and about Aboriginal People and Things*, North Sydney, NSW: Australian Film Commission.

Lansing, S. (1991), *Priests and Programmers: Technologies of Power in the Engineered Landscape of Bali*, Princeton, NJ: Princeton University Press.

Laumann, E. (ed.) (2004), *The Sexual Organisation of the City*, Chicago: Chicago University Press.

Layton, R. (1989), *Uluru: An Aboriginal History of Ayers Rock*, Canberra: Aboriginal Studies Press.

Lefkowitz, D. (2001), 'Negotiated and Mediated Meanings: Ethnicity and Politics in Israeli Newspapers', *Anthropological Quarterly*, 74(4): 179–89.

Leggewie, C. (2003), *Transnational Movements and the Question of Democracy*, http://www.eurozine.com/articles/2003-02-03-leggewie-en.html.

Liebow, E. (2002 [1995]), 'Inside the Decision-Making Process: Ethnography and Environmental Risk Management', in J. McDonald (ed.), *The Applied Anthropology Reader*, Boston: Allyn & Bacon, pp. 299–308.

Little, P. (2005), 'Anthropology and Development', in S. Kedia and J. Van Willigen (eds), *Applied Anthropology: Domains of Application*, Westport, CT: Praeger, pp. 33–59.

Luetchford, P. (2005), 'Brokering Fair Trade: Relations between Coffee Cooperatives and Alternative Trade Organisations – A View from Costa Rica', in D. Mosse and D. Lewis (eds), *Development Brokers and Translators: The Ethnography of Aid and Agencies*, Bloomfield, CT: Kumarian Press, pp. 127–45.

Lupton, D. (ed.) (2003), *Medicine as Culture*, Cornwall: Sage Publications.

Luhrmann, T. (2002), 'Dissociation, Social Technology and the Spiritual Domain', in N. Rapport (ed.) *British Subjects: An Anthropology of Britain*, Oxford: Berg, pp. 121–38.

MacClancy, J. (ed.), (2002), *Exotic No More: Anthropology on the Front Lines*, Chicago: Chicago University Press.

MacClancy, J. (2005), 'The Literary Image of Anthropologists', *Journal of the Royal Anthropological Institute*, 11(3): 549–75.

MacDonald, J. (2003), 'Crossing the Minefield: Politics of Refugee Research and Service', in A. Podolefsky. and P. Brown (eds), *Applying Anthropology: An Introductory Reader*, 7th edn, London: McGraw-Hill, pp. 308–12.

Macdonald, K. (2004), '"Developing 'Nature": Global Ecology and the Politics of Conservation in Northern Pakistan', in J. Carrier (ed.) *Confronting Environments: Local Understanding in a Globalizing World*, Walnut Creek, CA: Altamira Press, pp. 71–96.

Mackay, E. (2005), 'Universal Rights in Conflict: Backlash and "Benevolent Resistance" to Indigenous Land Rights', *Anthropology Today*, 21(2): 14–20.

Magowan, F. (2007), *Melodies of Mourning: Music and Emotion in Northern Australia*, Oxford: James Currey.

Malefyt, T. and Moeran, B. (eds) (2003), *Advertising Cultures*, Oxford: Berg.

Malpas, J. (1999), *Place and Experience: A Philosophical Topography*, Cambridge: Cambridge University Press.

Margry, P. and Sanchez-Carretero, C. (2007), 'Memorializing Tragic Death', *Anthropology Today*, 23(3): 1–2.

Mariampolski, H. (2006), *Ethnography for Marketers: A Guide to Consumer Immersion*, Thousand Oaks, CA: Sage Publications.

Marquez, P. (1999), *The Street is My Home: Youth and Violence in Caracas*, Stanford: Stanford University Press.

Marshall, P., Thomasma, D. and Darr, A. (1996), 'Marketing Human Organs: The Autonomy Paradox', in *Theoretical Medicine and Bioethics*, 17(1): 1–18.

Martin, E. (1996), 'Interpreting Electron Micrographs' in H. Moore (ed.) *The Future of Anthropological Knowledge*, London: Routledge, pp. 16–35.

Martin, E. (2006), 'Flexible Survivors' in W. Haviland, R. Gordon, R. and L. Vivanco (eds), *Talking about People: Readings in Contemporary Cultural Anthropology*, Boston: McGraw-Hill, pp. 84–6.

Marvin, G. (2006), 'Research, Representations and Responsibilities: An Anthropologist in the Contested World of Foxhunting', in S. Pink (ed.) *Applications of Anthropology: Professional Anthropology in the Twenty-first Century*, London, New York: Berghahn Books, pp. 191–208.

Mauzé, M., Harkin, M. and Kan, S. (2004), *Coming to Shore: Northwest Coast Ethnology, Traditions, and Visions*, Lincoln, NB: University of Nebraska Press.

May, D. (1994), *Aboriginal Labour and the Cattle Industry: Queensland from White Settlement to the Present*, Cambridge: Cambridge University Press.

Maybury-Lewis, D. (1985), 'A Special Sort of Pleading: Anthropology at the Service of Ethnic Groups,' in R. Paine (ed.), *Advocacy and Anthropology*, St John's Newfoundland: Institute of Social and Economic Research, pp. 130–48.

McCarty T. and Watahomigie, L. (2002), 'Indigenous Education and Grassroots Language Planning in the USA', in J. McDonald (ed.) *The Applied Anthropology Reader*, Boston: Allyn & Bacon, pp. 353–63.

McCay, B. (2000), 'Sea Changes in Fisheries Policy: Contributions from Anthropology', in E. Durrenberger and T. King (eds), *State and Community in Fisheries Management: Power, Policy, and Practice*, Westport, CT: Bergin & Garvey.

McCay, B. (2001), 'Environmental Anthropology at Sea', in C. Crumley (ed.), *New Directions in Anthropology and Environment: Intersections*, Walnut Creek, CA: AltaMira Press.

McDonald, J. (2002), *The Applied Anthropology Reader*, Boston: Allyn & Bacon.

McFall, L. (2004), *Advertising: A Cultural Economy*, London: Sage.

McGuire, T. (2005), 'The Domain of the Environment', in S. Kedia and J. Van Willigen (eds), *Applied Anthropology: Domains of Application*, Westport, CT: Praeger, pp. 87–118.

McLaren, C., (2002), 'Shopping Spies', in J, McDonald, (ed.) *The Applied Anthropology Reader*, Boston: Allyn & Bacon, pp. 419–21.

Messer, E. (1996), 'Hunger Vulnerability from an Anthropologist's Food Systems Perspective', in E. Moran (ed.) *Transforming Societies, Transforming Anthropology*, Ann Arbor, MI: University of Michigan Press, pp. 241–64.

Metcalf, P. (2005), *Anthropology: the Basics*, New York, Oxford: Routledge.

Metge, J. (1976), *The Maoris of New Zealand: Rautahi*, London: Routledge & Kegan Paul.

Mills, D., Babiker, M. and Ntarangwi, M. (eds) (2006), *African Anthropologies: History, Critique and Practice*, London: Zed Books in association with CODESRIA, Dakar, Senegal.

Milton, K. (ed.) (1993), *Environmentalism: The View from Anthropology*, London: Routledge.

Milton, K. (2002), *Loving Nature: Towards an Ecology of Emotion*, London, New York: Routledge.

Milton, K. (2008), 'Global Warming as a By-Product of the Capitalist Treadmill of Production and Consumption: The Need for an Alternative Global System', *Australian Journal of Anthropology*, 19(1): 57–8.

Milton, K and Svasek M. (eds) (2005), *Mixed Emotions: Anthropological Studies of Feeling*, Oxford: Berg.

Moeran, B. (2007), 'A Dedicated Storytelling Organization: Advertising Talk in Japan', *Human Organization*, 66(2): 160–71.

Moore, P. (1999), 'Anthropological Practice and Aboriginal Heritage: A Case Study from Western Australia', in S. Toussaint and J. Taylor (eds), *Applied Anthropology in Australasia*, Nedlands: University of Western Australia Press, pp. 229–54.

Morais, R. (2007), 'Conflict and Confluence in Advertising Meetings', *Human Organization*, 66(2): 150–60.

Moretti, D. (2006), 'Osama Bin Laden and the Man-eating Sorcerers: Encountering the "War on Terror" in Papua New Guinea', *Anthropology Today*, 22(3): 13–17.

Morphy, H. (1998), *Aboriginal Art*, London: Phaidon.

Morphy, H. and Perkins, M. (eds) (2006), *The Anthropology of Art: A Reader*, Oxford: Blackwell.

Morris, B. and Bastin, R. (2004), *Expert Knowledge: First World Peoples, Consultancy, and Anthropology*, New York: Berghahn Books.

Mosse, D. (2005), *Cultivating Development: An Ethnography of Aid Policy and Practice*, London: Pluto Press.

Mosse, D. and Lewis, D. (eds) (2005), *The Aid Effect: Giving and Governing in International Development*, London: Pluto.

Mtika, M. (2001), 'The AIDS Epidemic in Malawi and its Threat to Household Food Security', *Human Organisation*, 60(2): 178–88.

Munger, F. (2002), *Laboring Below the Line: The New Ethnography of Poverty, Low-wage Work, and Survival in the Global Economy*, New York: Russell Sage Foundation.

Myers, F. (2002), *Painting Culture: The Making of an Aboriginal High Art*, Durham, NC: Duke University Press.

Myers, F. (2006), 'Representing Culture: The Production of Discourse(s) for Aboriginal Acrylic Paintings', in H. Morphy and M. Perkins (eds), *The Anthropology of Art: A Reader*, Oxford: Blackwell, pp. 495–512.

Nagengast, C. and Vélez-Ibáñez, C. (2004), *Human Rights: The Scholar as Activist*, Oklahoma City: Society for Applied Anthropology.

Nash, J. (1979), 'Anthropology of the Multinational Corporations' in M. Léons and F. Rothstein (eds), *New Directions in Political Economy; An Approach from Anthropology*, Westport, CT: Greenwood Press, pp. 173–200.

Nash, J. (ed.) (2005), *Social Movements: An Anthropological Reader*, London: Blackwell.

National Association for the Practice of Anthropology (2001), 'Careers in Anthropology: Profiles of Practitioners', *National Association for the Practice of Anthropology Bulletin*, 20, www.anthrosource.net.

Nigh, R. (2002 [1995]), 'Animal Agriculture for the Regeneration of Degraded Tropical Forests', in J. McDonald (ed.) *The Applied Anthropology Reader*, Boston: Allyn & Bacon, pp. 310–27.

Nixon, S. (2003), *Advertising Cultures: Gender, Commerce, Creativity*, London, Thousand Oaks, CA: Sage.

Nolan, R. (2002), *Development Anthropology: Encounters in the Real World*, Boulder, CO: Westview Press.

Nolan, R. (2003), *Anthropology in Practice: Building a Career Outside the Academy*, Boulder, CO: Lynne Rienner Publishers.

Norman, J. (1970) *Ghost Dance: The Last Great Days of the Sioux*, New York: Ballantine Books.

Nyíri, P. (2006), 'The Nation-State, Public Education and the Logic of Migration: Chinese Students in Hungary', *The Australian Journal of Anthropology*, 17(1): 32–46.

Ocasio, R., Kilbane, T. and Hermanson, J. (1995), 'An Urban Environmental Sanitation Loan Programme in Honduras', in B. Bradford and M. Gwynne (eds), *Down to Earth: Community Perspectives on Health, Development and the Environment*, West Hartford, CT: Kumarian Press, pp. 23–4.

Okely, J. (1983), *The Traveller-Gypsies*, Cambridge: Cambridge University Press.

Olivier de Sardan, J.-P. (2005), *Anthropology and Development: Understanding Contemporary Social Change*, New York: Zed Books.

Omohundro, J. (2000), *Careers in Anthropology*, London: McGraw-Hill Humanities.

Ong, A. (2002), 'Flexible Citizenship among Chinese Cosmopolitans' in Vincent, J. (ed.), *The Anthropology of Politics: A Reader in Ethnography, Theory and Critique*, Oxford: Blackwell, pp. 338–55.

Orlove, B. and LeVieil, D. (1989), 'Some Doubts About Trout: Fisheries Development Projects in Lake Titicaca', in B. Orlove, M. Foley, and T. Love (eds), *State, Capital, and Rural Society*, Boulder, CO: Westview Press, pp. 211–46.

Painter, M. and Durham, W. (1995), *The Social Causes of Environmental Destruction in Latin America*, Ann Arbor, MI: University of Michigan Press.

Pawluch, D. Shaffir, W. and Miall, C. (eds) (2005), *Doing Ethnography: Studying Everyday Life*, Toronto: Canadian Scholars' Press.

Peace, A. (2001), 'Discourses of Ecotourism: the Case of Fraser Island, Queensland', *Language and Communication*, 21(4): 359–80.

Peace, A. (2002), 'The Cull of the Wild: Dingoes, Development and Death in an Australian Tourist Location', *Anthropology Today*, 18(5): 14–20.

Peacock, J. (1986), *The Anthropological Lens: Harsh Light, Soft Focus*, Cambridge: Cambridge University Press.

Pelletier, D. (2000), 'The Potential Effects of Malnutrition on Child Mortality: Epidemic Evidence and Policy Implications', in A. Goodman, D. Dufour and G. Pelto (eds), *Nutritional Anthropology: Biocultural Perspectives on Food and Nutrition*, Mountain View, CA: Mayfield Publishing.

Pelletier, D. (2005), 'The Science and Politics of Targeting: Who Gets What, When and How', *Journal of Nutrition*, 135: 890–93.

Perez-Escamilla, R. and Himmelgreen, D. (1999), 'Promoting Better Dietary Habits Through Nutrition Education in an Impoverished USA Community: the PANA Program and the Salud Campaign', *United Nations Newsletter*, 17: 31.

Phillips, R. (2006), 'The Collecting and Display of Souvenir Arts: Authenticity and the "Strictly Commercial"', in H. Morphy and M. Perkins (eds), *The Anthropology of Art: A Reader*, Malden, MA: Blackwell, pp. 431–53.

Pink, S. (2006), *Applications of Anthropology: Professional Anthropology in the Twenty-first Century*, London: Berghahn Books.

Pitt, D. (ed.) (1976), *Development From Below: Anthropologists and Development Situations*, The Hague: Mouton.

Podolefsky, A. and Brown, P. (eds) (2003), *Applying Anthropology: An Introductory Reader*, 7th edn, Boston, MA: McGraw-Hill.

Popkin, B. (2001), 'The Nutrition Transition and Obesity in the Developing World', *Journal of Nutrition*, 131 (3): 871S–873S.

Posey, D. (1989), 'Alternatives to Forest Destruction: Lessons from the Mebengokre Indians', *The Ecologist*, 19(6): 241–4.

Posey, D. (2002), *Kayapó Ethnoecology and Culture*, in K. Plenderleith (ed.). New York: Routledge.

Posey, D. and Plenderleith, K. (2004), *Indigenous Knowledge and Ethics: a Darrell Posey Reader*, New York: Routledge.

Postrel, V. (2003), *The Substance of Style: How the Rise of Aesthetic Value is Remaking Commerce, Culture, and Consciousness*, New York: HarperCollins.

Power, D. and Scott, A. (2004), *Cultural Industries and the Production of Culture*, London, New York: Routledge.

Purdie, N. (2008), *Indigenous Languages in Australian Schools*, http://www.languageseducation.com/purdie0708.pdf.

Ramos, A. (2004), 'Advocacy Rhymes with Anthropology', in B. Morris and R. Bastin (eds), *Expert Knowledge: First World Peoples, Consultancy, and Anthropology*, New York: Berghahn Books, pp. 56–66.

Ranson, G. (2005), '"I'm Looking Forward to hearing what You Found Out": Reflections on a Critical Perspective and Some of its Consequences', in D. Pawluch, W. Shaffir and C. Miall (eds), *Doing Ethnography: Studying Everyday Life*, Toronto: Canadian Scholars' Press, pp. 104–15.

Rapp, R. (1989), 'Chromosomes and Communication: the Discourse of Genetic Counselling', *Medical Anthropology Quarterly*, 2(2): 143–57.

Rasbridge, L. (1998), 'Role Transformation in a Refugee Health Program', in G. Ferraro (ed.) *Applying Cultural Anthropology: Readings*, Belmont, CA: Wadsworth, pp. 28–31.

Rathje, W. (2001), 'Integrated Archaeology: A Garbage Paradigm', in V. Buchli, G. Lucas and M. Cox (eds) (2001), *Archaeologies of the Contemporary Past*, London: Routledge, pp. 63–76.

Raz, A. (2004), *The Gene and the Genie: Tradition, Dedicalization, and Genetic Counselling in a Bedouin Community in Israel*, Durham, NC: North Carolina Academic Press.

Reeves-Ellington, R. (2003), 'Using Cultural Skills for Cooperative Advantage in Japan', in A. Podolefsky and P. Brown (eds), *Applying Anthropology: An Introductory Reader*, 7th edn, Boston: McGraw-Hill, pp. 247–58.

Reid, D. (2003), *Tourism, Globalization and Development*, London: Pluto Press.

Reyhner, J., Trujillo, O., Carrasco, R. and Lockard, L. (eds) (2003), *Nurturing Native Languages*, Flagstaff, AZ: Northern Arizona University.

Rhoades, R. (2005), 'Agricultural Anthropology', in S. Kedia and J. Van Willigen, (eds), *Applied Anthropology: Domains of Application*, Westport, CT: Praeger, pp. 61–85.

Richard, M. and Emener, W. (2003), *I'm a People Person: A Guide to Human Service Professions*, Springfield, IL: C. C. Thomas.

Rival, L. (ed.) (1998), *The Social Life of Trees: Anthropological Perspectives on Tree Symbolism*, Oxford: Berg.

Robbins, J. (2007), 'Continuity Thinking and the Problem of Christian Culture; Belief, Time and the Anthropology of Christianity', *Current Anthropology*, 48(1): 5–38.

Roberts, S. (2006), 'The Pure and the Impure? Reflections on Applying Anthropology and Doing Ethnography', in S. Pink (ed.) *Applications of Anthropology: Professional Anthropology in the Twenty-first Century*, London: Berghahn Books, pp. 72–89.

Robertson, J. (2005), *Same-Sex Cultures and Sexualities: An Anthropological Reader*, Malden, MA: Blackwell.

Robinson-Pant, A. (2004), *Women, Literacy, and Development: Alternative Perspectives*, New York: Routledge.

Rodgers, S. (2006), 'Feminine Power at Sea', in W. Haviland, R. Gordon and L. Vivanco (eds), *Talking about People: Readings in Contemporary Cultural Anthropology*, Boston: McGraw-Hill, pp. 231–3.

Rodríguez-Piñero, L. (2005), *Indigenous Peoples, Postcolonialism, and International Law: The ILO Regime, 1919–1989*, Oxford: Oxford University Press.

Roethlisberger, F. and Dickson, W. (1939), *Management and the Worker: An Account of a Research Programme Conducted by the Western Electric Company, Hawthorne Works*, Chicago: Harvard University Press.

Ronsbo, H. (2003), 'The Embodiment of Male Identities: Alliances and Cleavages in Salvadorean Football', in N. Dyck and E. Archetti (eds), *Sport, Dance and Embodied Identities*, Oxford: Berg, pp. 157–71.

Rosenberger, N. (2002), 'Business Anthropology in a Work Subculture: Korean and Japanese Young, Single, Working Women', in J. McDonald (ed.) *The Applied Anthropology Reader*, Boston: Allyn & Bacon, pp. 403–13.

Rosenfeld, G. (1971), *Shut Those Thick Lips*, Prospect Heights, IL: Waveland Press.

Rumsey, A. and Weiner, J. (eds) (2001), *Mining and Indigenous Lifeworlds in Australia and Papua New Guinea*, Hindmarsh, South Australia: Crawford House Publishing.

Rylko-Bauer, B., Singer, M. and Van Willigen, J. (2006), 'Reclaiming Applied Anthropology: Its Past, Present, and Future', *American Anthropologist*, 108(1): 178–90.

Sabloff, P. (2000), *Careers in Anthropology: Profiles of Practitioner Anthropologists*, NAPA Bulletin 20, Washington, DC: American Anthropological Association.

Sachs, C. (1996), *Gendered Fields: Rural Women, Agriculture, and Environment*, Boulder, CO: Westview Press.

Sampson, S. (2003), 'From Forms to Norms: Global Projects and Local Practices in the Balkan NGO Scene', *Journal of Human Rights*, 2(3), 329–37.

Scheper-Hughes, N. (2002), 'The Global Traffic in Human Organs', J. Inda and R. Rosaldo (eds), *The Anthropology of Globalization: A Reader*, Malden, MA: Blackwell, pp. 270–303.

Schuler, S., and Hashemi, S. (2002), 'Credit Programs, Women's Empowerment, and Contraceptive Use in Rural Bangladesh', J. McDonald (ed.), *The Applied Anthropology Reader*, Boston: Allyn & Bacon, pp. 278–97.

Schwandner-Sievers, S. (2006), 'Culture in Court: Albanian Migrants and the Anthropologist as Expert Witness', in S. Pink (ed.) *Applications of Anthropology: Professional Anthropology in the Twenty-first Century*, New York: Berghahn Books, pp. 209–28.

Schwartzman, H. (1987), 'The Significance of Meetings in an American Mental Health Center', *American Ethnologist*, 14, pp. 271–94.

Senior, K. and Chenhall, R. (2008), 'Walkin' About at Night: The Background to Teenage Pregnancy in a Remote Aboriginal Community', *Journal of Youth Studies*, 11(3): 269–82.

Serpell, J. (1996), *In the Company of Animals: A Study of Human-animal Relationships*, Cambridge: Cambridge University Press.

Shackel, P. and Chambers, E. (eds) (2004), *Places in Mind: Public Archaeology as Applied Anthropology*, London: Routledge.

Sheets, P. (2003), 'Dawn of a New Stone Age in Eye Surgery', in A. Podolefsky and P. Brown (eds), *Applying Anthropology: An Introductory Reader*, London: McGraw Hill, pp. 108–10.

Sherry, J. (ed.) (1995), *Contemporary Marketing and Consumer Behavior: An Anthropological Sourcebook*, Thousand Oaks, CA: Sage.

Shimkin, D. (1996), 'Culture Change and Health: Third World Perspectives', in E. Moran (ed.) *Transforming Societies, Transforming Anthropology*, Ann Arbor, MI: University of Michigan Press, pp. 265–300.

Shore, C. (1996), 'Anthropology's Identity Crisis: The Politics of Public Image', *Anthropology Today*, 12(2): 2–5.

Shore, C. (2000), *Building Europe: The Cultural Politics of European Integration*, London: Routledge.

Shore, C. and Nugent, S. (2002), *Elite Cultures: Anthropological Perspectives*, London, New York: Routledge.

Shore, C. and Wright, S. (eds) (1997), *Anthropology of Policy: Critical Perspectives on Governance and Power*, London: Routledge.

Shrestha, C. (2006), 'They Can't Mix Like We Can: Bracketing Differences and the Professionalization of NGOs in Nepal', in D. Lewis and D. Mosse (eds), *Development Brokers and Translators: The Ethnography of Aid and Agencies*, Bloomfield, CT: Kumarian Press, pp. 195–213.

Sillitoe, P. (1998), 'The Development of Indigenous Knowledge: A New Applied Anthropology', in *Current Anthropology*, 39(2): 223–52.

Sillitoe, P. (2003), *Managing Animals in New Guinea: Preying the Game in the Highlands*, New York: Routledge.

Sillitoe, P., Bicker, A. and Pottier, J. (eds) (2002), *Participating in Development: Approaches to Indigenous Knowledge*, London: Routledge.

Sillitoe, P. Dixon P. and Barr J. (2005), *Indigenous Knowledge Inquiries: A Methodologies Manual for Development*, Dhaka: The University Press.

Singer, M., Irizarry, R. and Schensul, J. (2002), 'Needle Access as an AIDS Prevention Strategy for IV Drug Users: A Research Perspective', J. McDonald (ed.) *The Applied Anthropology Reader*, Boston: Allyn and Bacon, pp. 194–215.

Sinha, R. and Sinha, S. (2001), *Ethnobiology: Role of Indigenous and Ethnic Societies in Biodiversity Conservation, Human Health Protection and Sustainable Development*, Jaipur: Surabhi Publications.

Smart, B. (2005), *The Sport Star: Modern Sport and the Cultural Economy of Sporting Celebrity*, London: Sage.

Smith, C. (1996), 'Development and the State: Issues for Anthropologists', in E. Moran (ed.) *Transforming Societies, Transforming Anthropology*, Ann Arbor, MI: University of Michigan Press, pp. 25–56.

Solway, J. (2004), 'Reaching the Limits of Universal Citizenship: "Minority" struggles in Botswana', in B. Berman, E. Dickson and W. Kymlicka (eds), *Ethnicity and Democracy in Africa*, Oxford: J. Currey, pp. 129–47.

Sommer, B. (1972), '*Kunjen* Syntax: A Generative View', *Australian Aboriginal Studies*, 45, Canberra: Australian Institute for Aboriginal Studies.

Squires, S and Byrne, B. (eds) (2002), *Creating Breakthrough Ideas: The Collaboration of Anthropologists and Designers in the Product Development Industry*, Westport, CT: Bergin & Garvey.

Stanton, J. (1999), 'At the Grass-Roots: Collecting and Communities in Aboriginal Australia', in S. Toussaint and J. Taylor (eds), *Applied Anthropology in Australasia*, Nedlands: University of Western Australia Press, pp. 282–94.

Stephens, R. (2002), *Careers in Anthropology: What an Anthropology Degree Can Do for You*, Boston: Allyn & Bacon.

Stewart, P. and Strathern, A. (eds) (2005), *Anthropology and Consultancy: Issues and Debates*, New York: Berghahn Books.

Stone, D. (ed.) (2000), *Banking on Knowledge: The Genesis of the Global Development Network*, London: Routledge.

Stone, G. (2002), 'Biotechnology and Suicide in India', *Anthropology News*, 1(4), http://grain.org/research_files/biotechandsuicide.pdf.

Stone, G. (2007), 'Agricultural Deskilling and the Spread of Genetically Modifed Cotton in Warangal', in *Current Anthropology*, 48(1): 67–103.

Strang, V. (1995), 'Quantifying Human Behaviour', in *Proceedings of the 1995 ECEEE Summer Study: Sustainability and the Reinvention of Government – a Challenge for Energy Efficiency*, ed. A. Persson, Stockholm, Sweden: The European Council for an Energy Efficient Economy.

Strang, V. (1997), *Uncommon Ground: Cultural Landscapes and Environmental Values*, Oxford: Berg.

Strang, V. (2001a), 'Negotiating the River: Cultural Tributaries in Far North Queensland', in B. Bender and M. Winer (eds), *Contested Landscapes: Movement, Exile and Place*, Oxford: Berg, pp. 69–86.

Strang, V. (2001b), 'Of Human Bondage: The Breaking In of Stockmen in Northern Australia', *Oceania*, 72(1) September, pp. 53–78.

Strang, V. (2004), *The Meaning of Water*, Oxford: Berg.

Strang, V. (2007 [2009]), 'Integrating the Social and Natural Sciences in Environmental Research: A Discussion Paper', *Journal of Environment, Development and Sustainability*, 11(1) pp. 1–18.

Strang, V. (2009), *Gardening the World: Agency, Identity, and the Ownership of Water*, Oxford: Berghahn Books.

Strathern, M. (ed.) (2000), *Audit Cultures: Anthropological Studies in Accountability, Ethics and the Academy*, London: Routledge.

Street, B. (1975), *The Savage in Literature: Representations of 'Primitive' Society in English Fiction 1858–1920*, London: Routledge.

Sukkary-Stolba, S. (1998), 'Development Anthropology: A Rewarding Career for Middle East Anthropologists', *Anthropology Newsletter*, April 1998: 47. Cited in Gwynne, M. (2003), *Applied Anthropology: A Career-oriented Approach*, Boston: Pearson Education, p. 123.

Sullivan, R., Allen, J. and Nero, K. (2007), 'Schizophrenia in Palau: A Biocultural Analysis', *Current Anthropology*, 48 (2): 189–231.

Sunderland, P. and Denny, R. (2008), *Doing Anthropology in Consumer Research*, Walnut Creek, CA: Left Coast Press.

Sutton, P. (1989), *Dreamings: the Art of Aboriginal Australia*, New York, Adelaide: The Asia Society Galleries and George Braziller Publishers.

Szala-Meneok, K. and Lohfeld, L. (2005), 'The Charms and Challenges of an Academic Qualitative Researcher Doing Participatory Action Research (PAR)' in D. Pawluch, W. Shaffir and C. Miall (eds), *Doing Ethnography: Studying Everyday Life*, Toronto: Canadian Scholars' Press, pp. 52–64.

Tan, Y., Hugo, G. and Potter, L. (2001), 'Rural Women, Displacement and the Three Gorges Project', *Development and Change*, 36(4): 711–34.

Taylor, K. (1988), 'Physicians and the Disclosure of Undesirable Information', in M. Lock and D. Gordon (eds), *Biomedicine Examined*, Dordrecht: Kluwer, pp. 441–63.

Theodossopoulos, D. (2002), *Troubles with Turtles: Cultural Understandings of the Environment in a Greek Island*, New York: Berghahn Books.

Thompson, C. (2006a), 'Strategic Naturalizing: Kinship in a Fertility Clinic', in E. Lewin (ed.), *Feminist Anthropology*, Malden, MA: Blackwell, pp. 271–88.

Thompson, R. (2006b), 'Yoruba Artistic Criticism', in H. Morphy and M. Perkins (eds), *The Anthropology of Art: A Reader*, Malden, MA: Blackwell, pp. 242–69.

Tilley, C. (1994), *A Phenomenology of Landscape: Places, Paths and Monuments*, Oxford: Berg.

Tishkov, V. (2005), 'The Anthropology of NGOs', in *Eurozine*, www.eurozine.com/articles/2005-06-01-tishkov-en.html.

Totten, M. and Kelly, K. (2005), 'Conducting Field Research With Young Offenders Convicted of Murder and Manslaughter: Gaining Access, Risks and "truth status"', in D. Pawluch, W. Shaffir and C. Miall (eds), *Doing Ethnography: Studying Everyday Life*, Toronto: Canadian Scholars' Press, pp. 77–89.

Toussaint, S. (ed.) (2004), *Crossing Boundaries: Cultural, Legal, Historical and Practice Issues in Native Title*, Carlton, Victoria: Melbourne University Press.

Toussaint, S. and Taylor, J. (eds) (1999), *Applied Anthropology in Australasia*, Nedlands: University of Western Australia Press.

Trigger, D. and Griffiths, G. (eds) (2003), *Disputed Territories: Land, Culture and Identity in Settler Societies*, Hong Kong: Hong Kong University Press.

Trisolini, M., Russell, S., Gwynne, M. and Zschock, D. (1992), 'Methods for Cost Analysis, Cost Recovery and Cost Control for a Public Hospital in a Developing Country: Victoria Hospital, St Lucia' *International Journal of Health Planning and Management*, 7: 103–13.

Trosset, C. (1993), *Welshness Performed: Welsh Concepts of Person and Society*, Tucson: University of Arizona Press.

Turner, V. (1982), *From Ritual to Theatre: the Human Seriousness of Play*, New York: Performing Arts Journal Publications.

Turner, V. (1992), 'Defiant Images: the Kayapo Appropriation of Video', *Anthropology Today*, 8(6): 5–16.

Turton, D. (2004), 'Lip-plates and "The People Who Take Photographs"', *Anthropology Today*, 20(3): 3–8.

Tylor, E. B. (1873) *Primitive Culture: Researches into the Development of Mythology, Philosophy, Religion, Language, Art and Custom*, London: John Murray.

Urla, J. (2006), 'Euskara: the "Terror" of a European Minority Language', *Anthropology Today*, 19(4): 1–3.

Van Willigen, J. and Channa, V. (1991), 'Law, Custom, and Crimes Against Women: The Problem of Dowry Death in India', in J. McDonald (ed.) (2002), *The Applied Anthropology Reader*, Boston: Allyn & Bacon, pp. 116–30.

Vigil, J. (2002), 'Streets and Schools: How Educators Can Help Chicano Marginalized Gang Youth', in J. McDonald (ed.) *The Applied Anthropology Reader*, Boston: Allyn & Bacon, pp. 363–78.

Villenga, M. (2005), 'Anthropology and the Challenges of Sustainable Architecture', *Anthropology Today*, 21(3): 3–7.

Von Sturmer, J. (1981), 'Talking With Aborigines', *AIAS Newsletter*, New Series, 15 pp. 13–30.

Wade, P. (2002), *Race, Nature and Culture*, London: Pluto Press.

Wallace, B. (2006), *The Changing Village Environment in Southeast Asia: Applied Anthropology and Environmental Reclamation in the Northern Philippines*, London, New York: Routledge Curzon.

Walker, R. (2004), *Ka whawhai tonu matou: Struggle Without End*, London: Penguin.

Waterston, A. (1998), 'Interpreting Audiences: Cultural Anthropology in Market Research', in G. Ferraro (ed.) *Applying Cultural Anthropology: Readings*, Belmont, CA: Wadsworth, pp. 106–9.

Wedel, J. (2004), 'Accountability in International Development Advising: When Individual Conscience is Not Enough', in B. Morris and R. Bastin (eds), *Expert Knowledge: First World Peoples, Consultancy, and Anthropology*, New York: Berghahn Books, pp. 12–21.

Werbner, P. (1996), 'The Enigma of Christmas: Symbolic Violence, Compliant Subjects and the Flow of English Kinship', in S. Edgell, K. Hetherington and A. Warde (eds), *Consumption Matters: The Production and Experience of Consumption*, Oxford: Blackwell, pp. 135–62.

Whitaker, E. (2003), 'Ancient Bodies, Modern Customs, and our Health', in A. Podolefsky and P. Brown (eds), *Applying Anthropology: An Introductory Reader*, 7th edn, London: McGraw-Hill, pp. 38–47.

Whiteford, L. and Bennett, L. (2005), Applied Anthropology and Health and Medicine, in S. Kedia and J. Van Willigen (eds), *Applied Anthropology: Domains of Application*, Westport, CT: Praeger, pp. 119–47.

Whiteford, L. and Vitucci, J. (1997), 'Pregnancy and Addiction: Translating Research into Practice', in *Social Science and Medicine*, 44(9): 1371–80. Cited in S. Kedia and J. van Willigen (eds) (2005), *Applied Anthropology: Domains of Application*, Westport, CT: Praeger, p. 130.

Whitehead, H. (1981), 'The Bow and the Burden Strap: A New Look at Institutionalised Homosexuality in Native North America', in S. Ortner and H. Whitehead (eds), *Sexual Meanings: The Cultural Context of Gender and Sexuality*, Cambridge: Cambridge University Press, pp. 80–115.

Whorf, B. (1938), *Some Verbal Categories of Hopi*, Indianapolis, IN: Bobbs-Merrill.

Williams, B. (2006), 'Owning Places and Buying Time: Class, Culture and Stalled Gentrification', in W. Haviland, R. Gordon and L. Vivanco (eds), *Talking about People: Readings in Contemporary Cultural Anthropology*, Boston: McGraw-Hill, pp. 181–90.

Wilhite, H., Nakagami, H., Masuda, T., Yamaga, Y. and Haneda, H. (2001), 'A Cross-cultural Analysis of Household Energy Use Behaviour in Japan and Norway', in D. Miller (ed.) *Consumption: Critical Concepts in the Social Sciences. Volume IV. Objects, Subjects and Mediations in Consumption*, London: Routledge, pp. 159–77.

Winarto, Y. (1999), 'Creating Knowledge: Scientific Knowledge and Local Adoption in Rice-integrated Pest Management (A Case Study from Subang, West Java, Indonesia)', in S. Toussaint and J. Taylor (eds), *Applied Anthropology in Australasia*, Nedlands, Western Australia: University of Western Australia Press, pp. 162–92.

Wolfe, A. and Yang, H. (eds) (1996), *Anthropological Contributions to Conflict Resolution*, Athens, GA: University of Georgia Press.

Worth, S. and Adair, J. (1997 [1972]), *Through Navajo Eyes*, Albuquerque, NM: University of New Mexico Press.

Wright, S. (ed.) (1994), *Anthropology of Organisations*, London: Routledge.

Xing, J. and Hirabayashi, L. (2003), *Reversing the Lens: Ethnicity, Race, Gender, and Sexuality through Film*, Boulder, CO: University Press of Colorado.

Yang, H. (1998), 'Practicing Anthropology in the Carter Presidential Center', in G. Ferraro (ed.) *Applying Cultural Anthropology: Readings*, Belmont, CA: Wadsworth, pp. 201–3.

Yearley, S. (2005), *Cultures of Environmentalism: Empirical Studies in Environmental Sociology*, New York: Palgrave Macmillan.

FILMS

De Heer, R. (dir.) (2006), *Ten Canoes*, Palace Films.

Faiman, P. (dir.) (1986), *Crocodile Dundee*, Paramount Pictures.

Noyce, P. (dir.) (2002), *Rabbit Proof Fence*, Miramax Films.

Roeg, N. (dir.) 1971. *Walkabout*, 20th Century Fox.

Singer, A. and Lansing, S. (1989), *The Goddess and the Computer*, Film. Channel 4 'Fragile Earth Series'. London: Royal Anthropological Institute.

Uys, J. (dir.) (1980), *The Gods Must Be Crazy*, Jensen Farley Pictures.

INDEX